# PSYCHOLOGY AS M

# PSYCHOLOGY AS METAPHOR

A.J. Soyland

**SAGE Publications**
London • Thousand Oaks • New Delhi

First published 1994

All rights reserved. No part of this publication may be reproduced, stored in a retrieval system, transmitted or utilized in any form or by any means, electronic, mechanical, photocopying, recording or otherwise, without permission in writing from the Publishers.

 SAGE Publications Ltd
6 Bonhill Street
London EC2A 4PU

SAGE Publications Inc
2455 Teller Road
Thousand Oaks, California 91320

SAGE Publications India Pvt Ltd
32, M-Block Market
Greater Kailash – I
New Delhi 110 048

**British Library Cataloguing in Publication data**

A catalogue record for this book is available from the British Library.

ISBN 0 8039 8957 1
ISBN 0 8039 8958 X (pbk)

**Library of Congress catalog card number 94–065555**

Typeset by Photoprint, Torquay, S. Devon

Printed in Great Britain by The Cromwell Press Ltd, Broughton Gifford, Melksham, Wiltshire

Making plans. – To make plans and project designs brings with it many good sensations; and whoever had the strength to be nothing but a forger of plans his whole life long would be a very happy man: but he would occasionally have to take a rest from this activity by carrying out a plan – and then comes the vexation and the sobering up.

(Nietzsche, 1878/1986: 231)

The book is dedicated to Ian, without whom it would never have started, and Felicity, without whom it would never have been completed.

# Contents

Preface                                                                    ix

1   Introduction                                                            1
    *Opening remarks*                                                       1
    *The distinction between philosophy and rhetoric*                       3
    *The rhetoric of anti-rhetoric*                                        13
    *What is this thing called psychology?*                                15
2   Metaphor, Rhetoric and Analysis                                        21
    *Science and literature*                                               21
    *Studying the rhetoric of science*                                     24
    *Final words*                                                          31


**Part I  Metaphor**
3   Memory after Lashley: Metaphors as Promissory Notes                    35
    *Introduction*                                                         35
    *The description of the problem in 1950*                               38
    *An 'older type of theory'*                                            41
    *A problem and its answer*                                             43
    *Promises currently outstanding*                                       45
    *Conclusions*                                                          51
4.  Comparing Concepts of Development: Metaphor and
    Presupposition                                                         56
    *Wundt*                                                                59
    *Psychoanalysis*                                                       61
    *Behaviourism*                                                         68
    *Piaget*                                                               74
    *Vygotsky*                                                             77
    *Merleau-Ponty*                                                        81
    *The conceptual child*                                                 84
    *Conclusions*                                                          86
5   Accounting for Emotion: Metaphor as System                            91
    *The thesis of metaphors of emotion*                                   94
    *The instinct account*                                                 95
    *The behavioural account*                                              96
    *The learning account*                                                 99
    *The choice account*                                                   99
    *Conclusions*                                                         101

6   The Theory of Metaphor: The Extension of Discourse        105
       *Enrolling Heidegger*                                   107
       *Towards an account of metaphor*                        110
       *Derrida on philosophical discourse*                    112
       *Reconciling Black and Wittgenstein*                    117
       *The thesis of metaphor as extension of discourse*      119

**Part II   Rhetoric**
7   The Rhetoric of Validity in the IQ Debate                  123
       *A case-study of the IQ debate*                          123
       *Historical background*                                  124
       *'Sketch of the skeleton of the mind'*                   127
       *The repetition of numbers*                              129
       *More on the present debate*                             131
       *Analysing the critic*                                   133
       *Conclusions*                                            135
8   James and Freud on the Mind: Metaphor and Rhetoric
    as Enrolment                                               138
       *An overview of two metaphors of the mind*              140
       *Enrolling the reader*                                   142
       *Promissory notes*                                       149
9   Describing Psychological Objects: Concluding Discussion    154

Appendix: 'Proofs that P'                                      162
Bibliography                                                   164
Index                                                          179

# Preface

Before this project, I was working on mental health professionals' discourse: amongst other things, this taught me to look carefully at the way things were phrased, and how persuasive cases were constructed. Beyond that, I began reading 'classic' works in the history of psychology: I was taken in by clever writing, mentally nodding at each proposition, making various metaphors my own. But, later, as I thought more about the topic being discussed, I began to think about how I had been persuaded: I read conflicting accounts which undermined each other, and I read more of the sociology of scientific knowledge literature which put their premises into doubt, and their style of argument under scrutiny. At the back of my mind were examples in history of large groups of people being persuaded by arguments which are no longer taken seriously, which are the object of ridicule, or even disgust. I came upon a basic question: how and why does a case become persuasive? With this general question as an overriding concern, I began writing and presenting material on metaphor and rhetoric. Psychology and philosophy are my areas of enquiry, the late nineteenth century to the present is my period of interest: with such criteria the present book was written. My hope is that others will find this book interesting and useful in future work.

I have had lots of help of various kinds. I am very grateful to the following: Charles Antaki (for comments on other things), Julia Barossa (for arguing), Mick Billig (for examining and arguing), Alan Collins (for comments), Susan Condor (for goading), Kurt Danziger (for reading), Rob Farr (for listening), Neil Gasgoine (for annoyance), Felicity Forster (for everything), Graham Hitch (for reading), Jeff Hughes (for arguing and commenting), Myles Jackson (for talking big), Gavin Kendall (for arguing and commenting), Mike Michael (for talking), Greg Myers (for many comments and for publishing), Nick Jardine (for being Nick Jardine and publishing), Ian John (for starting everything and reading a late version), David Leary (for writing back), Mark Levine (for comments), Peter Lipton (for letting me teach on related topics), Janet Low (for comments on e-mail), Iwan Morus (for being dismissive), David Papineau (for early reading and arguing), Jonathan Potter (for too many comments on other things), Jim Russell (for surprised comments), Simon Schaffer (for examining, arguing and publishing), Roger Smith (for serious reading, and for publishing), Henderikus Stam (for serious editing), Tim Thornton (for arguing), Jamie Whyte (for laughing, and saying I should do something serious), Steve Woolgar (for motivation when it mattered) and Brian Wynne (for conversation). My debt to the number of people who gave lectures and seminars in Cambridge (1988–1991) is difficult to quantify, however, two lecture series deserve mention: Michael Tanner (on Nietzsche, 1989), and Julian Roberts (on Heidegger, 1990). My warmest thanks go to John Forrester (listening, arguing, publishing): not only did he read several drafts of the book, provide numerous opportunities for discussion, use of his private library, and a variety of other ideas, references and motivations, he was also extremely tolerant of requests to read and comment on other papers and reviews not included here. Perhaps best of all, for the present book, he never suggested that an academic area was 'off limits' – and with that the present book appeared.

I gratefully acknowledge the following sources of financial support: the Cambridge Commonwealth Trust (and members of the Cambridge Commonwealth Society), the British Government for an Overseas Research Student Scheme grant and the University of Adelaide for a George Murray Travel Grant. More generally, I am grateful to the members of the Lancaster University Department of Psychology and the members of the Culture and Communication degree scheme; the staff of the University of Cambridge Library, the Whipple History and Philosophy of Science Library, the Library of the Psychological Laboratory, the Faculty of Social and Political Sciences Library, Cambridge, and the University of Lancaster Library for assistance with references. Finally, thanks to Ziyad Marar, my editor at Sage: he made the completion of the project an enjoyable process.

A.J.S.

# 1
# Introduction

You will have heard it said, I expect, that over-simplification is the occupational disease of philosophers, and in a way one might agree with that. But for the sneaking suspicion that it's their occupation.

(Austin, 1956/1979: 252)

He is a thinker; that means, he knows how to make things simpler than they are.

(Nietzsche, 1887/1974, sec. 189)

The more abstract the truth is that you teach, the more you have to seduce the senses to it.

(Nietzsche, 1886/1966, sec. 128)

## Opening remarks

This book, like any other piece of academic writing, broadly consists of an invitation to regard something in a particular way. The 'object', in this case, is the way some of the referents of psychological discourse have been described and constructed since psychology began to gain its status as a modern discipline of enquiry. There are two fundamental tasks in this endeavour. The first is to show how the rhetoric of psychology assembles its own objects of enquiry using texts. The second is to persuade the reader of the book that the arguments presented here are at least plausible (if not convincing). Within academic writing, statements of aims such as the second one are at least left tacit or, more typically, denied altogether. That is, most academic writing is structured so as to conceal the aim to persuade; more specifically, the rhetoric of most texts is used to convince the reader that it is the object under discussion (in the last resort: Nature) which is the agent of persuasion, and the text is either an adequate or inadequate means of communicating information about that object. However, in this case, no object from Nature is being discussed; there is only the discussion of textual construction. So, the opening sentence above and the statement of the two broad aims are being used here to signal two things: first the sole concentration on rhetoric; and second, the concern with the rhetoric of *this* text. These two concerns can be rather antagonistic, so the discussion of the second one has been kept to a minimum. To enter into it now would be to tell the punch-line without the preceding story; if that happens, the persuasive force of the book will be lost. So, to tell the tale in its most persuasive form, the present account should start with some preliminaries: first the distinction between philosophy and rhetoric (Chapter 1), then some of the methodological background to the book (Chapter 2). When those two things are out of the way, the book will proceed through the use of five case-studies (Chapters 3–5, 7–8), each one contributing to the overall argument, but each one developing it through a discussion of a different debate from the literature of Anglo-American experimental psychology.

Philosophy and rhetoric are usually portrayed as opposites: philosophy being about the world,[1] and rhetoric being about the manipulation of the reader through language. In Ancient Greece, rhetoricians tended to be regarded as dangerous because of the concern that they could make the weaker of two arguments appear the stronger. This tendency persists to this day (and will probably do so in the future; see also Billig, 1987; Simons, 1989; Beer and Martins, 1990; McCloskey, 1990; Peters and Rothenbuhler, 1989). But suppose that a reader (or listener) had no 'certain', or even 'reliable', knowledge of which arguments really *were* the stronger. In that case, the reader would simply be faced with two opposing agents, each claiming that they were the only one talking about the world. Then imagine that they each claimed to be philosophers (or psychologists, or scientists for that matter), and each claimed their opponent to be 'merely' be a rhetorician (or some 'wrong-headed' person trying to convince the reader of the merits of a falsehood). Now imagine that this is not a thought-experiment, but an integral aspect of daily life. That is exactly what has been done here; so, at least for the purposes of this book, everything will be labelled as rhetoric – just to be on the safe side. In any case, because this book is about the way language has been used in a variety of technical debates, no claims are going to be made concerning the world beyond the texts under discussion, and no claims are going to be made about which way psychology *ought* to describe an object. No experiments were performed during the course of this research, and no new ones will be suggested here for the working experimental psychologist. Of course, if one were to be suggesting new or revised descriptions of psychological objects, then performing a set of experiments is still an appropriate way of going about it. But that is just a different sort of task.

If everything presented here is about rhetoric – and it is – then the first step in the analysis should be about how the distinction between philosophy and rhetoric is described and maintained. It will be argued that this distinction is itself a rhetorical one; that people use it to perform actions akin to 'ruling' each other 'out of court'. So, in order to present a whole book about rhetoric, the first thing to be achieved is ruling this major distinction 'out of court' by declaring everything to be rhetorical. Along the way, a number of philosophers will be shown to have done the same thing in the opposite direction: ruling themselves 'in' by arguing that their opponent is merely using rhetoric. Thus the whole book will rule itself 'out' of philosophy, by siding with the rhetorician, and will not claim to be discussing 'the world' at all. Towards the end of the book it will be argued that even this (potentially damaging) manoeuvre does not by any means render the book irrelevant to psychology, science in general, or even the task of constructing a philosophy about the world. The issuing of this promissory note closes the introductory remarks, and turns attention to the first task.

## The distinction between philosophy and rhetoric

Philosophical discourse (and also discourse on theoretical psychology) consists, in part, of a number of rhetorical tools used to construct an issue or problem in a particular way. The list of devices will be familiar to readers of philosophical texts: drawing distinctions, identifying inconsistencies, invoking laws of identity and non-contradiction, giving counter-examples, using Ockham's razor, reductions to aporia, considering thought-experiments, appealing to scientific facts, labelling something as counter-intuitive, distilling formalisms, accusing something of being circular or leading to regress, imposing an 'is versus ought' distinction, labelling something as a 'category mistake', or giving diagrams and models.[2] The list is not definitive, but there should not be a need to multiply examples. These are the tools which, I suggest, would be most readily agreed as being the legitimate stock-in-trade of philosophy. But they are not the only tools. Another group of tools, which for convenience may be divided into two subsets, can be identified. This second group of tools may not be so easily taken as legitimate, but they remain as prevalent: labelling something as being naive, out of date or marginal, building a straw-man, accusations of wilful obscurity, of being too Continental or (conversely) plainly essentialist, assigning a derogatory label such as being fashionable, conservative or reactionary.[3] In this subset, the method is to ridicule an idea with the aim of eliciting laughter from those then more easily identifiable as being sympathetic to the speaker (see also Myers, 1990b). The second subset consists of more specifically *ad hominem* arguments: the most extreme case being to cast doubt on someone's sanity. But milder forms exist, such as identifying a personal idiosyncrasy as the cause of a belief: financial, political or sexual practices being the most frequent.[4] Three points for discussion arise concerning this second group of rhetorical tools.

### Philosophers using rhetoric

Examples of the use of such tools are most readily found in verbal (rather than textual) disputes where affect levels may be rising and the motivation to win the day is at its highest (see the next section). But examples from the

literature are also identifiable: Paul Feyerabend (for example 1984) often
calls on them; David Stove wrote a book about such techniques (1982),
although he claimed that the book was non-philosophical (but see Stove,
1984); Larry Laudan prefers to keeps such tools hidden in footnotes (for
example 1977: 241: 'Foucault has benefited from that curious Anglo-
American view that if a Frenchman talks nonsense it must rest on a
profundity which is too deep for a speaker of English to comprehend');
Russell wrote some into his *History of Western Philosophy* (see the section
on Nietzsche, for example: 'Nietzsche's superman is very like Siegfried,
except that he knows Greek. That may seem odd, but that is not my fault'
(Russell, 1948/1961: 728); Rorty's (1989) quasi-Freudian analysis of
analytic philosophy as being motivated by a hangover from a religious
outlook is another. Or consider Gellner's attack on Chomsky as someone
who, along with others, are 'a dreadful sight . . . shaking their paradigm
like a coxcomb . . . the confident and strutting social scientist' (Gellner,
1982/1985). Further examples may be given where an author complains of
such treatment at one point in a text, only to use the same rhetorical forms
themselves: Kaufmann, for instance, quotes (with disdain) a reference to
Nietzsche as someone who wrote on 'crackpot subjects' (1974: v); later
Kaufmann says (dismissively) that Heidegger's 'bulky' works *on* Nietzsche
are 'important for those who want to understand Heidegger' (1974: 500).

   Still more examples can be found in the texts of people who have also
been on the receiving end: Jerome Bruner recounts Jean Piaget labelling a
question concerning the possibility of enhancing the speed of childhood
development as '*la question américaine*' and thus dismissing it (Bruner,
1983: 141; see also Cohen, 1983: 22; and Chapter 4, pp. 74–77); William
James recounts early objections to pragmatism saying:

> You may not follow me wholly in these lectures; and if you do, you may not
> wholly agree with me. But you will, I know, regard me as serious, and treat my
> effort with respectful consideration. You will probably be surprised to learn,
> then, that Messrs. Schiller's and Dewey's theories have suffered a hailstorm of
> contempt and ridicule. All rationalism has risen against them. In influential
> quarters Mr Schiller, in particular, has been treated like an impudent schoolboy
> who deserves a spanking. (James, 1907/1978: 38)

Here is a master philosopher at work: assuming the kind of audience he
wants and then heaping scorn upon previous audiences who have come in
contact with the kind of ideas he is developing. Such textual devices are
examined further in Chapter 8.

   There is even an interesting analysis of various illegitimate tactics used
by philosophers called 'Proofs that P' (attributed to Hartry Field, see
Appendix). This text gives an account of the common rhetorical forms of a
particular philosopher (sometimes by merely quoting them directly) in a
bid to create humour. More than that, it is not difficult to hear philosophers
quote examples from such texts as a way of dismissing an opponent's
argument. However, *textual* evidence of this is sometimes hard to find (but
see Myers, 1990b, 1991a, 1991b).

The point of reeling off the examples is to show that such tools are certainly being employed in philosophical discourse; other examples will be found in the discussion which follows. It is, of course, possible to claim that such devices should be ruled out of philosophy, but the assumptions and rhetorical structure of making (and maintaining) such a claim is exactly what is being discussed here.

## Maintaining the boundary

The first group of rhetorical tools (drawing distinctions, etc.) was labelled as legitimate because there are some accounts of philosophy which maintain that the second group (attacking a writer's character, etc.) is not to be taken seriously. One *Dictionary of Philosophy*, for example, defines one sense of *ad hominem* argument as fallacious because 'it shows nothing about the truth or falsity of [a] thesis' (Flew, 1979: 5). This is to suggest that something non-philosophical is being attempted whenever one of the second group of tools is in use. Here an exchange from the history of philosophy may be invoked: A.J. Ayer, in his highly influential book *Language, Truth and Logic*, proposed what he called the Principle of Verification:

> The principle of verification is supposed to furnish a criterion by which it can be determined whether or not a sentence is literally meaningful. A simple way to formulate it would be to say that a sentence had a literal meaning if and only if the proposition it expressed was either analytic or empirically verifiable. (Ayer, 1936/1946: 7)

This is an example of an attempt to decide what will or will not count as meaningful: if a sentence was not either analytic or empirical it was to be considered as literally meaningless. It will be assumed here that many sentences which could be included in the second group of rhetorical devices would be meaningless according to this principle. This is a kind of refutation through the use of a form of 'reflexive' argument. As a working definition, this term refers to arguments which are self-referring and, therefore, circular.[5] But the object here is certainly not to refute Ayer, or to use Ayer to refute Austin.

Instead, John Austin will be cast as reacting against the 'positivist' (an abusive term in some contexts) philosophy developed by Ayer. But first some background on J.L. Austin as a philosopher. Isaiah Berlin says of Austin's early career (in the 1930s):

> In private he used no rhetorical tricks of any kind, and displayed an extra-ordinary power of distinguishing what was genuine or interesting in what his collocutor said from what was not – from ideological patter, or nervous confusion, or the like. This was not always so in public: opposition made him combative, and in classes or meetings of societies he plainly wished to emerge victorious. But this did not happen, so far as my own experience goes, in private conversation, at any rate not in the presence of those with whom he felt comfortable and unthreatened. I do not mean to say that he was not by temperament dogmatic: he was. But he argued patiently and courteously, and if

he failed to convince one, returned to the topic over and over again, with new and highly imaginative examples and first-hand arguments which were intellectually exhilarating whether they produced conviction or not. (Berlin, 1980: 105)

Here Berlin develops a characterisation of an 'ideal' theoretician: someone who does not engage in rhetoric (which is being relegated to a collection of 'tricks'). The account of Austin is couched in terms of suffering from a personal failing in not always living up to this ideal. Notice Berlin does not regard returning 'over and over again' as a rhetorical device, in the same way that he does not regard producing 'highly imaginative examples' as one. Further, Berlin is being persuasive in this passage; he is attempting to divide rhetorical tools into 'good' and 'bad'. This account has a prescriptive tone: go thou, do likewise in order to be a good philosopher.

Berlin's essay also provides an account of a debate between Ayer and Austin which is relevant here:

It was, I think, in the course of these skeptical onslaughts, after four or five formulations of the reductionist thesis of pure phenomenalism had been shot down by Austin, that Ayer exclaimed: 'You are like a greyhound who doesn't want to run himself, and bites the other greyhounds, so that they cannot run either.' There was certainly something of this about Austin. (Berlin, 1980: 109)

Applying the 'principle of verification' to Ayer's comment shows it could not be a candidate proposition for having meaning (in Ayer's terms) until it had been translated into 'literal' terms (and it would be possible to do this). But such a strategy misses the point: it makes good rhetorical sense to engage in such an act in order to achieve a certain outcome in the debate. But to view the debate in this way is to ask: 'What is it that philosophers are doing with words?', rather than enquiring about a particular meaning. A short discussion of Austin's ideas will be useful in explaining the theoretical framework used within the present study.

Austin's philosophical works amount to three short volumes, the most famous being *How to Do Things with Words* (1962/1975; originally delivered as the William James Lectures, in Harvard in 1955). Around that time, Austin characterised the recent history of philosophy thus:

First of all people began to say: 'Well, if these things are true or false it ought to be possible to decide which they are, and if we can't decide which they are they aren't any good but are, in short, nonsense'. . . . However . . . we set some limits to the amount of nonsense we talk, or at least the amount we are prepared to admit we talk; and so people began to ask whether after all some of those things which, treated as statements, were in danger of being dismissed as nonsense did after all really set out to be statements at all. Mightn't they perhaps be intended not to report facts but influence people in this way or that, or to let off steam in this way or that? (Austin, 1956/1979: 232–234)

Austin went on to propose a distinction between Constatives and Performatives, claiming that the first group described a state of affairs while the second group were used to perform particular discursive functions (see also Austin, 1962/1975: 1–24). However, he went on to claim that the distinction was not very successful because there appeared to be performative and constative components in every statement. He described his strategy in the following way:

> What we need to do for the case of stating, and by the same token describing and reporting, is to take them a bit off their pedestal, to realise that they are speech-acts no less than other speech-acts that we have been mentioning and talking about as performative. (Austin, 1956/1979: 249–250)

In the Harvard lectures he went on to argue for a new distinction: between locutionary, illocutionary and perlocutionary aspects of speech-acts (Austin, 1962/1975: 94–164). The first is the meaning of what is actually said, the second the function which the speech-act performs, the third the consequences arising from such a function. Austin's claim was that, in saying things, people are always doing things, and that there are no special classes of utterances which are exempt or purely descriptive. That claim will be extended in the present book in considering all of the texts analysed in the case-studies.

The argument here, using Austin as an example, is that any attempt to decide what counts as a legitimate move in philosophy (such as only discussing statements which pass the Principle of Verification) will be at the expense of ignoring some aspects of philosophical discourse; aspects, for example, of the process of persuasion by argument. Although the distinction between 'legitimate' and 'illegitimate' rhetorical devices is a highly useful one for maintaining one particular version of what is referred to as 'philosophy', it is not made or used in the present book because what is at issue is the use of language ('illegitimate' or not). This point may be expanded by making an additional comment on the use of the term 'fallacy'.

In the example from Flew (1979), the description of the term 'fallacy' is being used to fulfil a particular rhetorical end: it suggests that it is possible to decide what means of persuasion will count as philosophical; that certain people have a sense of what is 'genuinely' as opposed to 'merely' persuasive: there is a presupposition here which holds that it is possible (or at least will be possible – of which more in a moment) to know what parts of discourse ought to be persuasive because true, and those parts which ought not because false. Thus, to label an argument as fallacious is to suggest that there are correct and incorrect ways of engaging in philosophical discourse: lots of arguments might be persuasive but only some arguments should be so. If this distinction were to be given diagrammatically, it would involve a Venn diagram consisting of two slightly overlapping circles; one labelled 'philosophy' and the other 'rhetoric'. In such a diagram, the overlap would be labelled as 'bad philosophy'; that is, persuasive for the 'wrong' reasons. It is important to remember that certain types of philosophical discourse presuppose such a distinction without argument. (In the next section I will examine some discussions which argue for this type of distinction.)

One realist or essentialist way of 'cashing out' (to use part of the jargon from such literature) this presupposition would be to correlate truth and success. Thus, those arguments which ought to be persuasive are those which result in certain beliefs which are true, and beliefs which are true are those which are successful according to a particular index: the favourite ones being either the fulfilment of desires, or the level of evolutionary survival value (for references to both approaches to this area, see Papineau, 1988). An *ad hominem* argument, on this account, should only be persuasive if it reliably leads to someone holding beliefs which are true; here assuming that true beliefs are just those things which reliably lead to fulfilment of desires or have survival value, depending on the index of success.

The rhetorical force of this argument comes from our being able to observe the continuation of life in one case and to survey the level of fulfilled desires in the other. These two indices form an interesting rhetorical manoeuvre because they function as a way of shifting the burden of the need to be persuasive: on this account, biology will be the area of enquiry which will furnish persuasive evidence in one case, and psychology will supply the evidence for being persuasive in the second case. Thus, in this particular variety of realist argument, the philosophical debate concerning which arguments ought to be persuasive comes to a temporary (but deliberate) halt, pending further empirical evidence. I want to treat this as an example of a rhetorical move which I will call 'issuing a promissory note'. This move is discussed in detail in Chapters 3 and 8.

Meanwhile, while some of us wait for more empirical evidence, philosophical arguments continue and people continue to be swayed as a result of the influence of a whole battery of discursive tactics.[6] The distinction between legitimate and illegitimate tactics may be regarded, and is regarded in this book, as simply another rhetorical strategy to be employed in the service of a particular interested position.[7]

## *The distinction between philosophy and rhetoric in history*

It is possible to give an historical account of the emergence of attempts to divide the range of rhetorical tools into two groups. A review of the history will show how much rhetorical work goes into maintaining such a distinction. One of the earliest attempts to divide rhetorical tools into two groups is the early Socratic dialogue, the *Protagoras* (Plato, 1956; see also *The Republic*, book X: 607b [1974: 438], in which Plato states that 'we banished poetry from our state'), in which Plato purports to record the exchange between the philosopher Socrates and the sophist of the title.

The dialogue proceeds, after a number of introductions, along question-and-answer lines; the topic under discussion is whether it is possible to teach virtue. At one point, Socrates is acting as questioner and Protagoras is shown not to be doing very well ('Protagoras was beginning to bristle', 333E). The sophist resorts to using a quick speech (of 19 lines) rather than a short answer (of, say, 1 to 3 lines), and the audience bursts into applause. Socrates replies:

> I'm a forgetful sort of man, Protagoras, and if someone speaks at length, I lose the thread of the argument. If I were a little deaf, you would recognise the necessity of raising your voice if you wanted to talk to me; so now since you find me forgetful, cut down your answers and make them shorter if I am to follow you. (Plato, 334D)

This account is given as a matter of fact concerning the biological limitations and requirements of Socrates: Protagoras should recognise the 'necessity' of cutting his answers down. Later, as Protagoras resists having to answer in the manner Socrates prescribes, Socrates gets up from the group and threatens to leave. This rhetorical strategy results in Socrates again becoming dominant in the argument, although, by the end, both parties are highly complimentary towards each other.

Several points may be raised in order to undermine the strength of Socrates' demand. At one point a character (Alcibiades) refers to Socrates' remark about being forgetful as a 'little joke' (336D). Second, Socrates can be shown to have made some very long speeches and a sustained analysis of a poem within the dialogue. Third, the entire dialogue is structured as being an account rendered by Socrates to an unnamed friend: all of the speeches are given as recounted from memory. From this it is possible to conclude that Socrates is shown as having engaged in a rhetorical ploy worthy of a sophist. Having said that, it should be pointed out that Plato goes out of his way to distinguish between philosophy and rhetoric. As Billig notes:

> Like the word 'rhetoric', the word 'sophist' has a derogatory implication. . . . The young Hippocrates, who intended to attach himself to Protagoras as a pupil, admitted, under pressure from Socrates, that he would be ashamed to present himself to his countrymen as a Sophist (Protagoras, 312A). (Billig, 1987: 36)

Plato's characterisation of sophistry develops the derogatory implication and, having said that sophistry is a bad thing, he must ensure that Socrates is seen as involved in some other enterprise: the more respectable discipline of philosophy. However, by analysing the argument in terms of the rhetorical devices used, it may be seen that this attempt fails (see also Enos, 1991).

What the sophists (and poets) were suspected of was shifting people's opinions through the eloquent use of language. Philosophers, on the other hand, often describe their own project as being to persuade on the basis of logic, reason and truth. Thus, as Paul de Man points out, 'metaphors, tropes and figural language in general have been a perennial problem and, at times, a recognised source of embarrassment for philosophical discourse' (1978: 13). As a result, philosophers may be shown to have worked very hard at persuading the reader that their texts are a straightforward description of reality. This claim to be 'speaking plainly' can be undermined by developing an analysis of the rhetoric of philosophical discourse.

Such a project has recently been undertaken by a number of people (see Nehamas, 1985; Ree, 1988, and the bibliographical essay in Ree, 1987). Paul de Man (1978), for example, gives accounts of the rhetoric used by Locke, Kant and Condillac. Jonathan Ree (1987), having analysed some of the texts of Descartes, Hegel, Bentham, Mill, Kierkegaard and others, says at one point:

> Philosophy, it is commonly supposed, is not just one intellectual speciality amongst others. . . . It is the attempt (possibly doomed to fail) to appreciate the serious, primordial truths, without looking over your shoulder at anyone else, and with no vanity, compromise or circumlocution. . . . But in that case, it is disconcerting that the philosophical canon should contain a curious collection of elaborate literary devices which have more to do with telling tales than with stating facts, and which keep author, narrators and characters endlessly circling each other, seemingly oblivious to their obligation to any ultimate truth. The philosophical classics look back at their readers with the hesitant and ironic smile of a story-teller, nervously trying to engage our interest, rather than with the stern indifference of someone who knows it all already. (Ree, 1987: 96)

A further example may be taken from David Hume. In this case, the extract has been taken from the (at first anonymous; see Introduction by Macnabb in Hume, 1739/1962: 31–36) 'Abstract' which Hume (probably) published in an attempt to promote *A Treatise of Human Nature* (Hume, 1739/1962):

> He [the author of *A Treatise*] proposes to anatomize [sic] human nature in a regular manner, and promises to draw no conclusions but where he is authorized by experience. He talks with contempt of hypotheses; and insinuates that such of our countrymen as have banished them [hypotheses] from moral philosophy, have done more single service to the world, than *my Lord Bacon*, whom he considers as the father of experimental physics. He mentions, on this occasion, *Mr Lock, my Lord Shaftesbury, Dr Mandeville, Mr Hutchison, Dr Butler*, who, though they differ in many points among themselves, seem all to agree in founding their accurate disquisitions of human nature entirely upon experience. (in Hume, 1739/1962, emphasis original)

The quotation above poses a number of problems of interpretation. Scholars of Hume's work have noted the difficulty in understanding his use of irony (in Hume's *Dialogues Concerning Natural Religion*, for example; see Aiken's Introduction to Hume, 1779/1948: ix) which may be important here. For instance, having noted that Mr Lock et al. all agree upon the use of 'experience' as a method for 'authorizing' conclusions, Hume also notes that their various conclusions 'differ in many points'. It may be that Hume is suggesting that 'experience' is not a very reliable 'authority'; or, it may be that Hume is ironically referring to the variety of conclusions (previous to his own) in order to reduce the importance of texts by Mr Lock et al. If the former is the 'correct' interpretation, then doubts may be cast concerning the extent to which Hume's work has 'banished' hypotheses (for it may be asked how it is possible to have 'unreliable' authority as a source of validity, without using the term 'hypothesis' to describe the conclusions which result from it). However, if the latter is the 'correct' interpretation, it does at least allow Hume's text to be seen as a way of removing the inconsistencies between the texts of previous writers. Further, if the majority of the conclusions gleaned from Mr Lock et al. are taken to be based on experience, and therefore 'authoritative', what need is there for Hume's own text? Thus, irony may play a part in the interpretation of the extract from Hume.

The second difficulty is simply the status of the author: Hume's name did not appear on the 'Abstract'. Thus, if Hume was in fact the author, he may be seen as having employed the rhetorical conceit of adopting anonymity. There is an ambiguity in the extract: it is not clear whether all 'hypotheses' are being regarded with 'contempt', or just those contained in 'moral philosophy'. If the former is assumed, then one consequence of such a rhetorical move has been that many 'hypotheses' have been put forward concerning the name of the author (just as there has been much debate on which rhetorical character in the *Dialogues* corresponds to the views of Hume). Had Hume known that such rhetoric would see the creation of yet more hypotheses (and there is some reason to suppose he was aware of such possibilities), he would have been simultaneously 'banishing' and promoting the existence of the 'hypothesis'. Again, Hume's use of rhetoric raises questions concerning the extent to which a reader should take Hume's text 'literally'.

The third point is specific to the attack on the term 'hypotheses': in the quotation, 'experience' is being promoted at the expense of using 'hypotheses', and 'hypotheses', unlike 'experience', depend (at least in this context) on words. Thus, Hume argues against persuasion through words, and in favour of persuasion through the 'authority of experience'. At the same time, however, such an argument depends on words (and therefore, on rhetoric) in order to make such an argument persuasive.

These three points suggest that Hume was an ingenious manipulator of words. At the same time, the quotation (and, indeed, the *Treatise* as a whole) argues for the authority of 'experience' alone. Such a conclusion should reinforce the quotation from Ree (1987), whilst making a related point: the more carefully and strongly worded the argument against rhetoric, the more obviously the argument becomes a candidate for its own critique.

The final example for the present section is taken from Bertrand Russell's methodological essay, 'On Scientific Method in Philosophy' (1917/1986: 96–120). He discusses what ought to be considered as philosophy and (not surprisingly; see also Ramsey, 1925/1990; Quine, 1991) Russell concludes that philosophy should become 'indistinguishable from logic' (1917/1986: 109). This raises the reflexive problem of the topic of Russell's own essay: is it philosophical? Russell could have argued that it was 'about' philosophy rather than philosophy *per se*. But this would merely create the need to distinguish between 'meta-philosophy' and rhetoric. In any case, Russell continues to outline the problems which philosophy should be addressing:

> In some problems, for example, the analysis of space and time, the nature of perception, or the theory of judgment, the discovery of the logical form of the facts involved is the hardest part of the work and the part whose performance has been most lacking hitherto. It is chiefly for want of the right logical hypothesis that such problems have hitherto been treated in such an unsatisfactory manner, and have given rise to those contradictions or antinomies in which the enemies of reason among philosophers have at all times delighted. (Russell, 1917/1986: 109–110)

The danger for a book such as the present one is that its author could (objectively) be an 'enemy of reason' without realising it. But the criterion being given by Russell is whether one is treating a problem in a manner satisfactory to Russell. Putting this to one side, Russell saw a need to define what ought to be considered as philosophy, and could see that some philosophers were not writing philosophy within the boundaries Russell was giving in his essay. (Perhaps it is surprising that he did not label the 'enemies' as sophists.) Again, the object is to show the amount of rhetorical work that has been put into drawing the line between what will or will not count as philosophy.

It has been argued here that any attempt to draw a distinction between philosophy and rhetoric is itself a rhetorical act. Further, it is argued that there is, therefore, no firm foundation from which to decide what should or should not be persuasive, as opposed to being 'philosophical', and no ahistorical way to measure rhetorical power. Whether certain arguments were persuasive is a matter to be decided on the basis of historical accounts. It could be shown, for example, that particular philosophical arguments were persuasive in delineating what counts as a philosophical argument (see Ree, 1987, for a general discussion). That does not mean that those arguments were 'purely philosophical'; nor does it mean that it is possible to decide what will always be a 'good' (philosophical) or a 'bad' (rhetorical) argument. Discerning the level of persuasive force, therefore, is a matter to be evaluated and re-evaluated in different contexts.

I have placed this argument at the beginning of the book for a reason which I shall now spell out. The case-studies which follow examine particular theoretical debates within the psychological literature. They all focus on the way language has been used to fulfil certain rhetorical functions. Some of them focus more closely on the way particular scientific metaphors have been used within such debates. The case-studies, then, examine a wide range of rhetorical devices as they have been used in specific contexts. For methodological reasons, no attempt has been made to decide which side of an argument is the more persuasive, or the more empirically true. There will be no attempt to privilege one type of rhetorical device over another. This introductory argument has been used to suggest that a possible reader should approach the following material in the same way. Not to do so would be to deny the general argument in this section, and that would make reading the remainder of the book a futile exercise. Within the bounds of this book there is no distinction between rhetoric and 'mere rhetoric': everything is rhetoric.[8]

**The rhetoric of anti-rhetoric**

The present chapter has been concerned with the distinction between 'philosophy' and 'rhetoric' as it relates to the discipline of philosophy. However, there is also the possibility, as Beer and Martins (1990: 173) observe, that any discussion of 'rhetoric' and 'science' (rather than philosophy) may make some feel uneasy or even angry (see also McCloskey, 1990). The connection between rhetoric and science, and more particularly psychology, is the topic for discussion in the remainder of the chapter. The definition of 'psychology' will be discussed in the next section.

The connection between rhetoric and science will be treated here as a sub-section of the tradition of discourse in which 'persuasion' (rhetoric) is always opposed to 'knowledge'; and 'science' will be used here as a referent for fields of intellectual enquiry which have, historically, been demarcated from other academic disciplinary pursuits (history, philosophy and so on; see Fuller, 1991). This strong tradition, dating back to the works of Plato, was examined in the last section, and has been labelled by Finocchiaro as promoting a 'rhetoric of anti-rhetoric' (1990: 179). Such rhetoric may be observed most often when scientists discuss their own textual or discursive practices (as opposed to others which are rendered more problematic; see Gilbert and Mulkay, 1984, for a discussion). The object of this section is to examine such rhetoric as it relates to examinations of science (such as the present book).

Put in its most basic form, the rhetoric of anti-rhetoric suggests that any examination of rhetoric as a topic in its own right can only serve to degrade the status of the science being analysed. Borrowing from Nietzsche, the result may be expressed in the following way:

> To the disappointed of philosophy. If you have hitherto believed that life was one of the highest value and now see yourself disappointed, do you at once have to reduce it to the lowest possible price? (Nietzsche, 1879/1986: 215)

If one substitutes 'science' or 'psychology' for 'life' in the quotation above, one reads an account of one of the largest dangers in discussions of rhetoric and metaphor. It may appear all too easily as if such discussions are only (or merely) critical or destructive.

When Alan Gross's book *The Rhetoric of Science* (1990) was reviewed in the *Times Literary Supplement*, it was strongly criticised for claiming that rhetoric was all there was; was all that influenced the pursuit of research goals.[9] Such a conclusion will be resisted in the present book. What Gross claimed (despite what the reviewer suggested) was that the use of language was his only interest in writing the book (1990, 1991); that the ontological status of the theories he examined were simply beyond his jurisdiction. The same claim will hold for the remainder of the book.

The view that propositions in science should not rely on words alone is nicely captured by the motto of the Royal Society: *Nullius in verba* (literally: 'nothing by the mere authority of words').[10] The rhetorical force of such a phrase in the history of science (in both senses) can hardly be underestimated. And yet the implication of the phrase, that something could be taken on merely verbal grounds, has hardly been broached.[11] Perhaps ironically, the verbal force of such a phrase has excluded attempts to call it into question.

In many ways the study of scientific rhetoric is in its infancy, so claims to its overall significance to studies of science, or even to the processes of science itself, are at best premature. Moreover, any attempt to try to gauge the match between the persuasiveness of a given text and the ontological entities to which it purports to refer is fraught with methodological difficulties (see also Star, 1989: 2); difficulties which are probably insurmountable. Such an attempt would, in any case, be very different from the one presented here, and such a difference could not be overstated.

Having made a number of claims concerning what the study of scientific rhetoric involves (and does not involve), some examples from texts in the history of psychology will serve to show what rhetorical devices have been employed in the task of placing a distance between 'good science' and 'mere words'.

Fish notes (with heavy irony) the claim made by James Strachey (one of Freud's English translators) that Freud was 'never rhetorical' (Fish, 1988: 184). Similarly, Claparède introduced an early work of Jean Piaget with the claim that Piaget's 'only aim in collecting, recording, and cataloguing . . . different types of behaviour is to see the assembled material in a clearer light. . . . Our author has a special talent for letting the material speak for itself, or rather for hearing it speak for itself' (in Preface to Piaget, 1926/1959: xv). Such rhetoric stresses the role of objects of analysis in deciding which descriptions are to be assigned; at the same time it serves to diminish the role and practice of constructing a particular text. The 'facts' are claimed to simply 'speak for themselves'.

A more detailed example may be taken from Karl Lashley, who introduced an early experimental report of his own by suggesting that the 'inferences drawn from the experiments seem to be for the most part clearly indicated. Their uncertainty lies rather in the lack of complete statistical reliability of the data and in the limited number of situations studied' (Lashley, 1929/1963: xviii). Here, the stress on the role of inference (a set of rules which somehow 'govern' or 'dictate' the conclusion which may be taken from observations or premises) reduces the role Lashley played in drawing the inference. Conclusions are thus a matter of mechanical procedure, rather than persuasion. Further, the lack of 'complete statistical reliability' is made responsible for any uncertainty remaining about the status of such inferences. Again, the role of the author in constructing the descriptions made within the text is rhetorically diminished.[12] In this case, the steps involved in making an inference are claimed to be so obvious that the application of a set of rules for reasoning was sufficient for the construction of Lashley's text.

One further example will serve as an illustration of the rhetoric of anti-rhetoric. In this case, however, it involves a direct discussion of the topic of rhetoric and the process of writing a psychological text. It is taken from the short autobiography B.F. Skinner published in 1967 (that is, before such texts as *Beyond Freedom and Dignity*, 1971, but after his novel *Walden Two*, 1948/1976):

> I avoid rhetorical devices which give unwarranted plausibility to an argument (and I sometimes reassure myself by making lists of the devices used by others). I avoid the unwarranted prestige conferred by mathematics, even, I am afraid, when mathematics would be helpful. I do not spin impressive physiological theories from my data, as I easily could do. I never convert an exploratory experiment into an experimentum crusis by inventing a hypothesis after the fact. I write and rewrite a paper until, so far as possible, it says exactly what I have to say. (Skinner, 1967: 407)

In this passage, Skinner tries to persuade the reader that his texts are free of rhetorical devices, and that, in contrast, other people endeavour to give their arguments 'unwarranted prestige'. Part of this process of persuasion is the list of declarative terms ('I avoid' [twicc], 'I do not', 'I nevei . . .' and so on). Further, Skinner's suggestion that it was possible to employ the rhetorical devices (in Skinner's account: mathematics, physiology, crucial experiments) used by others helps to create an account of his own texts as 'anti-rhetorical'. Nevertheless, this passage is itself a rhetorical construction aimed at persuading the reader to read (or to continue reading) Skinner in a particular way. The same can be said of all such texts which claim to be avoiding, and exhorting others to avoid, the use of rhetoric (see also Rose, 1985: 1–3).

The reader of a psychological text may come to form a judgement about the truth of the claim made within a text, but the reader only does so as a function of the degree to which they find the text persuasive. Or, put more bluntly: the 'facts' do not simply 'speak for themselves'; they are presented in a particular form, in a given style, and using a specific number of 'descriptions' of the 'evidence' on which the arguments contained in the text are based. Each of these aspects of a text is rhetorical. So, in studying the rhetoric of science it is necessary to regard all discourse as rhetorical, and not to try to sort it into the 'merely rhetorical' and the 'true'. The outcome of this form of enquiry will consist of some suggestions concerning the ways in which discourse is (or has been) organised to achieve particular rhetorical functions. That is, it should add to an understanding of how scientific texts persuade(d) the reader.

**What is this thing called psychology?**

The next chapter is devoted to a discussion of methodological issues. But before the present chapter is closed, several points should be raised concerning the rhetoric employed in the present study. First, because the book maintains that 'everything is rhetoric',[13] the use of authoritative quotations has been avoided, especially in dealing with the case-study material. No particular accounts of memory, development, emotion, intelligence, consciousness or the mind are being promoted within the book. Thus, extracts from various texts have not been employed with any interest in the closure of a particular debate within psychology. In any case, such a rhetorical manoeuvre may be so 'well worn' as to have almost lost the rhetorical force once accorded to it within the humanities (although the sciences are a different matter).

Second, I have found no successful way of mitigating the possible charge of using an eclectic methodology, other than claiming that the study of the rhetoric of psychology is relatively novel (or recent).[14] As a result, the present book faces a potential rhetorical difficulty: the aim is to discuss the 'form' and 'function' of the rhetoric employed in psychological texts, whilst claiming (in a manner consistent with studies described as 'ethnomethodology') that descriptions of 'psychology', and descriptions of objects in psychological texts, vary with each description. However, this potential inconsistency need not be regarded as a dramatic one. The use of the terms 'form' and 'function' does not necessarily imply a universal conception of either, and the body of the following text should work against giving such an 'essentialist' impression.[15] Rather, because the present study is a constructive (rather than simply critical) one, such 'functionalist' terms are employed throughout the text in order to suggest that the study of scientific rhetoric itself has an object of enquiry. But such an object remains a contingent (historically specific) entity (and not some possibly Platonic universal or 'natural kind').

Third, a point on the 'archive' of psychological texts used as a 'data base' throughout the book. The object of the study is neither to endorse nor call into question the existence of the field of enquiry 'psychology' as it is described by 'psychologists'. That, in both cases (confirmation or denial), would simply be a different kind of study. Instead, the term 'psychology' will be used throughout to refer to a field of enquiry or 'discipline', which has been described (for example Smith, 1988; Leary, 1987, 1990a; Koch and Leary, 1985) as existing from around 1880. Further, texts published after that time which refer to 'psychology' (or contain descriptions in which 'psychology' is used in a self-referring manner), will be assumed to be 'psychological texts'. That is, for the purposes of the present study, 'psychology' is held to be constituted by various texts (rather than by the position of Psychology Departments in various universities, or through the existence of professional organisations, or through the existence of people who refer to themselves as 'psychologists').[16]

## Notes

1. 'Welcome to the Notes. . . . Quite a lot will be going on here and it would be a shame to miss it all' (Ashmore, 1989: 227, Note 1). 'Philosophy' is defined throughout the book as the activities of a list of authors normally referred to by the reading public as 'philosophers' (see Roberts, 1988: 3–5; Rorty, 1991b: 122). Definitions of 'the sciences' and 'psychological texts' will be made later in the present chapter.

2. Discussions of 'is versus ought' come from Hume (e.g. 1739/1962); discussions of 'category mistakes' come from Ryle (1949/1973). For an attack on 'is versus ought' (and much else), see Stretton (1987: 167–174).

3. Another potentially unacceptable tool in philosophy seems to be the practice of hiding self-damaging material in the Notes to an essay. That will not be the practice here, however this seems to work most successfully where humour can be invoked. Consider the following from Daniel Dennett:

> A defender of Skinner, in response to this sentence [in a paper called 'Skinner skinned'], sought to explain and justify this curious behavior of Skinner's by suggesting that the reason Skinner overlooked this crucial vacillation is that he had no idea he was conducting any such argument. . . . If so, I've *vastly overestimated* Skinner. However, if I understand the principles of the new hermeneutics (*a dubious antecedent!*), I am entitled to ignore refractory biographical details like these and press ahead with my interpretation of the texts' (1979: 329, Note 34, emphasis mine).

4. Any similarity between this division of rhetorical tools and Gilbert and Mulkay's (1984) distinction between 'empiricist' and 'contingent' repertoires is intentional. The relevant sociology literature is discussed in Chapter 2.

5. Reflexivity is frequently defined in this way (see Ashmore, 1989; Woolgar, 1988a), where the terms 'self-reflexive' and 'self-referring' are considered to be interchangeable. However, this need not always be the case. Consider the two sentences: (1) If this sentence is true, then it is false, and (2) All Cretans are liars (said by a Cretan). What these sentences have in common is that they are circular. But a distinction between forms of circularity may be usefully forged if (1) is considered merely self-referring, whereas (2) is considered self-reflexive. The difference, on this account, is that (1) is a sentence which, in grammatical terms, is sealed in a self-referring structure. On the other hand (2) is only known to be self-reflexive given a knowledge of the subject uttering the sentence. The difficulty to be overcome by this distinction is that 'self' may refer to either the sentence (on the page) or the agent uttering it. In the sciences (in particular), self-referring sentences are not likely to be common. But potentially self-reflexive sentences are likely to be frequent and subtle. Consider the prototype: 'scientists/philosophers frequently engage in rhetoric and that is deplorable', said by a scientist/philosopher. This is not obviously self-referring (as a sentence), but can be made to be self-reflexive by stressing its subjectivity. This is exactly the manoeuvre employed later in the present chapter. Finally, it should be noted that the distinction between the two different forms of reflexive propositions is not made in texts such as that of Bradley and Swartz (1979: 341), although the claim in that case is made to give a full definition of reflexivity.

6. The 'meanwhile' comment here is being used as a comic or ironic dismissal. I am aware that this has some rhetorical force.

7. Evidence supporting a distinction between philosophy and rhetoric in the literature is fairly easy to come by, and more of it will be covered in this chapter. In *The Development of Logic*, Kneale and Kneale say: Eubulides 'invented the Liar [paradox] and several other well-known sophisms which . . . are of considerable logical interest' (1962/1984: 16). Their argument seems to be that philosophers (or at least that sub-variety, logicians) should sometimes dirty their hands by examining Sophistic rhetoric. That is, 'rhetoric' is held to be something in which the philosopher/logician should not normally engage.

8. It could legitimately be claimed that the manoeuvre being used here is blatant 'side-stepping'. It is. There are two reasons for this. First, I think it is important to side-step some issues which otherwise tend to get bogged down in debating legitimate but well-worn dichotomies (realism versus anti-realism, physical versus social construction, objective versus relativist accounts of truth and so on). This amounts to another promissory note: if one agrees to side-step certain issues, other important conclusions will be forthcoming. In Chapter 3, I will claim that promissory notes are crucial for a research project to continue; without them, an academic endeavour loses much rhetorical force. Second, the term 'side-stepping', in any case, only maintains its own rhetorical force if one assumes that certain objective problems and issues exist, and that one must come to grips with any set of them in order to say anything

meaningful on the topic at hand. That is, it incorporates a metaphor (such as that used by Edwin Boring, 1963: 5, viz. 'The seats of the train of progress all face backwards . . .') of intellectual progress as a train following a certain (pre-existing) track. The implication, of course, is that were one to side-step, one would derail the train. Such an assumption is to be resisted. One way of doing this would be to pay attention to ethnological studies of science (Lynch, 1985, for example) which make a strong case for the claim that (continuing the metaphor), the track of science is constantly being laid down – even to the point of laying the rails on which the engine sits. Other sociological studies of science which have investigated areas of controversy (Collins, 1985, for example), have shown that, even if the tracks were already laid (something Collins would deny), the choice concerning which one to follow is highly problematic. For an analysis of the rhetoric of conflicting views in science, see Gilbert and Mulkay (1984) which shows that it is always the views of the researcher doing the talking which are 'on the right track'; for an analysis of rhetorical accounts of scientific 'discovery', see Woolgar (1976) which shows that researchers are able to call on a large variety of rhetorical devices to support the claim that finding the 'right track' is simply a matter ot time, and 'enginuity' (my candidate for the world's most convoluted pun).

9.  For the original review of Gross (1990), see Durant (1991a). For replies and responses, see Weatherall (1991), Hirschon (1991), Gross (1991), Lawrence and Shapin (1991) and Durant (1991b). After the reply from the reviewer, the correspondence ceased (enforced rhetorical closure). Durant (1991b) did not modify his original points of criticism concerning the text by Gross (1990).

10.  The motto comes from a line in Horace's *Epistles* (I,1, line 14); it is fully translated as: 'Not under the bond to abide by any master's authority' (Stimson, 1949: 35, Note 2). This phrase is sometimes (unfortunately) translated as 'nothing by mere authority' (Flew, 1979: 48). Both of these would seem to lose the concentration on the power of words. 'Authority' could, for example, come from physical reality, divine inspiration or almost anything else. Nevertheless, the assumption that 'mere authority' could only be verbal is an interesting one. The phrase is said to encapsulate the views of Robert Boyle, a founder member of the Royal Society. For analyses of Boyle's rhetoric, see Dear (1985), Shapin and Schaffer (1985) and Shapin (1984).

11.  Such a claim needs qualification. Some writers have suggested that the study of rhetoric has reached a stage in which it is possible to claim: 'we have begun to unravel the insidious power of discourse to generate its own forms of truth, to shape the future of human bodies, not through genetics, but through politics. . . . In a word, we have become postmodernists' (Keller, 1991). Keller may perhaps intend to address an audience only made up of those interested in rhetoric. However, the present book does not include the use of the term 'postmodernist', and it should not be assumed that the book ought to be described in that way. Nor should it be assumed that the present book propounds the claim that scientific discourse has any (inherent) 'insidious power' (see also Foucault, 1975/1977: 194; Soyland, 1994a). Some points which will be raised in Chapter 6 bear on (at least some brand of) postmodernism.

12.  The object of the present section is not to suggest that the role of the author is always diminished by every author, in every text. For example, Konrad Lorenz introduced one of his own texts with the claim that: 'My book would be really convincing if the reader reached the same conclusion as myself solely on the basis of the facts which I set before him. But . . . I cannot expect him [sic] to follow such a thorny path . . .' (1963/1966: xi–xii). However, it should be noted that even this form of rhetoric imposes a distinction between 'the facts' on one side, and the 'conclusion' on the other. Thus, the *descriptions* which Lorenz offers of the 'facts' are immune from rhetorical construction on his account – such a division is to be resisted.

13.  'Everything' is an important qualifier. It has already been noted that, within the context of this book, the claim that 'everything is rhetoric' does not entail that the claim 'ontology is nothing' should be 'applied' beyond the context of the book. Further, this study only presents an examination of words. However, other studies have given accounts of the rhetoric of visual representation (e.g. Gilbert and Mulkay, 1984; Myers, 1988, 1990a; Jordanova, 1989), the

rhetoric of statistics (Gigerenzer and Murray, 1987; Gephart, 1988; Signorile, 1989), and the textual representation of odours (Corbin, 1982/1986). (Whilst Corbin deals with texts and not odours, his account is worth citing here as few studies have attempted such a project.)

14. This mitigating claim was used in the previous section in the following sequence: studies of rhetoric are not concerned with ontology, the claim that science is never only concerned with words has had a powerful rhetorical effect (and one which continues; see references cited earlier), discussions of ontology and rhetoric are methodologically difficult, and the significance of studies of scientific rhetoric are difficult to consider because such studies are 'in a stage of infancy'. The metaphorical use of the term 'infancy' in this case is being used to persuade the reader that such studies should be allowed to 'grow'. A discussion of such metaphors of 'development' (also a metaphor), as they have been used in psychological texts, is given in Chapter 4. Second, the present Note is highly reflexive: discussions of such 'reflexivity' are made throughout the book – in small doses.

15. That such terms might refer to 'universal' entities (or, at least, to entities which were ahistorical or transcultural) was a possibility explored by researchers of/in 'structural anthropology'. For an introductory account of this area, see Leach (1976). For an important consideration of such issues and case-studies, see Lévi-Strauss (1958/1967). This form of 'structuralist' (or, sometimes, 'functionalist') approach, and that of the 'ethnomethodologists', is criticised in Potter and Wetherell (1987: 9–31) and Papineau (1978: 95–107). Unfortunately, the terms 'structuralist' and 'post-structuralist' can be difficult to define consistently, partly as a result of inconsistencies in secondary (and historical) accounts (between texts such as Manicas, 1987, Rorty, 1989, Ricoeur, 1978, and others). Sartre, for example, has, on occasion, been labelled either a 'structuralist' or an 'anti-structuralist'. As a result, the present study will attempt to label particular writers as little as possible.

16. The methodological problem which the present section attempts to avoid may be seen as follows. The definition of 'psychology' has been a matter of dispute at least since the appearance of university departments of Psychology. Such a dispute is an ongoing one (e.g. Staats, 1983; McGovern et al., 1991). James (1890/1950) defined psychology as 'the science of mental life'. It is sometimes maintained (e.g. Boring, 1933/1963, 1950) that this definition was undermined with the rise of behaviourism (around 1913 with the publication of a single paper by J.B. Watson), or that behaviourism became 'the "normal science" of psychology' (Buckley, 1989: ix). Some writers have developed philosophical critiques of psychology whilst assuming it is largely behaviouristic (e.g. Shotter, 1975; Eacker, 1983). Other writers have suggested that psychology has been defined using one of these two definitions, but not both; that only recent developments in psychology have suggested a return to the Jamesian definition (Valentine, 1991); or even that behaviouristic accounts of psychology have now been made part of the publication process of psychological texts (e.g. Bazerman, 1988: 257–277). However, other psychological texts from the period after 1913 noted such a redefinition in passing, before dismissing it (e.g. Spearman, 1923: 23–32), or simply gave an account of psychology without noting behaviourist definitions at all (e.g. Burt, 1923). Similar evidence has led some historians to argue against the importance of the behaviourist definition (e.g. Rose, 1985: 1–10) for some sections of 'psychology' (the 'mental testing movement'), while others produce historical accounts without mentioning changes in the continuity of definitions (e.g. Chapman, 1988). If other areas of 'psychology' are examined, the simple 'after Watson' account may be undermined further. For example, some texts noted the existence of 'Watson's language' (Murphy et al., 1931/1937 – social psychology), employed it for a short section, then passed on to other forms of description; L.S. Vygotsky (1896–1934) published work on thought and development, citing Watson's work, but dismissing it on theoretical grounds (Vygotsky, 1978: 58–60); Kellogg and Kellogg (1933) produced a comparative account of humans and primates without using behaviourist terms or definitions; and Piaget's account of thinking and language (e.g. 1926/1959) is, if not 'anti-behaviourist', given without reference to 'psychology after Watson'. Later psychological texts attempted to return to the definition proposed by James (e.g. Miller, 1962/1966 – cognitive psychology); developed anti-behaviourist accounts (e.g. Bruner, 1962/1979: esp. 131–148) (Miller and Bruner were colleagues of Skinner at Harvard); or simply gave an alternative definition (e.g. Luria, 1973/

1984: 16 – neuropsychology). Further, not all academic departments producing 'psychological texts' have the title 'Department of Psychology' (the department at MIT, for example, is a 'Department of Behavioural and Brain Sciences'), and not all 'psychologists' have been affiliated with departments of psychology (Cyril Burt, for example, was employed to carry out research by the London County Council; see Chapter 7). Such a list of examples should indicate that giving a non-textual definition of 'psychology', or of the archive of 'psychological texts', is at least highly problematic.

# 2

# Metaphor, Rhetoric and Analysis

When a human being resists his whole age and stops it at the gate to demand an accounting, this *must* have influence.

(Nietzsche, 1887/1974, sec. 156)

We should restrict ourselves to questions like 'Does our use of these words get in the way of our use of those words?' This is a question about whether our use of tools is inefficient or not, not a question about whether our beliefs are contradictory.

(Rorty, 1989: 12)

## Science and literature

Begin with a particular problem: what does it take to persuade someone of a particular view? This is a question that may be tackled in any number of ways. If the object was to persuade someone of something in the future, one would want to know about the components which go to make up a persuasive case; one could then shape a collection of information so as to ensure that a number of people were, in the end, persuaded. But to pursue the question in this manner would be to engage in the practices of psychology: communication would become the means through which persuasion was achieved, discourse would be seen as a strategy for attaining the desired goal, and then questions of the level of effectiveness of discourse would become paramount. That is not what is required here: this is not a book relevant to the psychology of advertising (or, for that matter, to the stylistics of scientific writing; but see Bazerman, 1988); I make no claims concerning prescriptions for effective future discourse. But what if the object was to be able to claim that a particular view ought to be persuasive? In that case the truth of a particular view would need to be defended from counter-attack: this is the business of philosophy, and of science. This way of tackling the question was ruled out in the last chapter: the purported 'truth' of a particular view will not be used to explain why it should be persuasive.

Two other general alternatives remain: the historical and the sociological ways of tackling the question. People have been persuaded of particular views in the past, and they are persuaded of particular views in the present. How does such a thing happen? Any number of alternatives may be pursued: institutional practices, social networks, historical and economic 'forces'. Each of these deserves consideration but, supposing such influences exist, how are they transferred from one individual to the next? At least one major method involves the comprehension of discourse, of the written word: a form of persuasion, used in an attempt to bring about a change in a reader. Texts perform actions: they encourage people to believe certain things, to behave in certain ways. One of the claims of the present book is that detailed analyses of texts serve to augment both historical and sociological approaches; the analysis of text cannot stand apart from either history or sociology, but it should deliver some understanding of persuasion through writing.

It will be useful to review some recent methodological developments in a number of disciplines to indicate the framework within which the present analysis is situated. For a book as methodologically eclectic as the present one, this is not such an easy task to perform because it involves the construction of a 'disciplinary history' for a methodological orientation in its infancy (but see Simons, 1989; Gross, 1990; Myers, 1990a). Moreover, the citation here of any particular text is likely to suggest a kind of 'master discipline' from which all others may be attacked. That is not the intention. Nevertheless, some account must be given of the background to the present approach.

Casting the present book in the present way could render all sorts of disciplinary methods as relevant. The entire book is given in historical terms, yet it incorporates aspects of sociolinguistics, presuppositions are teased out in a manner akin to both philosophy and ethnomethodology, texts are placed in a sociological context although they are described largely in their own terms, and texts are described in terms of being forms of literature, yet none of the objects described in such texts are treated as if they were fictional. The present chapter, then, fulfils the role of making such an approach seem legitimate. This will be done by examining some methodological arguments, regardless of their disciplinary affiliations.

Researchers in the sociology of scientific knowledge, for example, have often been interested in controversies in science because it has been assumed that disagreements over new knowledge-claims will expose the ways in which such claims come to be established (see, for example, Collins, 1985). The sociologists observe such disputes in order to develop their own account (as opposed to giving a critical examination of the construction of the accounts produced by the scientists) of the various factors which influence the outcome of debates in science. Such an approach has yielded a variety of conclusions (for a summary, see Woolgar, 1988a), but not without a lot of methodological disputes; for example, what status should the words of a scientist have for the analyst? As Gilbert and Mulkay (1984) examined this issue, a dilemma came about in the following way:

> As we travelled, in train compartments and airport departure lounges, and especially in Howard Johnson motel rooms, we discussed together what we were hearing [in interviews], and realized that although we were being given quite

different accounts of what 'really was happening' by different interviewees, they all seemed to be plausible and, indeed, convincing. (Gilbert and Mulkay, 1984: vii)

The dilemma was this: should they ignore the variability of the accounts they heard in order to generate their own, sociologically informed, account of what 'really happened' (as was the case in previous research in the sociology of knowledge;[1] see Gilbert and Mulkay, 1984: 2)? Or should they attempt to treat such variability as the site of investigation? They chose the second option and described the aim of their version of 'discourse analysis' as focusing on the ways 'accounts are organized to portray . . . actions and beliefs in contextually appropriate ways' (Gilbert and Mulkay, 1984: 14). As a result they turned away from attempting to get 'beyond' the words used in the interviews they conducted, and started to become interested in the words themselves:

> Discourse analysis, then, is the attempt to identify and describe the regularities in the methods used by participants as they construct the discourse through which they establish the character of their actions and beliefs in the course of interaction. (Gilbert and Mulkay, 1984: 14)

The result of this methodological change was that the results they produced were purely concerned with talk, and this is the common, if not mandatory, methodological initiative to be examined here. The present study is broadly consistent with that of Gilbert and Mulkay (1984; but see criticisms in Myers, 1990a): discourse is the site of investigation (see also Potter and Wetherell, 1987; Wooffitt, 1992; Soyland, 1991a, 1994a, forthcoming b).

There has also been an increase in works dedicated to the examination of philosophical texts in terms of trying to understand what the author of the text was attempting to achieve. In such works similarities are frequently drawn with Wittgenstein's descriptions of 'language-games' (with particular rules and assumptions), or with Austin's emphasis on language as a functional process, one in which saying/writing something is also construed as performing an action (doing something). Richard Rorty (1980, 1989, 1991a, 1991b) has promoted interest in such a project, and he has also published more general discussions of 'philosophy as a kind of writing' (see Rorty, 1982). But here I am more concerned with mentioning works which have concentrated on an examination of particular philosophical texts. Alexander Nehamas (1985), for example, examines Nietzsche's works: the general argument shows how an understanding of Nietzsche's style (that is, the rhetoric and construction of Nietzsche's texts) contributes to an understanding of Nietzsche's substantive (perhaps metaphysical) points; that knowing where a particular thesis is developed in a book, and where in Nietzsche's development the books fits in, is important in understanding Nietzsche's use of irony and narrative form. Such an approach is different from the one often employed in philosophy (for example Kaufmann, 1974), in which arguments are extracted from texts, and then evaluated on the basis of how valid or invalid they may be.

Such an enquiry has been taken up by Jonathan Ree[2] (1987, 1988) in an examination of the texts of Descartes, Hegel, Kierkegaard, J.S. Mill, Bentham and Spinoza. Similar, though more historically oriented, work has been undertaken by Quentin Skinner (for example 1984) and Nicholas Jardine (1991). For present purposes, all of these studies point in the same direction: they show that paying attention to the way a philosophical text is structured, and that asking what the author in question was doing with their words, contributes greatly to the general understanding of a text. That is, they claim that, if the form of the text is ignored and a general proposition is merely extracted from the text, then the original text has been only understood in terms of the current context. To emphasise the analysis of the language, on the other hand, results in a different understanding of what the original author was trying to achieve: such writers may be regarded as reacting against the way philosophy is ordinarily examined. The present study undertakes a similar examination of psychological texts.

## Studying the rhetoric of science

This book is intended as a contribution to debates in the history and philosophy of psychology, but it is neither history or philosophy as the terms are normally applied. Rather, the subject under discussion is the rhetoric of science. One of the claims of this book is that history and philosophy have much to gain from the study of scientific rhetoric. In some quarters, this is hardly a controversial claim given that there is now a diverse body of literature which fruitfully examines the rhetoric of a range of different sciences. Topics for analysis have included behaviourist assumptions underlying the *APA Publication Manual* (Bazerman, 1988), assumptions underlying aspects of social psychology (Billig, 1987, 1991) and other human sciences (Nelson, Magill and McCloskey, 1987), the use of experiment (Cantor, 1989; Schaffer, 1989; Gieryn and Figert, 1990), the construction of biology (Myers, 1990a), accounts of the end of physics (Schaffer, 1992), claims of scientific discovery (Woolgar, 1976), accounts of laboratory practice (Latour, 1987; Latour and Woolgar, 1986), disagreement and controversy (Gilbert and Mulkay, 1984; Mulkay, 1985), the use of scientific dialogues (Myers, 1992), and the works of Newton (Bazerman, 1988; Gross, 1990), Darwin and James Watson (Gross, 1990) and others (see essays in Pera and Shea, 1991). Gillian Beer's work (for example 1983, 1989) has inspired a lot of the work in this area (for example essays in Christie and Shuttleworth, 1989). In *Darwin's Plots*, for example, she examined the ways in which Darwin's great work was influenced by works of fiction, and how the narrative of *On the Origin of the Species* was shaped accordingly. Second, Beer examined the impact Darwin had on fiction written by contemporaries such as George Eliot and Thomas Hardy, as they came to terms with the novel forms Darwin developed and the ideas he propounded. Other researchers in the history of science interested in textual construction are reviewed in the next section. The present study is also broadly consistent with studies such as Beer's (1983): scientific texts are treated as a form of literature.

It is not necessary to rehearse the detail of such studies here, but, by way of introduction, two methodological rules for the study of scientific rhetoric should be outlined: the principles of symmetry and reflexivity.

### Symmetry

What was first labelled by Bloor (1973, 1976) as the 'principle of symmetry', originally formed part of his four tenets of the 'Strong Programme'. Stated simply, it is a methodological rule which demands that a researcher treat each aspect of each actor's discourse seriously, irrespective of the supposed truth-value it may have according to contemporary science (for a longer discussion, see Latour, 1987). Bloor (esp. 1976) introduced the Strong Programme, and particularly the principle of symmetry, in reaction to previous forms of enquiry, especially that of Merton (for example 1973), which was regarded as restricting the focus of the sociology of scientific knowledge to explaining why a scientific theory had been wrong (Myers, 1990a: 20–25).[3] It was claimed that earlier studies of science had assumed that, where science was 'correct', it was guided by a correspondence with the world, and sociological explanations were only required to account for mistakes. This assumed a prior knowledge of the absolute truth or validity of a scientific theory (which could only be based on conclusions from the writer's scientific era).

Such criticisms have often been mounted against work by Evans-Pritchard (see Latour, 1987), but he is not the only writer to be castigated on this point. In a preface to a collection of essays on social anthropology, Douglas (1975, in which she cites Bloor, 1973) develops an argument relevant to Bloor's when she castigates Durkheim for making a similar mistake (again, see Note 3). Durkheim's account of a distinction between the sacred and the profane was applied only to 'primitive' societies; he stopped short of applying his own arguments to Western society:

> With one arm he brandished the sabre of sociological determinism, and with the other he was protecting from any such criticisms the intellectual achievements of his own culture. He believed in things, in 'the world as it is', in an unvarying reality and truth. The social construction of reality applied fully to them, the primitives, and only partially to us. (Douglas, 1975: xxi)

That is, in the account by Douglas it is suggested that Durkheim was not fully reflexive in the application of his own methodology (a point to be examined in a moment), and that the 'refusal to privilege one bit of reality as more absolutely real . . . [and] one intellectual process more valid, allows the original comparative project dear to Durkheim to go forward at last' (Douglas, 1975: xviii). Thus, Douglas argues for the application of a symmetrical form of analysis in cross-cultural studies as well.

The principle of symmetry has come to mean different things to different groups of researchers. At one extreme it has been incorporated into Actor–Network Theory (largely through the work of Latour, 1987, and Callon, 1986). Callon's account of a fisheries project in St Brieuc Bay, for example, gave equal status to scientist, fishermen and scallops, by according each group a set of interests, and the goal of enrolling as many of the other participants as possible (Callon, 1986). This has led recently to the charge of 'hylozoism' (Schaffer, 1991), but this form of 'radical symmetry' is not the one used here, nor could it be, given that it would be difficult to assign interests to memories, brains and emotions in them-selves.[4]

Despite the large scope of the project Bloor proposed, and the amount of philosophical criticism it attracted (see Papineau, 1988, for example), it is difficult to point to a study which actually incorporates all of the tenets of Bloor's Strong Programme. One that comes fairly close is the study by Travis (1981) of 'replication' in worm running and memory transfer. Such a study is best described as one which develops a form of Interest Theory. Such an approach purports to account for the outcome of a scientific controversy in terms of the interests of the participants. Studies of this sort include Collins (1985), Shapin (1979) and MacKenzie (1978). Interest Theory has been criticised for promoting a form of social (as opposed to natural) realism, and Woolgar (1981) criticised it for turning the agents of a scientific controversy into 'interest dupes'. Proponents of Interest Theory have not been *primarily* concerned with the detailed analysis of texts and argument forms produced by scientists (although this is changing; see, for example, Shapin, 1984; Shapin and Schaffer, 1985), and while the present book has benefited from a reading of such sources, it does not attempt to explain historical developments in terms of interests. The argument here with Interest Theory is not that it turns scientists into 'interest dupes' (which it does, but that may be regarded as a useful rhetorical move under some circumstances),[5] but that it relies on and promotes an ontological system (social determinism) which, for present purposes, is unacceptable. Further, this book is not held to be a contribution to debates on ontology, but on epistemology. It seems that, so far as the effects which rhetoric may or may not have, the question is still undecided, and can only be approached through an examination of (a) rhetorical construction in its own right (as in the present book, and also Bazerman, 1988; Gross, 1990; Myers, 1990a), leading perhaps to (b) the impact of rhetoric on the history of intellectual development.

A third direction taken by researchers who have claimed some form of the principle of asymmetry is Discourse Analysis, as exemplified by Gilbert and Mulkay (1984), Potter, Stringer and Wetherell (1984), Potter and Wetherell (1987), Ashmore, Mulkay and Pinch (1989), Soyland (forth-coming b) and others. In this case texts (usually transcripts of conver-sations or newspaper accounts in the studies cited above) are treated symmetrically in order to examine the discursive structure of utterances, and the ways in which accounts are developed of topics such as professional identity, medical economics, attitudes to race and gender, feminist rhetoric and so on. Gilbert and Mulkay's (1984) study of biochemists, for example, examined two distinctive discursive repertoires scientists used to account for work performed by others and work performed by themselves. Later, they examined how discrepancies were negotiated by the scientists, and how juxtaposing examples from the two repertoires (identified, more formally, by Gilbert and Mulkay) were used by scientists to create humour. However, it needs to be pointed out that the Discourse Analysis approach is also not without its own interest (as a quick glance at the topics of their target discourse will show). Nevertheless, of the three approaches to the principle of symmetry, the present study most closely resembles discourse analysis.

Some scholarly work has begun to appear which does attend to the genre of academic writing. Notable under this heading are books by Ashmore (1989), Bazerman (1988), Bazerman and Paradis (1991), Beer (1983, 1989), Gross (1990), Jordanova (1989), Myers (1990a) and Star (1989). Further relevant papers will be discussed in the body of the text, but here it will be useful to examine some methodological points arising from such books.

While not using the term, Jordanova (1989) also provides an argument for a symmetrical methodology, this time from the perspective of the history of science. She criticises other historians whom she regards as falling into two camps. First, there are those who apply a form of 'use/ abuse' model (Jordanova, 1989: 16; on this see Foucault, 1975/1977: 194, and Soyland, 1994a) which attempts to distinguish between correct accounts of language usage, and incorrect ones. Thus, some historians, for example, have claimed to be able to distinguish what is to be regarded as the real phenomenon of hysteria from other 'misdiagnoses' in the past. Or, a target attacked by Jordanova (1989: 11–18), some have attempted to disentangle the 'real' social position of women, or the 'real' nature of sexuality (particularly) in the nineteenth century. Again, the methodological problem is the same: on what basis is it possible to decide on the decontextualised nature of some phenomena? What is correct and what is an error? What is science or myth? What counts as philosophy and what as rhetoric? A symmetrical approach avoids such dichotomies and methodological problems by refusing to maintain them.

Bazerman's book *Shaping Written Knowledge* (1988) is one of the most directly relevant to the present study as it attends to the construction of academic texts and calls attention to the persuasive power of some rhetorical forms over others. However, Bazerman's project is different from the present one in that he argues (a) that the reason for studying scientific rhetoric is to construct better linguistic representations of scientific objects,[6] (b) that persuasive rhetorical forms, when used to advance theories (such as Newton's) which are otherwise correct in some absolute sense, only serve to hasten the acceptance of such theories, and

(c) because of his reliance on (his version of) Mertonian and anti-
deconstructionist arguments.

In effect, Bazerman (1988) is being described here as promoting a
(perhaps mild) form of 'Whiggish' history, in which claims made by the
present scientific community are used *retrospectively* to legitimate certain
parts of particular historically situated texts. Although Kuhn (1962/1970:
1–9) didn't employ the term directly, he began his highly influential text by
criticising just such an approach and arguing that the 'errors' of the past
can only be regarded as errors if the current state of scientific knowledge is
regarded as the product of 'truths' brought about through a process of
'discovery'. However, if:

> . . . out-of-date beliefs are to be called myths, then myths can be promoted by
> the same sorts of reasons that now lead to scientific knowledge. If, on the other
> hand, they are to be called science, then science has included bodies of belief
> quite incompatible with the ones we hold today. (Kuhn, 1962/1970: 2)

Kuhn went on to promote his own account of how to deal with such
incompatibility, however the details of his argument are not relevant here,
nor is his theory of scientific progress being endorsed. Rather, what is at
issue is whether a symmetrical approach to historical texts can avoid the
sorts of methodological difficulties which Kuhn identified. That is, whether
historical accounts can be organised so as to avoid the systematic promotion of present-day 'bodies of belief'.

Ashmore (1989) claims that arguments against the sorts of Whiggish
historiography which are being criticised in this section are *themselves*
Whiggish. This form of argument will be examined in the next section (on
reflexivity). However, it will be worth attempting to reply to this particular
argument here. First, it needs to be pointed out that Ashmore's argument
is of a different order to the one developed by Kuhn: Ashmore is not so
much concerned with whether particular scientific bodies of belief are
being promoted in a historical account, but whether Kuhn's account of his
own methodology is in fact being promoted, at the expense of others, as
*methodologically* superior. For Ashmore, the Kuhnian methodology is
what may possibly be regarded by Kuhn as 'an advance' or 'a discovery'.
So, Ashmore's argument is about the methods of historiography Kuhn
employs, and not concerned with the possibility than Kuhn may be
promoting particular *scientific* bodies of beliefs.

Ashmore suggests that any claim to actually have a better method than
the Whiggish (or asymmetric) one, involves 'bringing off [sic] a distinction
between the realm of the observer and the realm of the observed' (1989:
91). Thus, for example, Kuhn (see 1962/1970) insists on 'limiting his thesis
to physics and similar "mature" sciences [which] acts to preserve the
boundary between his own practice and the practice he observes'. Ashmore then brands Kuhn with 'a certain lack of reflexive awareness' (1989:
91). For the purposes of argument, Ashmore will be assumed to be
persuasive on this issue, but it remains to be shown how many of the 'new
historiographers' fail on his account.

Two points need to be raised on the definition of the term 'Whiggish'. First, it might be claimed, as Ashmore does, that Kuhn, for example, is Whiggish because he uncritically asserts his own methodological stance as superior. That *might* be regarded as 'Whiggish' in some sense of the term. But, second, that does not entail that Kuhn regards his own methods as being a product of the present, which: 'was the cause of [this] historical change, pulling the past in conformity to it by some magnetic attraction, or perhaps pre-existing like some genetic code in the developing social organism . . .' (Barnes, quoted in Ashmore, 1989: 90). One way to avoid such criticisms is to incorporate a reflexive element into the analytical framework employed; that is, to recognise the role of the analyst in the text. To some extent that has been attempted in the present book. But even a non-reflexive, or not overtly reflexive, project should be immune to Ashmore's attack, so long as it was carefully symmetrical. That is, if an analyst did not claim to *know* which of an agent's statements were 'true', then they would not be a Whiggish historian. That in itself is a methodological improvement. Now, 'improvement' could mean one of two things: (a) 'better' in some absolute sense (in which case Ashmore's argument goes through), or (b) 'improvement' could be read as 'current reaction against a previous method'. This second form is the one intended here (and perhaps also the one intended by Kuhn). This seems to have two implications: that such a methodology is always regarded as revisable (changeable) in the light of further criticism, and that such an analysis could also be reflexive (especially in a debate on historiography).[7]

Finally, a further implication of symmetrical analyses: Latour (1988) claims that such studies should not attempt to offer the sorts of strongly causal stories (of the sort originally envisioned by Bloor, 1976), which give a kind of mechanised, scientific gloss on historical accounts (although it is possible to claim that this is exactly what Latour does do).[8] Instead, such studies should, according to Latour, 'search for non-scientific and weaker explanations' (1988: 176), and that is what is attempted here. For a start, the field of the analysis of scientific rhetoric is fairly new, and exploratory accounts are most appropriate under the circumstances. Further, the degree of influence that rhetoric (or social interests, or power structures, or obligatory passage points, or whatever) may have is, in the end, too complex for the development of a simple equation which arrives at the outcome of a scientific debate (such as the one Bazerman, 1988, appears to suggest, in which Newton's rhetoric + Newton's social influence + a discovered truth = a high degree of influence). The present study, then, offers rather modest suggestions relating to the effect particular texts may have had.

## Reflexivity

Bloor (1976) also proposed a principle of reflexivity, such that the explanations offered in studies of science should be applicable to those

studies: the position of the analyst should not be privileged or taken for
granted. This is the second methodological rule which is incorporated into
the present study. The topic of reflexivity is fast becoming a research area
in its own right (see, for example, essays in Woolgar, 1988b) and the
arguments involved have developed a high level of complexity. I will be
concerned here with a fairly basic methodological objection to the present
project. One of the frequent questions I faced when presenting material
from this book at seminars and conferences related to the problem of
reflexivity. It seems that (at least for some people) any enquiry into the
structure or form of a text in anything but the conventional philosophical
manner raises the issue of the rhetoric involved in talking about rhetoric.
This has been discussed at great length by Ashmore (1989) as the '*tu
quoque*' argument. One solution to the problems raised by such an
objection is that proposed by Mulkay in *The Word and The World* (1985).
In an early chapter involving the use of a second 'textual voice', he debates
the reflexive turn:

> You [the Textual Commentator] have chosen to comment on the present text as
> it is being formed. Your intervention makes this text more reflexive. You display
> some of the interpretive work on which it depends and you draw attention to
> parallels between its textuality and that of the biochemists' letters. But constant
> textual reflexivity is not obligatory. Textual reflexivity does not make a text any
> less reliant than other forms of discourse on the ordered interplay of signs. Nor
> does analysis of others' discourse necessarily imply a denial of one's own
> textuality. (Mulkay, 1985: 40)

Thus, texts concerned with rhetoric are inescapably rhetorical in themselves; to deny this would be to refute all the arguments presented here so
far. So, of course, the possibility is open for someone to point out my use
of a particular rhetorical form. Such an option is always open in principle,
but 'would it actually be analytically productive?' (Mulkay, 1985: 76). That
is hardly a question an author could be expected to answer.

But, if an objection is raised concerning a project which develops an
analysis of rhetoric, it is possibly not going to involve an examination of the
analyst's text, but the wholesale refutation of the entire project. This
would indeed be devastating were it to be persuasive. But notice that it
relies on exactly the distinction that the argument thus far has been
attacking. It occurs in the following form:

1   Texts concerned with rhetoric are themselves rhetorical.
2   All circular arguments are self-refuting.
3   Using rhetoric to examine rhetoric is viciously circular.

Therefore:

4   The study of rhetoric is self-refuting.

A number of strategies may be employed here. First, given the plausibility
of the first premise in the argument so far, the first should not be denied.
Thus, there would seem to be some commitment to a form of circularity.[9]

That is in fact what has been embraced above by the suggestion that, in principle, it will always be possible to re-analyse the analytical text. However, that claim was made without inferring the *necessity* of always doing so (see also Potter, 1988a). Thus, while this statement may look circular, it is not viciously circular: the circularity could be highly informative. Therefore the critic's argument does not go through.

A second, and more risky, solution would be to deny the second premise, and this is an implication of the argument in Chapter 1. It was argued there that it was merely a rhetorical, rather than an absolute, demand to adhere to the canons of logical validity. From the present perspective, there has not yet been a convincing argument given for the existence of some objective, context-dependent set of logical rules. If there were, it would be possible to decide, in advance (and analytically) what constituted a valid argument under all possible circumstances. If there is not, then although the second premise looks obvious in the current climate, there is no guarantee that it could not be overturned and rejected. If that is plausible, then the conclusion to the critic's argument may, again, be denied.

In giving the arguments above, I realise I am disagreeing with Ashmore who claims (insofar as his highly ironic text claims anything) that the 'power of the *tu quoque* cannot reside in its logic, however perfect, because logic in itself does not compel' (1989: 88) and that, *therefore*, he does not intend to put forward counter-arguments. My disagreement comes in two parts. First, I think it is worthwhile designing counter-arguments because if, as I claim, the discursive field of argument is only one of rhetoric, then counter-arguments ought to be produced in order to make the current case persuasive. Second, Ashmore backs up the quote given above by reference to the work of two sociologists (Barnes and Bloor). This use of the authoritative reference is rhetorically interesting; however, if the object is to convince more than the previously converted, then this is a little too quick, and arguments had better be presented on their own merits (in the present context) and not with reference to hardened reflexivists.[10]

## Final words

The form of the following case-studies is fairly straightforward: each one examines a range of texts from the history of psychology in some detail. As a result, texts were usually selected on the basis that they gave a fairly short or concentrated account of a particular position. Only those texts published in the form of a book or journal article were used. This is not to suggest that the same thing could not be done for unpublished sources; also, given that Bazerman (1988) had published a long account of the genre of the experimental journal article, texts were most often chosen for analysis if they were of a fairly theoretical nature. The quotations taken tend to be reasonably long in order to give a clearer account of the style and content of an author's work. More specific details of the methodology employed in the present book are given in the relevant case-studies.

A note on the use of translations: I will be paying attention to the detail of the language used in texts some of which originally appeared in a different language (French, German, Russian). Take the cases of Freud and Vygotsky: Freud wrote in German. Were it the case that the present study attempted to give an account of theories important to German psychology, the use of English definitions of terms would be redundant. However, the present study attempts to examine theories which have been important (frequently cited/influential) in Anglo-American psychology. Thus the use of English terms avoids the following problem: supposing that the great majority of Anglo-American psychologists (especially those after William James' generation) had read (and now read) the works of such authors in translation, then it will have been the English terms which affected Anglo-American thought and writing. Now suppose that a secondary study (such as the present one) begins to undermine the interconnection (the 'network' in Hesse's, 1980, terms) of words and phases read (by the reader of a translation), by giving an analysis of the German, French or Russian terms. The result would be at odds with the way the text had been previously read by the English-speaking psychologist. There is some suggestion, for example, that the Anglo-American world may have misunderstood Vygotsky's works, insofar as it was assumed (on the basis of the translations currently available) that Vygotsky's conception of the child was a social one (see Chapter 4). If it turns out, for example, that a more 'accurate' translation turned Vygotsky into a 'cognitivist' (a Chomsky, a Fodor or a Rumelhart, for example), it will still be the case that a large amount of work (experiments, texts, statistics, etc.) will exist in the 'archive' of psychology, and that work will have been influenced (perhaps initiated) by the 'anti-cognitivist' reading. Put more baldly: the discursive intentions of Freud, Piaget, Vygotsky and Merleau-Ponty are completely irrelevant to the present analysis. Thus, the maintenance of English would seem appropriate.

The quick or critical reader may already have begun to be sensitive to the rhetoric of the present text: such a reaction would be helpful in traversing the case-studies which follow. But, to the question of what action is being performed by the previous two chapters, the answer must be: establishing credentials. Of course, they set up the range of issues to be tackled; the rules to be followed; the background to the debate on the rhetoric of science. However, a great deal of interdisciplinary work must satisfy the requirements for each relevant form of enquiry: recent refer-ences must be given (with a few 'forthcoming's' and texts in press; Billig 1987: 1), footnotes must document the source for each historical claim, philosophical arguments have to be given in the strictest style, sociological references have to be made to the relevant 'classical' texts, the fleeting literary reference must be made, the appropriate citations and acknowledge-ments given (hey, Greg, this bit's for you). That's what's really going on in the previous two chapters but, from here on, things get serious: enter now into the world of the psychological literature.

## Notes

1. Some sociological studies have, for example, attempted to give accounts of the real status of scientific replication (e.g. Collins, 1985; Travis, 1981); that is, whether replication does in fact involve what the scientists say it does (see also Ashmore, 1989: 112–138). This sort of research programme is not being criticised here: it is simply a matter of distinguishing it from what was attempted by Gilbert and Mulkay (1984).

2. To some extent, the analysis provided by Roberts (1988) of texts from the German philosophical tradition is similar to the one attempted by Ree. But Roberts does not use the term 'rhetoric', and to that extent cannot be considered as having produced a text which is completely consistent with Ree's.

3. It needs to be stressed that this is a (very) particular reading of Merton's work – as will be the later reading of Durkheim. Especially in the generation of disciplinary histories, the process of reading a particular text to one's own advantage is a common occurrence. As Holub argues: 'In a certain sense one might say that a theory creates its own forerunners' (1984: 13), or even alters its own forerunners to its own advantage. See Kendall and Soyland (1993) for a similar story on the treatment of Foucault by later writers.

4. Difficult, but not impossible. The difference between Latour and Schaffer is largely in the use of the term 'interest'. Schaffer sticks to the ordinary (or dictionary) use of the term. Latour seems to be defending a revision of it in terms of a broader definition. Were this to go through, I would have no objection to saying 'memories have interests' or 'memories "will" their own stability'. Seen in this way, the debate has quite a history. Nietzsche wrote: '. . . even Schopenhauer's "will" has . . . through the philosophers' rage for generalisation turned out to be a disaster for science: for this will has been turned into a metaphor when it is asserted that all things in nature possess will' (1878/1986: 216). One could defend Latour using Nietzsche: 'Mankind has in all ages confused the active and the passive: it is their everlasting grammatical blunder' (1881/1982, sec. 120). That is, even though such a confusion may result from a 'blunder', it is not an unusual one.

5. However, there is a remaining unease in using it, put well by Nietzsche: 'Why the stupid are often malicious. When our head feels too weak to answer the objections of our opponent our heart answers by casting suspicion on the motives behind his objections' (1878/1986: 224). Having said that, let it not be thought that there is nothing very sensible underlying Interest Theory. Again, Nietzsche: 'Need is considered the cause of why something came to be; but in truth it is often merely an effect of what has come to be' (1887/1974, sec. 205). This would make the investigation of the relationship crucial.

6. Bazerman was a writing instructor employed to teach students just this aspect of academic writing. However, while this may be regarded as a 'sociological' explanation for Bazerman's perspective, that perspective is not reproduced by Bazerman's colleague Myers (1990a).

7. It might be supposed that anyone interested in examining rhetoric or discourse is attempting not to hold any views or opinions. That is not the case. Rather, they hold opinions on opinions (or, awfully, 'meta-views'); a good example is Billig (1991).

8. There seems to be an inconsistency between claims made by Latour (1988), and actual practice; in the essay cited, Latour argues that SSK should only offer stories concerning science, and not attempt to give even weakly causal accounts. However, Latour (e.g. 1987) and others who explicitly align themselves with Latour (e.g. Callon, 1986; Gieryn and Figert, 1990), would appear to apply the conclusions of one 'story' to a completely different area of scientific enquiry (scallops, electric cars, O-rings, etc.); that is, they utilise terms such as 'obligatory passage point' and 'enrolment' as explanatory devices – and ones important to causal stories. But, if Latour (1988) is to be taken seriously, this is exactly what should *not* be

done, because a 'story' (Little Red Riding Hood) is not normally assumed to provide an explanatory heuristic (a moral, but not an explanation).

9. On circularity and validity, see Grayling (1982: 56), Haack (1978: 11–27) and Bradley and Swartz (1979: 315–320). On self-refuting arguments see Ashmore (1989: 76). For a much more sophisticated account of circularity and the *reductio ad absurdum* argument, see Priest (1987: 128–133).

10. If there is an irony in my disagreeing with Ashmore on this, given the major arguments of this section, then it is to be grasped and not mitigated with an excuse.

# PART I  METAPHOR

## 3

# Memory after Lashley:
# Metaphors as Promissory Notes[1]

We must do away with all explanations, and description alone must take its place. And this description gets its light, that is to say its purpose, from the philosophical problems. These are, of course, not empirical problems; they are solved, rather, by looking into the workings of our language . . .

(Wittgenstein, 1958/1968, sec. 109)

When a promise is made, it is not the words that are said which constitute the promise but what remains unspoken behind the words that are said.

(Nietzsche, 1881/1982, sec. 350)

## Introduction

This is the first of the five case-studies to be presented in the book. It examines what happened to the work of a famous neuropsychologist, Karl Lashley (a professor at Harvard University)[2] after his death (in 1958). Since that time, the neurosciences have been reshaped, both in terms of investigative practice, and in the way such investigations are described. The present chapter initiates a discussion of such changes, but it does so only in terms of the rhetoric employed in published texts (rather than through the examination of laboratory practice). Thus, the chapter provides an examination of the use of metaphors of neural processing. However, the most important aspect of the chapter for the general argument of the book is the exploration of the use of 'promissory notes'. This particular rhetorical form will be examined through the ways in which it has been used in disciplinary histories, research outlines (summaries), and philosophical and experimental conclusions concerned with the activity of the brain. In the process, the chapter will itself stand as a promissory note for future work on the rhetoric of engaging the interest of the research community.

The debate concerned with 'memory' may be characterised as one in which 'holism' has been described in opposition to 'localisation': either the entire brain is important to specific functions, or particular areas are crucial for isolated forms of activity. If 'psychology' is defined as a separate discipline which began around 1880 (for example Koch and Leary, 1985), then the debate on the localisation of 'higher' brain 'processes', such as 'memory' or 'problem-solving' (to use some recent forms of description) may be described as pre-dating that carried out between 'psychologists'.[3] However, the present chapter is largely concerned with psychologists who published descriptions of 'memory' in the twentieth century. While some of the texts to be examined here attempt to describe the debate (and an author's own position within the debate) as a connected sequence of researchers and 'ideas', the present chapter does not depend on the adequacy of such an account: it need not be assumed that there exists a central truth to which some ideas and some research endeavours correspond. Instead, the focus here is upon the ways such accounts of disciplinary history are constructed.

## A view from the present

Take a passage in a fairly recent book by J.Z. Young, *Philosophy and the Brain* (1987). At one point, Young is summarising a number of models of memory and he includes a short section on holographic memory:

> This theory is difficult to explain shortly: it depends upon the analogy of holographic photography discovered by Dennis Gabor. . . . The analogy seemed especially appealing in the light of the work by the famous physiologist Karl Lashley. He thought he had proved that memory in a rat . . . was distributed all over its cortex and that the memory was retained so long as any small part was intact. This concept of non-localization of memory records has been steadily losing its hold as surgeons, physiologists and psychologists have explored the functions of the human cortex. . . . In a few cases quite specific memories have been awakened or suppressed in humans during electrical stimulation of particular points in the brain.
>   However, it would be a mistake to interpret these results as demonstrating that each item of memory is to be found pigeon-holed in a few cells of the brain. As has been emphasized, we do not understand how representations of complex situations are encoded. It may yet prove that local electrical and chemical processes in addition to those of nerve impulses and synapses are involved. Some such effects may be holographic. It will be exciting to find out. (Young, 1987: 160–161)

Here Lashley is described as a 'famous physiologist' who examined memory in rats (although he used a variety of animals, including higher primates). However, while Lashley 'thought he had proved' memory was 'distributed all over' the cortex, he was, on this account, plainly mistaken: Lashley's 'concept' has been 'steadily losing its hold' ever since. Young here provides a typical example of the way in which Lashley's research is currently being described (see pp. 43–50): Lashley is described as 'famous', and yet the 'concept' he produced is not to be taken as relevant to current research: the individual is praised at the same time in which his research is discounted. Instead, the prospect that memory may *be* 'holographic'[4] is held out as a promissory note in a debate which Young regards as undecided: 'we do not understand' the 'encoding' of complex situations, 'yet' the resolution of the debate will be 'exciting'. The hologram is used here as a way of answering questions posed by Lashley's arguments for a form of holism; if memories are distributed across the cortex, then the hologram may be the solution. But Young also mentions a group of (anonymous) professionals ('surgeons', etc.) whose research suggests that, 'in a few cases', localised memories have been discovered: the resolution may render 'holism' irrelevant or mistaken.

## Promissory notes

Using Young's account as a starting point, a number of questions will be addressed. In what ways was the invention of the hologram used to account for Lashley's results? What importance is given to Lashley's work in contemporary accounts of neuropsychology? And, what sort of rhetorical work is involved in describing Lashley's work? In beginning to answer these questions, an attempt will be made to examine the role of the promissory note in accounts of the field. This will lead to a discussion of the promises currently outstanding in the field.

A 'promissory note' shall be defined here as a rhetorical device which is used to postpone certain problems or questions by reference to some desired research goal. So, a promissory note is of the form: if you accept X for the moment, then desirable results Y will be attained in the future. Thus, if a promissory note is accepted, future research will be aimed at fulfilling the promise, at least until the prospects of such a fulfilment are described as 'unattainable', or perhaps 'misconceived'.

A famous passage will illustrate this device: in *The Origin of the Species* Darwin states:

> In the distant future I see open fields for far more important researches. Psychology will be based on a new foundation, that of the necessary acquirement of each mental power and capacity by gradation. Light will be thrown on the origin of man and his history. (Darwin, 1859/1968: 458)

This passage appears as the third-to-last paragraph of the book, and this position in the text is fairly typical of promissory notes (see pp. 50–51). In terms of classical rhetoric, the passage may be described as 'deliberative' insofar as it attempts to establish the course of future research. The promise of this 'important' research is that it will 'throw light' on the history and origin of man.[5] So it can be seen that, if the reader is persuaded of the factual status of Darwin's text (of the descriptions he gives), then one ought to pursue the line of enquiry he proposes: the promise stands as an end-point for Darwin's enquiry. It is the desire to obtain the promised outcome which dissuades the reader from trying to undermine Darwin's project, or the metaphor on which it is based (see also Beer, 1983). This is a working definition, not of the form, but of the function of a 'promissory note'.

It will be suggested that the metaphor of the hologram involved the issuing of a promissory note, and it will be shown that, in recent reviews, the assumption of modular processing (the 'boxes in the brain' metaphor) involves the issuing of other (alternative, perhaps contradictory) promissory notes. There have been some recent historical (for example Leary, 1987, 1990a; Gigerenzer and Murray, 1987) and philosophical texts which examine the role of metaphor in scientific theories. Richard Rorty, for example, has gone so far as to develop an 'account of intellectual progress as the literalization of selected metaphors' (1989: 44).[6] The present chapter will tell one of these stories, with a number of specific claims: (a) scientific metaphors function as promissory notes. An extension or corollary of this claim is that (b) such promissory notes act as motivators to direct or promote research in the direction suggested by a given author.[7] Finally, (c) promissory notes will continue to be issued, offering a range of inducements, because this aspect of the rhetoric of science has become an accepted trope, not only for the seduction of the reader but for financial support in an increasingly complex and competitive arena.

### The description of the problem in 1950

The case-study begins with the work of the neuropsychologist Karl Spencer Lashley (1890–1958), and the way accounts of his work have changed. This will involve examining a complicated debate, which has been described as having developed over a significant period.[8] Thus, writers and readers of this debate have been 'enrolled' (see Chapter 8; Callon, 1986; Latour, 1987) in particular ways of characterising the 'problems' posed by accounting for 'higher brain processes'. The aim, in the present context, will be to present this debate without attempting to enrol the reader; to examine the rhetoric involved without assuming that the reader maintains the background knowledge developed by those who pursue an interest in such a psychological object. This method will draw attention to the ways in which metaphors have been used to persuade psychologists of a particular description at a particular time. The starting point here was the account given by Young (1987). The contrasting accounts that follow begin with Lashley.

In his 1950 article 'In search of the engram', Lashley summarised a number of experiments on the localisation of memory:

> The psychological studies, like the more limited direct experiments on the brain, point to the conclusion that the memory trace is located in all parts of the functional area; that various parts are equipotential for its maintenance and activation.' (Lashley, 1950/1960: 492)

The term 'trace' (or, sometimes, 'engram') was applied to the physical entity assumed to be located within the brain when something is remembered. The 'psychological studies', in this case, involved teaching an animal (often rats or primates in Lashley's work) to perform a given task (running through a 'maze', or opening a 'puzzle box') until such behaviour could be described as forming a 'habit'. The criterion used to gauge the success of the animal's memory for the task was the number of errors the animal made: if the errors were infrequent, the habit had been established and the trace had become part of the brain. Surgery would then be performed during which some parts of the brain would be damaged (the neocortex, for example, could be cut or 'hatched' using a sequence of incisions). After surgery, the animals were allowed to rest and recover before being retested on the task learned earlier. Again, the number of errors would be used to describe the extent to which the 'trace' remained intact (see, for example, Lashley, 1929/1963). Such research relied on the assumption, frequently made in many areas of psychology, that the brains of animals (though less complicated) would be sufficient for drawing conclusions about the brains of humans[9] (an assumption often denied by some theorists; see also Chapter 4). The reference to 'direct experiments' characterises ('more limited') studies in which the brains of conscious human subjects are electrically stimulated (as in the extract from Young, 1987) in order to ascertain the location of specific memories (that is, in the part of the brain being stimulated). In the extract, then, Lashley draws conclusions from such studies to claim that all memories are located across all parts of the neocortex. As a result, the passage indicates continued support for the 'principle of equipotentiality': 'the apparent capacity for any intact part of a functional area [of the brain] to carry out, with or without reduction in efficiency, the functions which are lost by destruction of the whole' (Lashley 1929/1963: 25). Later, this principle was extended such that all parts of the neocortex were equally important to the process of memory and learning. The quotation also shows the conclusion that would affect accounts of the research to come: memory was not localisable.

Another account from the same period will show the extent of the claim against localisability. Donald Hebb's 1949 monograph, *The Organization of Behavior*, attempted to summarise much of the clinical and experimental work carried out in neuropsychology.[10] At the beginning of the book, in a way characteristic of accounts given at this time (see Pribram, 1969, discussed later), Hebb outlines the following puzzle:

> How can it be possible for a man to have an IQ of 160 or higher, after a prefrontal lobe has been removed, or for a woman to have an IQ of 115, a better score than two-thirds of the normal population could make, after losing the entire right half of the cortex? (Hebb, 1949: 1–2, references omitted)

The problem is posed in terms of general competence (IQ) after a given amount of brain damage (here, the removal of part of a human brain): given that damage has occurred, how is it possible to have a high intelligence quotient? Although the variation to the theory introduced by Hebb (1949) is not directly relevant, it is important to note the way in which general summaries of the localisation issue were given. In his final chapter, 'The growth and decline of intelligence', Hebb states:

> Animal experiments, anatomical studies, and studies in which the brain of the

fully conscious human patient is stimulated electrically have clearly localized a
number of sensory and motor areas. But, because of the difficulties of method
that have just been considered, about the only localization of high function that
has so far been achieved is that of the so-called speech area. . . . No other
localization of function in the human cerebrum has been established. I am aware
that this statement is not in accord with much of the literature, but a critical
evaluation of the evidence presented in support of various claims concerning
localization permits no other conclusion, so far as I can see. (Hebb, 1949: 284)

Hebb mitigates the conclusions made by noting that his account 'is not in
accord' with those of others on the subject, but he qualifies this dissent by
saying that a 'critical' evaluation 'permits no other conclusion'; this is
further qualified ('so far as I can see'), but the implication is that others
have been uncritical or hasty in their judgements. Thus, according to
Hebb, the localisation account is only possible for 'lower' functions
(sensation, motor control, speech). The whole tenor of Hebb's book is one
of grand overview, a kind of state-of-the-art summary from which to
criticise aspects of work in the field: statements of this kind were designed
to guide future research in the direction of Hebb's own theory, which was
in many ways an approved extension of Lashley's programme.

    In a similar way, Lashley's (1950/1960) article includes a number of
general conclusions. Before coming to these, Lashley made a remark
which many others (for example Miller, 1962/1966: 185; Pribram, 1990: 87–
88; and pp. 46–50) have since commented on. Reverting to a kind of
personalised account not typically favoured in scientific papers (see
Bazerman, 1988), Lashley confessed: 'I sometimes feel, in reviewing the
evidence on the localization of the memory trace, that the necessary
conclusion is that learning is just not possible' (Lashley, 1950/1960: 501).
This statement will be regarded as 'pessimistic' insofar as it offers no
guarantees of future success in this direction of enquiry. Moreover,
Lashley's general conclusions added to such an impression: he goes on to
say that the conditioned reflex theory is 'certainly false' (see also Lashley et
al., 1951; Pribram, 1982: 277–278). Second, while certain areas seem
necessary for the learning or retention of a particular activity, it is not
possible to demonstrate the localisation of the memory trace; the engram is
represented throughout (see Thompson, 1982; Rumelhart and McClelland,
1986: 41). Third, defects arising from damage to the 'so-called associative
areas' (visibly different from other parts of the brain) involve the inability
to form generalisations (a higher function) rather than the loss of certain
memories. Fourth, organic amnesia (in the form of brain damage) is most
likely to be accounted for in terms of a general reduction of attention
(reinforcing the principle of equipotentiality). Fifth, memories are reproduced throughout the functional area 'much as the surface of a liquid
develops an interference pattern of the spread of waves when it is disturbed
at several points' (Lashley, 1950/1960: 502). Sixth, all of the cells in the
brain are constantly active and single neurons must be involved in
countless other functions.

    'In search of the engram' was not Lashley's last publication (he produced nine further papers) but later researchers were to treat it as a final statement of Lashley's research endeavours, and the conclusions listed above were to set the challenge for theories attempting to come to terms with the localisation of higher functioning. Later models were to focus on Lashley's fifth point: memory might function as an interference pattern: like the surface of water disturbed at several points. The pond metaphor offered a simple analogy, obvious in its implications but without offering a technological link. But, rather than develop the pond metaphor, research concentrated on the newly developed hologram – thus giving another example of psychology using developments in a different field in order to foster its own enquiries (see chapters in Leary, 1990b).

## An 'older type of theory'

Before examining accounts of the metaphor of the hologram, it will be useful to review the ways in which a very specific rhetorical device has been used involving labelling an opposing view as 'old'. Examples of it may be found throughout the period in question.

Shepard Ivory Franz (1874–1933) was one of Lashley's teachers and, later, a co-researcher, and he had a significant influence on Lashley's research techniques, and surgery in particular (Bruce, 1986). He published an article in *Science* in 1912 'poking fun at the belief in exact localization, calling it the new phrenology' (Boring, 1950: 685). The paper opens by reviewing an account constructed by Gall (1758–1826),[11] who had argued for a high degree of localisation in the structure of the brain, in which one area of the brain had control over one type of brain function (at the level of the brain tissue; see Harrington, 1987). The rhetoric employed by Franz relies on a reader knowing that 'phrenology' was 'old' and (at the time Franz was writing) discredited:

> Thus was born a definite conception of centres in the brain for particular mental acts. This conception was naive and crude, to be sure, but it is the one which dominated neurology and nervous physiology for the past century, and which is still to be recognized in present-day teaching and writing. (Franz, 1912: 322)

Franz first establishes that phrenology was 'naive and crude', and then forms an association between the earlier account and 'present-day teaching and writing'. In this manner, Franz attempted to discredit more contemporary research (on credit, see also Schaffer, 1989). As a result, the rest of the article consists of a critique of proposals made by researchers who favour the localisation thesis and 'histological-phrenological reasoning' (Franz, 1912: 324). The conjunction of the terms 'histological' (here relating to types of brain tissue) and 'phrenological' (relating function to location) discredits a form of 'reasoning': Franz promotes his own 'holistic' account by associating 'old' and 'new phrenology' by suggesting a similarity of methods, an interest in types of brain regions (locations), *and* tissue types (for example white matter versus grey matter). Finally, Franz concludes:

> We have no facts which at present enable us to locate the mental processes in the brain any better than they were located fifty years ago. That the mental processes may be due to cerebral activities we may believe, but with what anatomical elements the individual mental processes may be connected we do not know. Notwithstanding our ignorance, it would appear best and most scientific that we should not adhere to any of the phrenological systems, however scientific they may appear to be on the surface. (Franz, 1912: 328)

The historical sweep here is important: Franz presents a comparison of old and discredited results with contemporary and misguided endeavours. By concentrating on 'anatomical elements' and relating them to 'mental processes', Franz concludes, in a mitigated form ('notwithstanding . . .'), that 'no facts' have been found (prefiguring Lashley's conclusion, above). Again the historical comparison is made: 'phrenological systems' old and new are only scientific 'on the surface'.

A similar device, from the same side of the argument, may be seen in Hebb (1949) where he states that theories which are concerned with discovering which part of the cortex contributes to which function: 'arise from an older type of theory, no longer entertained in psychological thought' (Hebb, 1949: 285). The neurologist Lord Brain used the same device in 1964:

> The older neurologists, and even some today, thought that the different varieties of aphasia produced by different lesions in different situations could be classified in psychological terms . . . but this presupposes first that in the nervous system speech is organized in such a way that anatomical centres correspond to psychological functions, and then that destruction of such a centre merely impairs a particular psychological element in speech. This view has largely been abandoned. (Lord Brain, 1964, quoted in Ellis and Young, 1988: 17)

The suggestion here is that an old view 'has largely been abandoned'; and again a connection is made between 'older neurologist' and 'even some today' suggesting some surprise at such old ideas still being maintained. Such rhetoric sits well with Anne Harrington's suggestion that unitary functioning was regarded as a touchstone of modern thinking (1987: 270). The irony is that the assumptions being dismissed by Lord Brain are again being made (see Fodor, 1983; discussed later).

It would be too simplistic to suggest that labelling a theory as 'old' is sufficient to ensure the demise of the theory.[12] But it quite often happens that, within a single text, the only time an alternative idea appears is when it is being dismissed as old. That is, labelling a theory as 'old' has often been regarded as sufficient reason to no longer discuss an idea within a particular text: 'old' in such cases implies 'worn out' (barren, or impotent). Although there is no a priori (or 'logical'; see Chapter 1) reason why the age of a thesis should affect its validity, it is possible to find many instances when authors cast doubt on an idea in just this manner. (Further examples of labelling a theory as 'old' will be found on pp. 46–52)

**A problem and its answer**

Pribram (1990: 92) states that 'holograms' (three-dimensional representations) were first described in 1948 (by Gabor). Patricia Churchland
(1986: 407) reports that the suggestion that the brain's information storage
system was holographic was first made by Van Heeden in 1963. By 1969 the
idea had gained enough credibility for the neurophysiologist Karl Pribram
to make it the main issue of his general paper on memory in *Scientific
American*. The extent of the problem posed by Lashley's work is still a
dominant feature of Pribram's article, and in a passage similar in form to
that by Hebb (quoted above), he states:

> The abuses that the brain can survive have been documented many times since
> Lashley's pioneering experiments. . . . In the laboratory the brain seems to
> mock the ingenuity of the experimenter. Robert Galambos of the University of
> California at San Diego has severed up to 95 percent of the optic tract of cats
> without seriously impairing the cats' ability to perform skillfully on tests
> requiring them to differentiate between highly similar figures. (Pribram, 1969:
> 75)

Here the brain is given as a kind of agent: something capable of mocking
the efforts of the experimenter. Again an example (using cats) is given of
general competence (test performance) after large amounts of brain
damage (the percentage of severed 'optic tracts'); the puzzle could still be
structured as it had been twenty years earlier. The term 'pioneering' here
suggests historical importance on the one hand, and being quaint, early
and out-of-date on the other. This description is similar to that given by
Young (1987: 161) of Lashley being a 'famous' researcher whose account
has been 'steadily losing its hold'.[13]

Pribram (1969) goes on to cite experiments which introduced sections of
mica, gold foil and aluminium hydroxide cream in to the cortices of animals
all to little effect.[14] Pribram then states that:

> I reasoned (much as Lashley had) that the neuronal events might interact in
> some way to produce complex patterns within the brain: the hologram now
> provided an explicit model. . . . The attractive feature of the hypothesis is that
> the information is distributed throughout the stored hologram and is thus
> resistant to insult. Even if a small corner of the hologram is illuminated by the
> appropriate input, the entire original scene reappears. Moreover, holograms can
> be layered on top of the other and yet be separately reconstructed. (Pribram,
> 1969: 76–77)

Note first the prestige associated with reasoning along lines similar to that
of a revered predecessor: Pribram depicts himself as following the path of a
master. Yet here Pribram discusses memory as if it *were* holographic. The
term 'insult' is typically applied to a case of cortical damage, but Pribram is
discussing damaging a hologram (not a damaged brain). This is a small
example of the way in which a metaphor becomes the object under
discussion; the text slides from the metaphoric to the literal (see also
Leary, 1987, 1990a; Sarbin, 1990).[15] Thus, terms used to describe one

object come to be applied (rhetorically) to a different object – in the
manner suggested by Aristotle (see Ricoeur, 1978: 13).

Pribram's 1982 article for the commemorative collection *Neuropsychology after Lashley* (published fifty years after Lashley's first book)
contains a long and complicated discussion of the mathematics involved in
holograms. The introductory discussion of the hologram is similar to that in
his 1969 article: he lists the essential properties of a hologram and then
points to their similarity to the characteristics Lashley demanded. The list
of materials introduced into various brains is still used as a way of
dismissing simplistic field theories. He begins modifying his enthusiasm
for the metaphor by saying that it does not account for all the data;
modifications are needed (Pribram, 1982: 281). Later in the article, he
admits: 'The multiplex hybrid nature of cortical holographic organization
serves as a warning that any simply conceived "global-Fourier-transform-
of-input-into-cortical-organization" is untenable' (Pribram, 1982: 289).
Here, 'global' application of the mathematics of holograms 'serves as a
warning': simply conceived the holographic metaphor 'is untenable'. This
may be regarded as an 'admission of failure' which creates other rhetorical
problems. Pribram's solution to such difficulties will be examined in the
next section.

The final account of the holographic metaphor to be examined comes
from Patricia Churchland's (1986) *Neurophilosophy*. This book was
intended to draw two different fields together: educating philosophers
about neuropsychology, and psychologists about philosophy. At one point,
she introduces a number of rival models of brain organisation:

> In coming to grips with the problems of getting a theory of brain function, I had
> to learn a number of general lessons. First, there are things that are advertized as
> theories but are really metaphors in search of genuine theoretical
> articulation. . . . [T]he holographic idea did not really manage to explain
> storage or retrieval phenomena. Although significant effort went into developing
> the analogy, it did not flower into a credible account of the processes. . . . Nor
> does the mathematics of the hologram appear to unlock the door to the
> mathematics of neural ensembles. (Churchland, 1986: 407–408)

This personalised account of Churchland's 'progress' involved learning
'general lessons': mere metaphors are sometimes 'advertised' (here a
degrading term) as 'theories', but have no 'genuine' (clear) 'articulation'.
The holographic metaphor is characterised in this extract as having run out
of promise: genuine theories are those which allow growth. So, by 1986 it
was possible to be fairly dismissive about the holographic metaphor;
however, this is inconsistent with the account by Young (1987) which
opened the chapter. The difference may lie in the amount of detail
incorporated into each account: Churchland gives extensive accounts of
the developments in a variety of areas, while Young offers a kind of
textbook summary. Young held out the promise of solutions to Lashley's
problems by referring to the holographic metaphor, and this could still be
done in 1987 without immediately being contradicted. Such a rhetorical

strategy could only be employed at that time by issuing the promissory note in the most general terms. Alternatively, it may be that the texts by Young and Churchland were being used to fulfil different rhetorical purposes: Young's account acting as a general summary of earlier work, Churchland's as a critique attempting to alter the debate.[16]

## Promises currently outstanding

The results of much of Lashley's work were reproduced in a 1978 textbook, *Physiological Psychology* (Swartz, 1978). A chapter on learning and memory states:

> The history of the search for CNS [central nervous system] loci in learning shows several trends. Initially, research design concentrated mainly on finding single, discrete, 'critical' structures. When this strategy failed to localize the engram, theoretical models based on the assumption that learning and memory involved the entire brain became popular. It would be premature to dispute this notion unequivocally but recent results offer another model. (Swartz, 1978: 449)

Here a textbook account suggests it was 'premature' to dismiss the sort of account given by Lashley. Nevertheless, even in such an introductory text, the 'offer' of an alternative account was possible by this time. Swartz goes on to postulate a 'model' which makes use of studies of 'subcortical' processes (below the cortex; see also Thompson, 1982); a model 'somewhere between conceptions that looked for discrete localization of the engram and conceptions that say localization is impossible' (Swartz, 1978: 449).

If the detail of Lashley's work was still relevant in the 1970s, a decade later this was no longer the case. The task of this section, then, is to show some of the ways in which Lashley's work is described and to examine some of the promissory notes on offer. First an examination of the way in which Pribram concluded his 1982 article. He lists a large number of rival proposals for the localisation of function (these include the model suggested by Hebb in 1949). He then says:

> The persistent puzzle that brain functions appear to be both localized and distributed is thus resolved. Memory storage is shown to be distributed; decisional operators involved in coding and retrieval are localized. . . . In short, there are 'boxes in the brain', each 'box' corresponds to a 'faculty of mind'. But these 'boxes' operate on a distributed matrix that is nonlocal and therefore available to all. (Pribram, 1982: 291)

Single quotation marks are used in this extract to suggest a temporary or 'pragmatic' status for the terms employed.[17] However, while memory is 'distributed' across the cortex, 'coding and retrieval' functions (the terms come from work in artificial intelligence) are held to be localized. At this stage in the text, no mention of the term 'hologram' appears; a new 'solution' has been constructed. In this case, objects such as memory are 'boxes' with 'functional' status: they are 'distributed' and not given specific anatomical locations. This is the first time the phrase 'boxes in the brain' appears in the article. Pribram then gives a 'Conclusion':

> There is a considerable intellectual distance between Lashley's despair in finding a localized engram in 1950 and the richness of data and theory on cerebral localization and distribution in 1980. To his credit, Lashley recognized the problem and specified it in sufficient detail so the generation of investigators standing on his shoulders could deal effectively with it. That so much progress has been made reflects the support given by society to the brain and behavioural sciences during this 30-year period. Should this support continue, the issue of localization–distribution that has mobilized such differing views over the past two centuries may yet be resolved before the end of the twentieth. (Pribram, 1982: 291–292)

Credit is being assigned to Lashley for 'recognizing the problem' despite his 'despair'; a generation stands on 'his shoulders' (see also Merton, 1965). Further, in the space of three paragraphs, a change has occurred: from the 'persistent puzzle is thus resolved', to the issue 'may yet be resolved', if current funding levels continue. This inconsistency makes a satisfactory interpretation difficult to find, but it will be assumed that this is not a straightforward proof-reading error. Rhetorically, there may be a problem for an author in trying to distance himself from the perceived failure of an earlier writer; to reject the holographic metaphor, without appearing to return to 'Lashley's despair'. The solution to this difficulty involved claiming to have resolved the issue of localization–distribution by standing on Lashley's shoulders (a standard trope; see Merton, 1965), without offering large amounts of detail concerning the solution. Thus, the conclusion contains yet another promise of results to come.

The promissory note offered by Pribram is slightly different from the others to be considered in this section. Pribram uses the 'boxes in the brain' account, but his final sentence does not refer to this metaphor. Instead, the promissory note is given in terms of the importance of the whole question, rather than some specific avenue of research. Pribram (1982) promises that, although the issue has been in debate for 'two centuries', the problem is resolvable and 'may yet' be resolved within twenty years.

This practice of incorporating historical material into contemporary accounts is fairly typical: many authors attempt to describe the particular 'origins' of the accounts they are expounding. One example of this is the work of Rumelhart and McClelland (1986), two researchers in the highly influential, computer-based, Parallel Distributed Processing perspective (PDP). They begin their account of the PDP approach with reference to Hughlings Jackson, the nineteenth-century neurologist, and to Luria.[18] They then state that:

> Two other contributors to the deep background of PDP were Hebb (1949) and Lashley (1950). . . . Lashley's contribution was to insist upon the idea of distributed representation. Lashley may have been too radical and too vague, and his doctrine of equipotentiality of broad regions of the cortex clearly overstated the case. Yet many of his insights into the difficulties of storing the 'engram' are telling, and he seemed to capture quite precisely the essence of

distributed representation in insisting that 'there are no special cells for special memories'. (Rumelhart and McClelland, 1986: 41)

As in the extract from Pribram (1982), Lashley's 'contribution' is stated in terms consistent with the general account by Rumelhart and McClelland (1986). The meaning of this 'deep background' metaphor is not entirely clear, but it may suggest that the details of Lashley's work are not worth considering. This is borne out by the description of his work as 'radical', 'vague', 'clearly overstated', the product of a 'doctrine'. Lashley is also described as having been precise (with 'many insights') insofar as he can be read as conforming to the PDP thesis. Rumelhart and McClelland go on to give credit to a long list of people including those (e.g. Longuet-Higgins) who were in part responsible for the popularity of the holographic model, although here they are described as having worked on 'distributed representational schemes' (Rumelhart and McClelland, 1986: 42).[19] Thus, the history of this discipline is being rewritten in order to show a particular thesis as the culmination of what has gone before (see also Fuller, 1991). Lashley's work is described as only part of the 'deep background' because, on this account, such work was itself 'vague' and 'radical'; Lashley's contribution was at once too vague, and full of precise insight. The section on origins ends, as may be expected, with a promissory note:

> The power of parallel distributed processing is becoming more and more apparent, and many others have recently joined in the exploration of the capabilities of these mechanisms. We hope this book represents the nature of the enterprise we are all involved in, and that it does justice to the potential of the PDP approach. (Rumelhart and McClelland, 1986: 43–44)

This promissory note offers 'power' and 'potential' and the possibility of working with 'many others' in a united research effort, for a common goal. The use here of the term 'becoming' suggests that the approach has some inner nature which is revealing itself, as does the expression 'exploration of the capabilities'. This is a frequent part of such texts: the rhetoric shifts the source of agency from the researcher to the phenomena in question. It is the 'potential' of the object of enquiry which is paramount; it is not the ingenuity of the writer which is the controlling factor.

Research in accordance with the PDP approach bears few similarities to the research programmes Lashley used. It involves such things as computer simulation and mathematical models of domain-specific tasks such as reading, learning, sequential processing and so on. The questions are often of the form: 'How could a process such as X be performed?' The answers given are often functional (rather than anatomical), and related to specific tasks (particular sorts of recall in humans, for example). Lashley's questions were typically of the form: 'Given that an action of a specific kind is performed, what sections of the brain are involved?' The answers given were in terms of general competence using a particular anatomical basis. Whilst these forms of question and answer could be related in some ways, each is tied to the methods the researcher has adopted. Thus, using a computer as both research tool and as a metaphor[20] (something which became more feasible from the 1970s), helped to shift research away from Lashley's programmes.

The development of computer technology can be broadly characterised as invoking a change from 'top-down' to 'bottom-up' research strategies (and the terms themselves come from the artificial intelligence field). Lashley's research, with its use of surgical damage, was a sort of top-down approach difficult to apply to a computer: it is, for example, unusual to describe an action as having inflicted damage to 93 percent of the computer's components (though, perhaps not impossible). Further, although the use of live subjects and the examination of the effects of damage to the brain is still being undertaken, several differences need to be noted. The subjects are typically human (rather than primate, feline or rodent); the form of cortical damage is not controlled by the experimenter (as it results from medical dysfunction, rather than experimenter intervention) and the detailed examination of a single case is regarded as a valid method (but was not for Lashley, who used groups of animals which were given the same pattern of injuries). This more recent general account will now be illustrated.

Ellis and Young in their textbook *Human Cognitive Neuropsychology* (1988), spell out what they take to be the assumptions made in contemporary accounts of studies done using single, human subjects. They identify four major assumptions which they regard as 'untestable':

1  *Modularity*: the mind is made up of a number of specialised or domain-specific modules, each of which is informationally encapsulated to the extent that processing is carried out 'in complete ignorance of, and isolation from, the processes going on elsewhere in the total cognitive system' (Ellis and Young, 1988: 14). The metaphor they use to explain this idea is that of a modular home-stereo system. This could also be described as the 'boxes in the brain' metaphor (although the number of boxes, and the extent of such modular architecture is currently a matter for debate).
2  *Isomorphism*: there is a correspondence between models of the mind and the organisation of the brain. This assumption is crucial: without it all such research is irrelevant.
3  *Transparency*: 'the pattern of errors shown by a patient after brain injury must be capable of leading us to valid conclusions about the nature and functions of the impaired processing components' (Ellis and Young, 1988: 17). That is, the pattern of errors must be stable, and not a product of the experimental situation.
4  *Subtractivity*: once an injury has been sustained, a mature brain is incapable of developing a new module. Without this assumption, credence would be given to Lashley's principle of equipotentiality, with alternative areas of the brain taking up functions of a damaged area.

Using the philosopher Imre Lakatos as a kind of authority figure, Ellis and Young argue that, although such assumptions are untestable, an indication of the validity of the assumptions can be taken from the success of the whole research enterprise. The argument is then made that the field is flourishing, therefore the assumptions must be correct. Each of these assumptions may be regarded as a promissory note; notes that will be paid off with the solution of brain organisation. All but the third assumption either rejects, or renders irrelevant, the account presented by Lashley (1950/1960).

Ellis and Young also give an historical account in which they explicitly align their approach with the one dominant between 1870 and 1910: 'there are several respects in which modern cognitive neuropsychology can justly be regarded as a return to this turn-of-the-century approach, though the theories and methods have become more sophisticated' (Ellis and Young, 1988: 10). The philosopher Jerry Fodor (1983) reaches back even further into history by beginning with a long discussion of the merits of the phrenological movement. In Fodor's account, the only 'mistake' Gall made was in assuming that developments in particular areas of the brain would be revealed in the contours of the skull (Fodor, 1983: 23). Gall was 'right' to suggest that the mind is made up of a number of vertical faculties, and those faculties are 'modular' in the sense described by Ellis and Young. But Fodor also admits, albeit without any explicit reference to the term 'equipotentiality', that it is possible that some aspects of the system are nonmodular (1983: 119). Thus, the extent of modular architecture remains a direction for future research. In his Introduction, Fodor deals with the possibility of 'nonmodularity' in the following way:

> I shall make some depressing remarks along the following lines: though the putatively nonmodular processes include some of the ones that we would most like to know about (thought, for example, and the fixation of belief), our cognitive science had in fact made approximately no progress in studying these processes, and this may well be because of their nonmodularity. It may be that, from the point of view of practicable research strategy, it is only the modular cognitive systems that we can have any serious hope of understanding. In which case, convincing arguments for nonmodularity should be received with considerable gloom. (Fodor, 1983: 38)

This claim, according to Ellis and Young (1988), was regarded as controversial: why should some parts of the brain *not* be modular? According to Fodor, if the brain did (at least in part) turn out to be nonmodular, then further research would be made very difficult (perhaps in the way implied by Lashley's account, though Lashley did not use the language of artificial intelligence); research would have no 'serious hope of understanding . . . thought, for example'. Recall Pribram's (1969) comment that the brain seemed to mock the ingenuity of the experimenter; such a prospect should indeed be received with considerable gloom – that indeed is the warning being issued here. That is, on this argument, if accounts were presented which suggested that the brain was nonmodular, promissory notes would be difficult to issue. Rhetorically, such an alternative evokes such words as 'gloom', 'depressing' and 'despair' (the last was used by Lashley, 1950/ 1960). Tim Shallice (1988) makes a similar point in a section called 'On Modularity':

> If Lashley's (1929) idea of mass action were valid, then neuropsychology would be of little relevance for understanding normal function. Any form of neurological damage would deplete by a greater or lesser degree the available amount of some general resource, say the mythical *g*. . . . If one considers the design principles that might underlie cognitive systems, a rough contrast can be drawn between systems based on equipotentiality . . . and more modular ones. At a metatheoretical level, some form of the 'modularity' thesis is probably the most widely accepted position in the philosophy of psychology today . . . (Shallice, 1988: 18)

Shallice has chosen one of the oldest references to Lashley (1929 rather than, say, 1950). Further, the idea of a general resource ('*g*') is referred to as 'mythical'.[21] The point given in favour of the modularity thesis is that it is the 'most widely accepted' position. In this passage it is claimed that, in terms of a practicable research project, the assumption that Lashley's work is 'valid' is no cause to celebrate because contemporary neuropsychology would then be of 'little relevance'.

Shallice later gives a substantial account directed against the notion of equipotentiality, and so does not dismiss the rival thesis as lightly as Rumelhart and McClelland (1986). However, he does state that: after 'the defeat of the diagram-makers [around 1905], neuropsychology became much less interesting' (1988: 13) – thus imposing a judgement from the present context, while making it a universal claim. Little information is provided about the reaction against the diagram-makers (a period Shallice gives as 1905 to 1940)[22] he states that the theoretical approach must have seemed outdated by 1920 'when conceptual frameworks like behaviourism, Gestalt psychology, and mass action were in the ascendance' (1988: 10). Each of these 'frameworks' is now largely discredited within the psychological literature (and 'mass action' was a term from Lashley). Shallice is able to construct his particular historical account partly through limiting the term 'neuropsychology' to human clinical studies (of individual defects and injuries), and Ellis and Young (1988) make the term function in the same way (and thus make Lashley irrelevant).

Shallice again adopts an historical perspective in the final paragraph of his book in order to issue a promissory note:

> Thirty years ago, except for certain seemingly outdated schools of neurologists, the modular view of the cognitive system that neuropsychology offers would have seemed as implausible as that provided by Gall. The answers that have been given for the variety of phenomena discovered and documented over many aspects of perception, language, memory, and cognition may not survive. The range of conceptual problems that these phenomena pose will, however, remain. When they can be adequately answered, psychology will have become a science. (Shallice, 1988: 404)

Here the promissory note rests less heavily on the success of the assumption of modularity; at the same time earlier 'conceptual problems' (from 'thirty years ago') are implied to have resulted from nonmodular accounts. Nevertheless, the suggestion is that the modularity thesis is no longer implausible. The pay-off for continuing to research the problems which Shallice poses in his book is an impressive one: the admission of psychology into the realm of science.

The final promissory note to be examined comes from Churchland's book (1986) which, in part, attempts to give a general account of the merits of various theories of brain functioning. Each of these modern theories depends on the assumption (or metaphor) of modularity. Without spelling out exactly which particular theory she prefers, Churchland concludes:

> [D]iscoveries in the neurosciences will undoubtedly change out of all recognition a host of orthodoxies beloved in philosophy. Barring a miracle (or calcified stubbornness), it will in particular transfigure epistemology, as we discover what it really means for brains to learn, to theorize, to know, and to represent. (Churchland: 1986: 482)

With prospects such as these, the arrival of which will only be delayed by a 'miracle', or 'calcified stubbornness', there remains little motivation for maintaining a research programme into Lashley's principle of equipotentiality: the roads of future funding seem to be lined with gold.

**Conclusions**

The present chapter has begun the task of opening up debates in psychology for analysis in terms of rhetorical construction: a task to be given in more detail in the remaining chapters. But the focus here on promissory notes is one intended for generalisation: the motivation of research to come is not by any means restricted to debates in neuro-psychology. A 'promissory note' was defined as a rhetorical device used to postpone certain problems or questions by reference to some desired research goal, no matter what psychological object is being investigated. It was then suggested that scientific metaphors function as promissory notes; that the metaphorical description of a psychological object (as a hologram, or as a computer program or component) may be used to invite further investigation in the direction suggested by the original study. Moreover, such an investigation will be consistent with a metaphor described as 'promising'. In order to illustrate these claims, the work of Lashley was briefly reviewed to show the way in which a problem was being character-ised in 1950. Some detail was then given concerning the way in which the holographic metaphor was used as a way of accounting for Lashley's results. It was then shown that such a metaphor could be regarded as an unfulfilled promissory note because recent reviews characterised it as an unfruitful avenue for research. The remainder of the chapter was then taken up with two things: first, how current reviews of the field account for Lashley's work. It was suggested that changes in the field have been so

great as to render irrelevant a direct argument against Lashley's conclusions. Second, a number of recent promissory notes were reviewed; notes
which claimed that, if funds continued, the debate would be resolved, that
continued research will reveal the power of a given approach, that human
neuropsychology will expand because the assumptions made are correct,
that further research will result in psychology becoming a science, and that
an epistemological revolution will occur unless a miracle stops it. Such
promises act as a way of motivating further research in a given direction,
towards the sort of goals listed above. Although many technological
changes have worked against the continuation of Lashley's research
programmes, it may also be the case that his ideas were not described as
providing the scope for promises of the sort currently being offered:
Lashley's 'despair' (1950/1960) was not rhetorically sufficient for motivating further research; not enough promises were made.

Lashley described himself as aware of the use of metaphors within his
area. At an American Neurological Association symposium in 1951 he
remarked:

> There has been a curious parallel in the histories of neurological theories and of
> paranoid delusional systems. In Mesmer's day the paranoid was persecuted by
> malicious animal magnetism, his successors by galvanic shocks, by the telegraph,
> by radio, and by radar, keeping their delusional systems up to date with the latest
> fashions in physics. Descartes was impressed by the hydraulic figures in the royal
> gardens and developed a hydraulic theory of the action of the brain. We have
> since had telephone theories, electric field theories, and now theories based on
> the computing machines and automatic rudders. I suggest that we are more likely
> to find out how the brain works by studying the brain itself and the phenomena
> of behaviour than by indulging in far-fetched physical analogies. (quoted by
> Cobb, 1960: xix)

Here a list of changes in the metaphors employed in accounting for the
brain is given, ending with the 'automatic rudder' (and perhaps producing
laughter). Rhetorically, this passage ridicules the use of physical analogy
by associating it with the practices of those certified insane. According to
Lashley, researchers should not fall prey to the sorts of 'delusional systems'
that psychiatric patients (the 'paranoid') 'suffer' from; they should,
instead, study 'the brain itself'. One reaction to such a claim has been to
argue that, even if new ideas come from the latest technology, this 'is
fashion, but not just fashion' (Oatley, 1985: 34). However, it may also be
that such a reaction constitutes the 'rhetoric of anti-rhetoric'; that changes
in accounts of psychological objects result from changes in rhetoric and
metaphor. It remains an open question for psychologists and philosophers
whether such a 'direct' examination of the brain is possible (and a question
for some historians and sociologists). But, to issue my own promissory
note, if psychology does proceed through what Danziger (1990) calls
'generative metaphors', and these metaphors are communicated through
texts, then we must abandon the rhetoric of anti-rhetoric and focus on the
way texts are constructed. It is only by doing this that we can begin to
understand the process of persuasion in psychology and science in general.

Finally, a note to any psychologists reading this text: be aware of being goaded by the latest theoretical pronouncement. The reading of a text, no matter how technical, is a form of seduction: it is used to offer inducements and issue warnings; a bright new future awaits those who devote their efforts to the pursuit of research in the direction favoured by the author you are reading. But with each promissory note comes a variety of presuppositions, theoretical and methodological; presuppositions which entail the closure of problematic questions, and alignment with concerns that render irrelevant forms of investigation originally regarded as urgent. In the next chapter, theories of development are used to illustrate the variety of presuppositions involved in the investigation of a psychological object, in this case, the child: each theory offers a number of promises while, at the same time, denying the pursuit of alternatives. With Kenneth Burke, it needs to be asserted that: 'All questions are leading questions. . . . Every question selects a field of battle, and in this selection it forms the nature of the answers' (1941/1973: 67; see also Bygrave, 1993: 58 ff).

**Notes**

1. A draft of the present chapter was given as a paper at the 4th Annual Conference of the History and Philosophy of Psychology Section of the British Psychological Society, 1990; a different version will appear as Soyland (1994g).

2. The role of Harvard University in the history of psychology should not be under-estimated. As well as being the centre of Lashley's research programme, it was (at different times) the work place of William James, Edward Thorndike, Edward Tolman (as a graduate student), Gordon Allport, Edwin Boring, B.F. Skinner, Jerome Bruner and George Miller. The William James Lectures, and other forums at Harvard, were used to introduce the ideas of Kohler, Lewin, Luria, Piaget, Chomsky, Lacan, J.L. Austin, Donald Broadbent, Tversky and Kahnemann, and others (see Bruner, 1983). Bruner and Miller established the first Centre for Cognitive Studies there (in 1960) and Thomas Kuhn worked there as a graduate student, having some contact with the cognitive group (Bruner, 1983: 85).

3. There is a methodological issue here concerning the way researchers before 1880 should be described. Harrington, for example, chooses to use such terms as 'psycho-physiologists' (1987: 63) to describe British researchers working in the nineteenth century – the label used in different cases is a reflection of theoretical framework (see also Smith, 1992 and O'Connor, 1988).

4. The excerpt from Young (1987) provides an example of what Leary (1987, 1990a) describes in a different context; that is, of a rhetorical shift between suggesting an 'analogy', and later suggesting something 'is' the same as the analogy. A more theoretical discussion of metaphor and related tropes (such as analogy) will be found in Chapter 6.

5. For discussions of Darwin's rhetoric, see Beer (1983) and Gross (1990) – Beer's text is a classic of the literature in this area. The promissory note given here allowed Darwin to avoid questions which he had discussed at length in an earlier manuscript, but which he thought would bring too much controversy; see Desmond and Moore (1991) for an account of the process of Darwin's writing (among other things).

6. The detail of the literature on metaphor will not be discussed until Chapter 6. For other accounts see, for example, Ricoeur (1978) and Cooper (1986). Cooper provides an account of both Continental and Anglo-American traditions (as does Ricoeur), but develops arguments on metaphor which concentrate on the Anglo-American tradition (but that is certainly not a dismissive description).

7. In Austin's (e.g. 1962/1975) terms, (a) is an illocutionary act and (b) is a perlocutionary act. This distinction was discussed in Chapter 1. I will maintain that (b) is to be a 'corollary' of (a) in that, if the rhetorical act of making a 'promise' is regarded (by the reader/listener) as significant, then the promise will have (perlocutionary) consequences. Alternatively, if the promise is dismissed or disregarded, then the consequences should not be connected to the original promise. If, for example, I suggested that 'memory is a banana' (an illocutionary act), then the perlocutionary consequences for psychological research are likely (in present circumstances, at least) to be fairly small, because the scope of the metaphor (and therefore of the promise) would not be regarded as significant (or relevant) to the research community of the 1990s. The present chapter will show that metaphors involving holograms and computers have had a significant rhetorical impact – to the extent that the latter are currently regarded as the end of the story.

8. A collection of Lashley's more important papers appeared in Beach et al. (1960); a commemorative collection of essays devoted to the significance of Lashley's work appeared in Orbach (1982). For accounts of Lashley's position in the history of psychology, see Bruce (1986), Boring (1950), Hoffman et al. (1990), and Hebb's Introduction to Lashley (Lashley, 1950/1960). For historical accounts of the background to Lashley's research, see Luria (1973/ 1984), Harrington (1987), Young (1970), Brazier (1988), Star (1983, 1989), Riese (1959) and Franz (1932).

9. Such an assumption is not always made. Miller, for example, closes an introductory chapter on 'Animal behaviour' thus: 'Why study animal psychology? Not to learn about man, even though we may. If we see ourselves mirrored there, it is good, but not necessary. The only true reason for studying animals is to learn about animals, about the lives and struggles of our fellow creatures' (1962/1966: 248). Here 'fellow creatures' should not imply any direct relation to be expanded upon by psychology. The antagonism in this passage may be seen with reference to Chapter 3, Note 2. Lashley worked for a time with J.B. Watson (Bruce, 1986). Thus, although Lashley and Skinner are not mentioned in Miller's chapter on animal behaviour, the possible targets are obvious (to some; see Myers, 1990b): 'some behaviourists claimed to pull the whole science of psychology out of a rat' (1962/1966: 238).

10. Aspects of Hebb's (1949) theory are still described as relevant in some of the current discussions. See, for example, Pribram's and Hebb's contributions to Orbach (1982) and Pribram (1990). This will be discussed later in the chapter. On the relationship between Hebb and Lashley, see Doty (1982). Doty notes that Hebb approached Lashley as a co-author at an early stage of producing the book. Hebb (1949) cites fifteen of Lashley's publications (author or co-author) – a high count in the field.

11. Gall's account of mind ('Phrenology') had been made popular partly through the efforts of Spurzheim (Harrington, 1987: 10). It is important to introduce this particular account here because the debate for and against localisation has been influenced by the term 'phrenology'. For various accounts of the importance of Gall, and of the 'Phrenology movement', see Star (1989), Young (1970), Boring (1950) and Brazier (1988). The impact of the phrenological account has received attention in sociology and literary studies: for a list of references to this literature, see Shuttleworth (1989).

12. What 'really' caused the downfall of Lashley's thesis is not the question addressed here – such a question is beyond the remit of the present enquiry, and would entail a different form of investigation.

13. Thompson (1982) sustains such rhetoric throughout his article: at once praising and reducing the importance of Lashley's work. This form of writing will be addressed in Chapter 9.

14. While such techniques were being reported in 1969, earlier reports are also frequent. Lashley et al. (1951), for example, described experiments involving the introduction of gold foil into the cortex of monkeys in order to argue against 'simple field theories'. Pribram (1982) also reported on 'field theories' and dismissed them; the most recent experimental report cited by Pribram in this case was 1963. More recently, Pribram (1990) included a discussion of work originally labelled 'field theory' using the 'holography' label, but in this case gave a more favourable characterisation.

15. It is perhaps now easier to understand how secondary texts such as Young (1987) can come to refer to memory as actually being holographic. More detailed accounts of the metaphor will show how it came to be regarded.

16. Hatfield's (1988) extended review of Churchland (1986) treats the latter as promoting a 'program'. This would support the second alternative given here, one in which the literature has a kind of 'leading edge' (the metaphor here suggests progress and a given direction). The first alternative, in which Young is left 'uncontradicted' as a result of brevity, would entail a more uniform or systematic literature within the neurosciences in which the texts of one author are vetted by a hierarchy of peers. The difference here cannot be pursued; it constitutes an avenue for further research.

17. Rather than to indicate, as in the present text, where a term is being 'mentioned' and not 'used'. This issue is mentioned in Chapter 9.

18. For an account of the work of Jackson, see Star (1989). Luria (1902–1977) gave an overview of his work (in relation to neuropsychology) in English in 1973 (with a Foreword by Pribram).

19. Pribram (1990: 88) cites Rumelhart and McClelland (1986), and also gives an account of the 'impact of holography (parallel distributed processing)'. By giving this form of title to a section of his text, he forms a rhetorical link similar to Rumelhart and McClelland. In both, the holographic metaphor *is* the PDP metaphor.

20. Connections between tools employed and metaphors developed are examined by Gigerenzer and Murray (1987) in an account of the use of statistics in psychology. In a related context, Billig (1987) and Billig et al. (1988) may be regarded as using rhetoric and dilemmas as metaphors for what happens inside the head.

21. The term '*g*' was associated with research into IQ, and used to label 'general' intelligence (see Spearman, 1923, 1927; and discussion in Chapter 7). A recent debate (Howe, 1990; Nettelbeck, 1990, and rejoinders) indicates that '*g*' may be used as an insulting label. Instead, generalised (innate) cognitive ability, at least according to Nettelbeck, no longer ought to be associated with 'a *g* model' (1990: 495).

22. This period is covered by the majority of the historical texts cited in earlier Notes; see also Forrester (1980), which concentrates in particular on the relation between this literature and psychoanalysis; some of this material is extended in Forrester, 1990a.

# 4

# Comparing Concepts of Development: Metaphor and Presupposition

> Mothers with babies are dealing with a developing, changing situation; the baby starts off not knowing about the world, and by the time they have finished their job the baby is grown up into someone who knows about the world. . . . What a tremendous development!
>
> (Winnicott, 1957/1964: 69)

> . . . this seems so outlandish a thing that one must needs go a little into the history and philosophy of it.
>
> (Melville, 1851: 358)

In Chapter 3, it was argued that metaphors function as promissory notes which allow assumptions to be maintained through offering desirable rewards. In this chapter it will be argued that metaphors may also be used as a way of bringing philosophical presuppositions into a text: with each presuppostion comes a particular view of a psychological object, a way of describing and analysing it, a lexicon to be assimilated; taking some assumptions for granted is the first step in rendering alternatives irrelevant; it is also to assume the very existence of the object being described. By giving a detailed account of various texts, many such presuppositions may be made explicit: this is the first step in making alternatives possible. The literature concerned with the psychological development of children was chosen for the present analysis because this is an area which is frequently regarded as philosophically 'unproblematic'.

The changes which occur from birth to adulthood are dramatic, but accounts of 'development' (whether influenced by 'genetic' *or* 'historical' *or* 'social' causes) will be shown to vary substantially (the differences between sorts of causes is a subject for the present discussion): children do not just 'grow' into 'adolescents' (the category itself is recent) and then 'mature' into adults. The method for showing such variations will be to juxtapose several theories, examining several (but certainly not all) of the conflicting views of development that there have been in the history of psychology. This will entail giving a short exposition of each theory, through the detailed analysis of a small number of texts: each text is an example from a larger corpus, but the generalisations will remain fairly implicit.

The great majority of the theories covered here are still being researched and expanded today: this is a complicating factor in the present analysis. The range of psychological texts which include discussions of the term 'development' is vast, and one important area in contemporary research (the 'cognitive' or, sometimes, 'nativist' approach) will not be covered at all. Moreover, there are post-Freudians, post-Piagetians, post-Vygotskians and so on, each of whom may (or will) claim to have refined aspects of some earlier theory. So, it should be stressed again (see Chapters 1–2) that the object is only to review texts in order to examine a variety of metaphors and presuppositions which have been related to conceptions of development (and not to find the most appropriate metaphor).

This chapter makes several theoretical claims which should not get lost in the large amount of case-study material which follows. One of the most important aspects of a theory of psychology is that it gives a reader (or writer) a way of characterising a phenomenon: the creation of a lexicon is an important part of the rhetoric. Talking and writing will depend on a number of presuppositions and, accordingly, different presuppositions will bring about different forms of discourse.[1] The main burden of the chapter, then, will be to show that even 'unproblematic' phenomena may be discussed in many different ways: the 'development' of the child will be used here to introduce a variety of theoretical perspectives and, by juxtaposing these perspectives, it will be shown how much they depend on presuppositions (and how often such presuppositions are revealed in the use of metaphor). So, the claim here will be that different metaphors give rise to different forms of rhetoric, and that such rhetoric is rendered 'invisible' insofar as it is successfully describes a phenomena as 'unproblematic'. The ultimate form of success, in this case, would be for a text to achieve a 'complete explanation' of a phenomenon (supposing such a thing were possible). Conversely, the rhetoric of the present chapter will be used to render discourse concerned with development less straightforward.[2]

At one point in his book, *Mental Illness and Psychology* (1954/1976), Foucault discusses what he regards to be two general conceptions of development:

> In psychological evolution, it is the past that promotes the present and makes it possible; in psychological history, it is the present that detaches itself from the past, conferring meaning upon it, making it intelligible. Psychological development is both evolution and history. . . . The original error of psychoanalysis and, following it, of most genetic psychologies is no doubt that of seizing these two irreducible dimensions of evolution and history in the unity of psychological development. (Foucault, 1954/1976: 30–31)

In a methodological chapter (written in the 1920s), Vygotsky also draws (*and* exemplifies) the distinction given by Foucault:

> Naturalism in historical analysis, according to Engels, manifests itself in the assumption that only nature affects human beings and only natural conditions determine historical development. The dialectical approach, while admitting the influence of nature on man, asserts that man, in turn, affects nature and creates

through his changes in nature new natural conditions for his existence.
(Vygotsky, 1978: 60)

In the present chapter, these two characterisations will be taken as a
starting point. Importantly, none of the texts analysed here present the
'history (nurture) versus evolution (nature)' dichotomy as an 'either/or'.[3]
Rather, the texts to be examined here all concentrate on the young child
(birth to around 10 years of age), and accounts which do invoke a 'nature/
nurture' dichotomy typically debate developmental issues using a much
wider age range (birth to adulthood). So, the point to be taken from the
quotations above (Foucault, Vygotsky) is that differences emerge in
the way one aspect of development is favoured (but not favoured at the
complete expense of the other).

Historically, very little attention has been paid to philosophical issues
related to developmental psychology (although there have been changes
recently).[4] A general text such as Valentine's *Conceptual Issues in
Psychology* (1982) does not discuss problems raised by theories of
development. Cairns and Ornstein (1979) point out that Boring's *History
of Experimental Psychology* (1950) does not list any terms related to
development in the index. Other general texts (for example Pratt, 1978;
Dennett, 1979; Eacker, 1983; Koch and Leary, 1985; Leary, 1990b) give
accounts of historical and philosophical issues relevant to psychology,
without treating 'development' as an issue of significance.[5] That is, while
much observation and experimental work has been undertaken, it is not
(typically) seen as problematic beyond the specialist literature on developmental issues.

The theories to be considered here do not all discuss the same aspects of
development. There is at least, then, the possibility of some unified theory
of development. Were such a thing possible it might take the following
form. Perhaps, for example, Piaget is right about the structure of logical
thinking and perspective, psychoanalysis right about the development of
the ego and the resolution of conflicting drives, Merleau-Ponty right about
the importance of the perspective of the 'other', Watson and Skinner right
about the level of flexibility in development and the importance of
reinforcement, Vygotsky right about the importance of the role played by
the teacher in developing a less able mind and so on. Here the image is of a
child whose development has many 'facets'; a given theory only 'casts light'
on one. Such an 'image'[6] will be discussed in the final section of the
chapter, 'The conceptual child'. But this ontological possibility is not at
issue here. Instead, it will be argued that the discourse of each account is at
best difficult to resolve into a common rhetoric, and such a resolution
would do violence to the respective metaphors and assumptions involved in
establishing a theory: while a 'unified' theory of cognitive development is
(of course) rhetorically possible, I will be suggesting that such a theory
would necessitate the invention of a new rhetoric, one that could not be
compatible with all of the components of the rhetoric used in previous
texts.

## Wundt

The majority of historical accounts of the development of the discipline of
psychology (for example Koch and Leary, 1985; Ash, 1982: 109–116) take
the work of Wilhelm Wundt, the founding of his laboratory, and the
publication of *Outlines of Psychology* (1897), to mark the start of scientific
psychology.[7] The book was described as a 'brief manual to supplement the
lectures' (1897, author's preface) which Wundt was giving in Leipzig and it
contains a brief account of the psychical development of the child (1897:
283–295). Thus, given its importance in disciplinary histories, it will be
worthwhile to begin the review of the discourse on development with this
text.

By the time Wundt comes to his discussion of 'psychical development' he
has already devoted many words to examining psychical 'elements' (pure
sensations, simple feelings), 'compounds' (intensive, spatial and temporal
ideas, composite feelings, emotions), and the 'interconnections of psychical
compounds' (consciousness, associations, apperceptive combinations).
Each could be examined in isolation, as a set of autonomous components.
Part 4 of the book, on 'Psychical development', is then given as three
sections: psychical attributes of animals, psychical development of the
child, and the development of mental communities. Part 5, finally, is titled
'Psychical causality and its laws'. Wundt, then, did not regard the study of
development as fundamental or prior to other areas of psychology (and the
pattern of topics presented by Wundt is largely repeated in most general
textbooks).

In Wundt's text, the topic of development is largely covered in his
discussion of animals:

> If we try to answer the general question of the genetic relation of man to the
> animals on the ground of a comparison of their psychical attributes, it must be
> admitted, in view of the likeness of psychical elements and of their simplest and
> most general forms of combination, that it is possible that human consciousness
> has developed from a lower form of animal consciousness. This assumption also
> finds strong support in the fact that the animal kingdom presents a whole series
> of different stages of psychical development and that every human individual
> passes through an analogous development. (Wundt, 1897: 280–281)

This promotes the doctrine that 'ontogeny recapitulates phylogeny'[8] which
I will discuss briefly in relation to Freud. Wundt goes on to say that the
differences between man and animal are 'after all more one of degree and
complexity . . . than of kind' (1897: 282). The use of the 'degree versus
kind' distinction (typical in philosophical texts) allows the connection or
continuity between animals and man to be inserted into the argument fairly
simply (using 'after all', here a kind of 'of course' clause). This part of
Wundt's argument thus leads on to the section on human development (as
it does not for Vygotsky; see later discussion).

Wundt states that development in man is slower than most animals
because of a 'gradual maturing of his sense functions'. Some movements

are the result of 'inherited reflexes' and the child's rather 'obscure sensations and feelings' with nothing 'clear' in consciousness until the end of the first month; even then mood changes are rapid and sensations 'limited'. It is then that the first 'symptoms of pleasurable and unpleasurable feelings' can be observed.[9] Towards the end of the first year comes the 'differentiation of feelings'. Memory, too, undergoes a process of development: babies rapidly acquire the 'ability to find the mother's breast' but these associations 'cover only very short intervals of time, at first only hours, then days'. Even at 3 or 4 years memory remains imperfect. Self-consciousness (a 'feeling' of the 'ego') is a development which is difficult to determine but probably occurs before 5 or 6, and traces may 'begin to appear in the first weeks'. With the 'growth of attention come the volitional acts'.

The ability to speak is a result of the 'influence of those about the child' who both imitate and are imitated by the child. Complex functions are the last to develop and include the 'activity of imagination' and the 'play impulse'. A child's games, starting in the first year with 'rhythmical movements of the arms and legs', are 'pure imagination' and 'untrammelled' by intellectual or aesthetic demands. Play later 'becomes gradually a voluntary imitation . . . often accelerated' through the influence of others. The 'processes of imagination are gradually curtailed' as the development of 'abstract thinking' has 'set in' (which does not happen in 'savages').

Wundt's account of development, then, is one in which various aspects of general cognitive ability change as a function of time. This is not true of language, however, in which Wundt stresses the role of the adult (as does Vygotsky). Nevertheless, the processes described are autonomous: things 'grow', 'begin to appear' and 'set in'. Wundt's account is presented in terms of a number of observations, drawing attention to methodological problems arising from not having direct access to what the child's thinking is like. Wundt offers no grand theory and posits few abstract entities (such as the 'play-impulse'). Unlike the other theorists to be reviewed here, he left no surviving 'school' of thought, yet his account presents (by no means for the first time) rhetorical elements which are still to be found in theories of development in the twentieth century.

The remainder of the chapter, then, is structured in roughly chronological order but, while the theories did not all start at the same time and were, in some cases, reactions against each other, they were all largely developed in the twentieth century; they are still taken seriously and put under investigation in some quarters, and they have all been popular during some part of the century is some countries.[10] Finally, in the sections which follow, the selection of texts for analysis was made according to length; short pieces which summarised an account of development were chosen simply because they could be analysed in detail without overly increasing the length of the chapter. This method of analysis leaves some room for debate as to whether it constitutes a form of conceptual history, an area of scholarship which claims to be able to extract from a text the essential elements of a writer's work. An analysis of rhetoric may not be directly in opposition to such an approach except insofar as it claims to describe a position beyond the one originally given by an author, a kind of 'what X *really* meant to say'.


## Psychoanalysis

### Freud

Freud (1856–1939) wrote a very concise summary of his views on development in the opening chapter of *Civilization and its Discontents* (1930/1961). For Freud development was something a child underwent alone, with a combination of learning (what I shall call a linear model) and a progression through phases or stages (what I shall call a sequential model).[11] This difference will be explained in a moment. But before any development begins, Freud postulates an 'ego' and claims this ego to be different at birth from that of an adult (1930/1961: 66); the ego is said to be undifferentiated (see also Mitchell, 1986: 15). To begin with, then, everything the child is aware of is part of the ego but, through interacting with the world, the child comes to understand some things to be not part of the ego. The things that are not part of the ego are, for the child, all objects. This world of objects is further divided into 'good' and 'bad' depending on the pleasure gained by the child from them. Similarly, the ego is divided into good and bad. In Freud's words:

> Some of the things that one is unwilling to give up, because they give pleasure, are nevertheless not ego but object; and some sufferings that one seeks to expel turn out to be inseparable from the ego in virtue of their internal origin. . . . In this way, then, the ego detaches itself from the external world. Or, to put it more correctly, originally the ego includes everything, later it separates off an external world from itself. (Freud, 1930/1961: 67–68)

In this manner Freud gives an account of the development from childhood to the adult ego. At first this seems to give a trial-and-error learning, or 'linear', model of development (see the discussion of behaviourism). That which cannot be escaped must be part of the ego (if beyond the ego's control) and that which cannot be maintained, though pleasurable, must be part of the world of objects. In this way, the ego becomes differentiated. This is a linear progression of learning what is and is not the ego, along with what is good and bad. But Freud's account is not so simple: there are also a number of 'stages' which the child goes through which are imposed from 'within' and yet beyond the control of the ego. A detailed account of such stages is contained in *Three Essays on the Theory of Sexuality* (1905/1953).

These essays were concerned not with development in general but sexuality in particular. However, 'sexuality' is central to Freud's general account. Juliet Mitchell points out: '. . . Freud's work can be subjugated to two central tenets: the formative importance of infantile sexuality and the existence of an unconscious mind that works on principles quite distinct from those of the conscious mind' (Mitchell, 1986: 12). In the Summary to the *Three Essays*, Freud alludes to a 'course of maturation' (1905/1953: 231) taken by the sexual 'instinct', but this 'course' or 'direction' is restricted by certain 'forces'. Freud emphasised 'shame, disgust, pity and the structure of morality and authority erected by society' (1905/1953: 231). The sexual instinct is 'necessarily complex' but by examining different perversions, the complex 'falls apart, as it were, into its components' (1905/1953: 231). Perversions divide into two groups: those aising from 'inhibitions' and others from 'dissociations' of normal development.

One of Freud's mechanisms, using a 'hydraulic' metaphor (see Bruner, 1986: 139; Gellner, 1985; McReynolds, 1990), is then called upon to explain the existence of perversions: 'a collateral filling of the subsidiary channels when the main current of the intellectual stream has been blocked by "repression" ' (Freud, 1905/1953: 232). There is something inside the child (an instinct) which forces or causes something to force its way upward (because in psychoanalysis the imagery is always so dependent upon things being 'hidden' or 'underneath'), and the direction of this force can be changed and is changed largely by the world around the child – the force from without.

Freud goes on to express regret concerning society's attitudes toward childhood sexuality; he assumes the child to possess a natural state (later he calls it an 'essence') which is disturbed by the artificial constraints set by society. But neither is the natural state static:

> The sexual activity of children, however, does not, it appeared, develop *pari passu* with their other functions, but, after a short period of efflorescence from the ages of two to five, enters upon the so-called period of latency. (Freud, 1905/1953: 232)

Sexuality is depicted as 'bursting into flower' (*OED* on 'efflorescence') before entering, again of its own accord, the period of latency: to lie 'dormant', 'existing but not developed' (*OED*). Growth, in this case, is a result of internal changes. Second, the instinct is 'not unified' and, being without object, is 'auto-erotic' (1905/1953: 233). Three phases are then outlined: first an oral eroticism, then a sadism with anal eroticism, to a third phase of 'a primacy of the phallus' (1905/1953: 233).[12]

Freud then says that one of his 'most surprising findings' was that the 2- to 5-year-old period: '. . . gives rise to the choice of an object. . . . Thus . . . the phase of development corresponding to that period must be regarded as an important precursor of the subsequent final sexual organiza- tion' (Freud, 1905/1953: 234). Here is an important part of the Freudian account: the postulation of a 'critical period' in which something is said to occur that determines the 'final' organisation; the start of the development of the 'ego' determines the finish. Therefore it becomes important to know what happens during the critical period. Freud claims that it is not possible (perhaps at the time he was writing, thus issuing a promissory note) to say how much sexual activity was normal in childhood, however 'premature sexual activity' as in the case of seduction[13] 'diminishes a child's educability' (1905/1953: 234). Here, then, is a link between sexual and cognitive development, the primacy of the first influencing the development of the latter. Again, it is the possible influence from without which may impinge upon and damage the normal development within, and the events in the critical period control the final outcome.

A 'further stage of repression is necessary' (1905/1953: 235) during puberty in order to differentiate between the sexes and this stage, too, is a natural occurrence initiated from within. Having outlined his developmental sequence, Freud goes on to account for further factors which include the 'innate variety of sexual constitutions' (1905/1953: 235) and the possibility of 'inherited degeneracy' (1905/1953: 236).[14] However, 'hereditary conditions in the case of positive perverts are less well known, for they know how to avoid investigation' (1905/1953: 236). Thus making Freud's task that much more difficult.[15] But not everything is completely decided by inheritance in Freud's account, as further possibilities emerge from 'the vicissitudes of the tributary streams of sexuality springing from their separate sources' (1905/1953: 237). Thus, there is an alternative for Freud between inherited and accidental factors:

> In theory one is always inclined to overestimate the former; therapeutic practice emphasizes the importance of the latter . . . The constitutional factor must await experiences before it can make itself felt; the accidental factor must have a constitutional basis in order to come into operation. (Freud, 1905/1953: 239)

Note here the importance and prior existence of the basic structure Freud is alluding to: constitution first, accident later. The most important accidents are those of early childhood: the accidents themselves become part of the constitution. However, not all accidents will become part of the constitution (see also Freud, 1911/1970: 292–294). The constitution will only be triggered by traumatic (non-trivial) accidents (Forrester, 1990a: 192–206). Thus, time is an important factor:[16]

> The order in which various instinctual impulses come into activity seems to be phylogenetically determined; so, too, does the length of time during which they are able to manifest themselves before they succumb to the effects of some freshly emerging instinctual impulse or to some typical repression. Variations, however, seem to occur both in temporal sequence and in duration and these variations must exercise a determining influence upon the final results. (Freud, 1905/1953: 241)

Here the terms 'manifest', 'succumb', 'emerging' and 'impulse' are all used to render an instinctual impulse as undergoing change in an autonomous and sequential manner. Further, this account suggests that the ontogenetic sequence is phylogenetically determined and this is in line with the arguments popular at the time which suggested that 'ontogeny recapitulates phylogeny' (Cairns and Ornstein, 1979: 461–464). In discussing Klein's work, I shall comment on the functional role of referring to phylogenetic inheritance in psychoanalytic accounts.

There is also a level of flexibility in this sequential model. The sequence is determined but variations are possible (an assumption not allowed by Piaget, for example); an instinct is 'able to manifest itself' before 'succumbing'; a certain number of universally determined things are at work, of their own accord, inside the individual, but different 'final' individuals emerge through possible variations. The possibility of variation emerges again, this time as a problem, under the heading of 'Pertinacity of early impressions':

> . . . it is necessary to assume that these early impressions of sexual life are characterized by an increased pertinacity or susceptibility to fixation in persons who are later to become neurotics or perverts. For the same premature sexual manifestations, when they occur in other persons, fail to make so deep an impression . . . (Freud, 1905/1953: 242)

This is indeed a problem and, ideally, Freud would have liked to know more about the 'biological processes constituting the essence of sexuality' (1905/1953: 169) to solve the problem.[17] But he notes again the possibility of a 'psychical factor' which is influenced by culture and education:

> In consequence of the inverse relation holding between civilization and the free development of sexuality . . . the course taken by the sexual life of a child is just as unimportant for later life where the cultural or social level is relatively low as it is important where that level is relatively high. (Freud, 1905/1953: 242)

Where the development of the culture is 'relatively low' sexuality is more flexible and closer to its 'essence'. However, Freud is interested in a world in which the cultural level is 'relatively high' and therefore the need to postulate inner, innate 'susceptibilities' is greater: civilization reveals a further component of human nature (of something inside the individual) which remains 'dormant' in less civilized societies. Such a suggestion accords with Wundt's (1897) ideas reviewed earlier.[18]

We leave Freud with the stage (rhetorically) set for individuals who contain a number of forces or drives, having their genetically determined sexualities emerging or being uncovered by the pressures of the civilizations into which they are born, or, as he described it in the *Introductory Lectures on Psycho-Analysis*:

> We [psychoanalysts] believe that civilization has been created under the pressure of the exigencies of life at the cost of satisfaction of the instincts; and we believe that civilization is to a large extent being constantly created anew, since each individual who makes a fresh entry into human society repeats this sacrifice of instinctual satisfaction for the benefit of the whole community.' (Freud, 1916–1917/1963: 22–23)

As Bruner (1986: 140) points out, the heroic Freudian individual is not one who overcomes such forces and pressures, but comes instead to understand them.[19]

*Klein*

The work of Melanie Klein (1882–1960) extended discourse in psycho-analysis, nevertheless discussions of Klein's work in relation to the texts by Freud work against parts of Klein's rhetoric, because her work is a variation often at odds with, rather than simply extending, Freud's theory. Two of Klein's essays are normally taken (for example Segal, 1975; Mitchell, 1986; Hughes, 1989) to have indicated a change in her general account: 'A contribution to the psychogenesis of manic-depressive states' (1935/1975) and 'Mourning and its relations to manic-depressive states' (1940/1975). Klein's texts, practice and teaching led to a 'school of thought' and controversial debates within the psychoanalytic community (especially in Britain; see Hughes, 1989; Appignanesi and Forrester, 1992). I shall focus on giving a detailed account of one of Klein's later essays: 'The origins of transference' (1952a/1975) because it contains a brief account of her views on development. Klein's main object in this paper was to argue that the processes involved in transference (of any kind, but the therapeutic one in particular) were the same as those which determined a child's object relations. In pursuing this argument, Klein gave a condensed version of her theory of development generally.[20]

The Kleinian mind is comprised of 'deep layers' (1952a/1975: 55; hereafter by page number) which are laid down both over time and in terms of structure. Using the Freudian lexicon, early experience affects the way later experiences are layered on top and, in a similar fashion, the Kleinian baby passes through a number of constitutionally ordered stages: children are described as having 'drives', 'compulsions' and 'impulses' similar to those described by Freud, but Klein also posits 'positions' which she maintains are developmentally important.

Klein begins her paper by citing Freud's definition of transference.[21] She then states that some form of transference 'operates throughout life', but that she is only concerned with the 'manifestations' which occur in psychoanalysis (48). This indicates a common rhetorical form in (but not only in) Klein's work: she claims that something exists within each person and that it is prone to later appearances; hence the use of terms like 'manifest' and 'revive'. An example taken from a chapter published the same year will serve as an illustration:

> . . . it takes years for the child to overcome his persecutory and depressive anxieties. They are again and again activated and overcome in the course of the infantile neurosis. But these anxieties are never eradicated, and therefore are liable to be revived, though to a lesser extent, throughout life. (Klein, 1952b/1975: 113, note 1)

In this case, words like 'activated' and 'revived' maintain that such anxieties always exist within a person rather than, for example, suggesting they are a product of a social situation. Klein develops a particular kind of causal story by using such a form.[22]

Klein (1952a/1975) goes on to state that a characteristic of 'psychoanalytic procedure' is that it 'begins to open up roads in to the patient's unconscious'. The term 'roads' suggests 'mapping' for later 'travel'. Therapy, then, ensures that the patient's past is 'revived,' thus positing its permanent existence. This may be regarded as a central tenet of psychoanalytic theory: as with Freud, the claim is made that none of the internal structures (memories, for example) are ever removed or completely by-passed. Development, then, is a process which may always be returned to (in therapy, for example; see Gellner, 1985; Forrester, 1990a), even though the 'crucial stages' of such a process are those 'undergone' early (in Klein's case, very early) in the life of the child.[23]

Next Klein posits an 'urge' the patient has to 'transfer his early experiences' which have been 'reactivated' through the use of 'mechanisms and defences' used in earlier situations. At the conclusion of the paper we are told that this 'urge to repeat fundamental experiences' (and they must be fundamental to be repeated) comes through pressure exerted' by 'the repetition compulsion' (56). The important word in the lexicon here is 'fundamental' because, for Klein, what was experienced first determines how one responds to 'pressures' later. Having performed that much rhetorical work, Klein can make the following deduction:

> It follows that the deeper we are able to penetrate into the unconscious and the further back we can take the analysis, the greater will be our understanding of the transference. Therefore a brief summary of my conclusions about the earliest stages of development is relevant to my topic. (Klein, 1952a/1975: 48)

In accordance with late Freudian thought, Klein assumes the existence of a 'death instinct within' (thanatos; see also Soyland, 1993) which 'gives rise to the fear of annihilation' which is in turn 'the primordial cause of persecutory anxiety' (48). Although Klein does not describe the way in which a child comes to (non-linguistically) have a concept of its own annihilation, a concept of 'self' (a reflexive ego) does not seem to be necessary for such a fear. Klein (1956/1986: 211) assumes that, ideally, a child wants the 'pre-natal unity' it has lost, and that the child longs for 'an inexhaustible and always present breast'. The latter is wanted not only as a supply of food ('drives' such as hunger are hardly ever the issue in psychoanalysis) but as a way of preventing 'destructive impulses and persecutory anxiety' (212). Because such things cannot be achieved, they are 'bound' to be the cause of 'unavoidable grievances'.

So, Klein posits 'life and death instincts' which give rise to love and hate. Internal conflict is a consequence of such instincts. It is the simultaneous love and hate of the breast which causes 'splitting' as a form of defence. Such 'feelings from inner sources are intensified by painful external experiences' which makes the child feel that 'he is being attacked by hostile forces' (48–49). External 'care and comfort' on the other hand 'are felt to come from good forces':

> In speaking of 'forces' I am using a rather adult word for what the young infant dimly conceives of as objects, either good or bad. The infant directs his feelings of gratification and love towards the 'good' breast, and his destructive impulses and feelings of persecution towards what he feels to be frustrating, i.e. the 'bad' breast (Klein, 1952a/1975: 49)

The importance of the breast may be seen in Klein's statement that the 'core of the super-ego' is the 'breast, both good and bad' (50). It is the relationship the baby has with this part of the mother's body which helps to form the child's personality.

By discussing 'splitting' as one of the child's defence mechanisms, Klein is adopting Freud's lexicon (see also Mitchell, 1986: 175), but there is a tension here between it being a 'stage' (something which is passed through) or a 'structure'. Klein suggests the former when she says that at 'this stage splitting processes are at their height' (49). Elsewhere she states that:

> I have often expressed my view that object relations exist from the beginning of life, the first object being the mother's breast which to the child becomes split into a good (gratifying) and bad (frustrating) breast; this splitting results in a severance of love and hate. . . . These processes participate in the building up of the ego and super-ego and prepare the ground for the onset of the Oedipus complex in the second half of the first year. (Klein, 1946/1975: 2)

Thus, the processes of 'splitting, denial, omnipotence, and idealization' are all 'prevalent during the first three or four months of life' which Klein 'termed the paranoid-schizoid position' (1952a/1975: 49): the metaphors suggest a sequential process in which 'processes' form part of the 'positions'. On the latter, Hanna Segal says:

> In some sense, the paranoid-schizoid position and the depressive position are phases of development. They could be seen as subdivisions of the oral stage, the former occupying the first three to four months and being followed by the latter in the second half of the first year. . . . Klein chose the term 'position' to emphasize the fact that the phenomenon she was describing was not simply a passing 'stage' or 'phase' . . . her term implies a specific configuration of object relations, anxieties and defences which persist throughout life. (Segal, 1975: viii–ix)

Klein is therefore attempting to give an account both of development, largely as a variation of the Freudian account, and of structure; she posits a number of entities which rise to a certain 'height' only to diminish, awaiting later 'manifestations'. Developments, then, occur thus:

> The ego's growing capacity for integration and synthesis leads more and more, even during the first few months, to states in which love and hatred, and correspondingly the good and bad aspects of objects, are being synthesized; and this gives rise to the second form of anxiety – depressive anxiety – for the infant's aggressive impulses and desires towards the bad breast (mother) are now felt to be a danger to the good breast (mother) as well. In the second quarter of the first year these emotions are reinforced, because at this stage the infant increasingly perceives and introjects the mother as a person. Depressive anxiety is intensified, for the infant feels he has destroyed or is destroying a whole object by his greed and uncontrollable aggression. Moreover, owing to the growing synthesis of his emotions, he now feels that these destructive impulses are directed against a *loved person*. (Klein, 1952a/1975: 50, emphasis original)

The two conflicting 'impulses', love and hate, are gradually 'synthesized', a process which itself 'gives rise to' a second form of anxiety in this developmental sequence.

Klein says that it is 'at this stage' that 'the Oedipus complex sets in' gaining 'powerful impetus' from anxiety and guilt (50), which in turn increases 'the need to externalize (project) bad figures and to internalize (introject) good ones' (thus echoing Freud, quoted above). Also following Freud, Klein posits a 'drive towards new aims' from 'oral desires towards genital ones'. Several 'factors' are involved:

> . . . the forward drive of the libido, the growing integration of the ego, physical and mental skills and progressive adaptation to the external world. These trends are bound up with the process of symbol formation, which enables the infant to transfer not only interests, but also emotions and phantasies, anxiety and guilt, from one object to another.' (Klein, 1952a/1975: 50–51)

In discussing the Freudian account I called attention to the emphasis on phylogenetic factors. Given that Klein has been held to have placed an even greater stress on 'nature' over 'nurture' (Hughes, 1989: 50), it is appropriate to examine an example of one such claim. In a long note Klein (1952b/1975) states:

> My psycho-analytic work has led me to conclude that the new born infant unconsciously feels that an object of unique goodness exists, from which a maximal gratification could be obtained, and that this object is the mother's breast. I furthermore believe that this unconscious knowledge implies that the relation to the mother's breast and a feeling of possessing the breast develop even in children who are not breast-fed. . . . The fact that at the beginning of post-natal life an unconscious knowledge of the breast exists and that feelings towards the breast are experienced can only be conceived of as a phylogenetic inheritance. (Klein, 1952b/1975: 117)

Klein describes newborn children as possessing a degree of 'unconscious knowledge' concerning the breast: the Kleinian baby arrives as a complicated entity with a predisposition to develop object relations. While many of the terms Klein uses came from Freud, they are often deployed in different ways (see Mitchell, 1986); it is the conflict between life and death drives rather than sexuality which act as the hydraulic force behind development.

As with all psychological discourse, the expansion of the lexicon helps to assert the reality of the objects being described: the psychoanalytic is perhaps one of the richest in the literature. As the novice becomes enrolled in the rhetoric (see also Chapter 8; Soyland 1994a), terms in the lexicon begin to refer unproblematically to the processes and objects being described: egos become split, channels become blocked, basic desires are frustrated, unconscious knowledge is assumed, anxieties are intensified. While the psychoanalytic vocabulary became more complex and childhood development more crucial, writers in the behaviourist tradition sought a simpler lexicon in which development was more easily overwritten by history.

**Behaviourism**

This heading has been used as a kind of 'catch-all' in the literature, used to refer to a number of different theorists from Pavlov and Watson to Skinner. In this context, it is useful to begin with a current textbook account of their major points:

Stimulus–response theorists emphasized the role of learning rather than any innate predispositions, processes or structures of intellectual development. They were not truly concerned with differences over age, but tried to apply the same principles of learning across all ages. Standard laws of conditioning, reinforcement, generalization and extinction were invoked to explain the behaviour of children of all ages as well as the behaviour of rats from which these principles were derived. (Heatherington and Parke, 1986: 339)

Age is invoked in this account as the truly important variable which these theorists did not investigate. In a moment I shall show why the behaviourists did not construct their accounts of development in age-related terms; this will be shown as central to the behaviourist programme. Single papers by Watson and Skinner have been selected to indicate some of the rhetoric of behaviourism.[24]

## *Watson*

John B. Watson (1878–1958) occupies an important position in histories of experimental psychology. The appearance of his article, 'Psychology as the behaviorist views it' (1913), has been described as marking the beginning of a methodological change.[25] It was largely an attack on introspection (repeated in *Behaviorism*, 1924/1930), but in stating his views on what a behaviourist psychology would look like, Watson knew he was suggesting a significant break with accepted practice. In a letter to Robert Yerkes (dated 26 March 1913, cited in Cohen, 1979: 73) Watson wrote: 'I am sending you a bunch of reprints. I understand [James] Angell thinks I am crazy. I should not be surprised if that was the general consensus of opinion.' And, indeed, Titchener, Angell, MacDougall, Munsterberg, Cattell, Woodworth and Thorndike 'all attacked Watson for being too extreme' (Cohen, 1979: 79; see also Buckley, 1989). Nevertheless it was in this essay that Watson gave a very influential blueprint for later work in some areas of psychology. The topic of development, and the method of investigation, for example, was broached in the following way:

In order to understand more thoroughly the relation between what was habit and what was hereditary in [the] responses [of birds], I took the young birds and reared them. In this way I was able to study the order of appearance of hereditary adjustments and their complexity, and later the beginnings of habit formation. (Watson, 1913: 167)

The assumption was that results from experiments with animals could be used to describe developments in children; Watson focused on the situation in which the animal was present, and examined changes in behaviour.

'What the nursery has to say about instincts' (1925/1926) was presented as a lecture in a series on theoretical psychology at Clark University in 1925. Like Klein, Watson was also interested in claiming that his developmental mechanisms were activated before birth:

. . . another fact only recently brought out by the behaviourists and other students of animal psychology, namely, that habit formation starts in all probability in embryonic life, and that even in the human young, environment

> shapes behaviour so quickly that all of the older ideas about what types of
> behaviour are inherited and what are learned break down. Grant variations in
> structure at birth and rapid habit formation from birth, and you have a basis for
> explaining many of the so-called facts of inheritance of 'mental' characteristics.
> (Watson, 1925/1926: 6–7)

Here the 'fact' of 'habit formation' is described as having 'recently' been
'brought out' by behaviourists. Most important, for the present study, is
Watson's claim that the 'environment shapes behaviour'. First, this places
stress upon the role of the environment in development. Further, while
placing emphasis on the environment, a number of 'older ideas' are
claimed to 'break down'.[26] Such rhetoric is being used here to promote the
importance of Watson's 'recently brought out [revealed] facts'. Finally, the
use of the term 'shaping' is important to Watson's account; this will be
examined in the next quotation.

While the psychoanalytic metaphors are often described as 'hydraulic' or
'economic' (amongst other terms; see Gellner, 1985; McReynolds, 1990),
the behaviouristic ones are exclusively described as 'mechanical' (L.D.
Smith, 1990a; Buckley, 1989). The following example should demonstrate
that such a characterisation of behaviourism is appropriate. Frequent
targets of behaviourist writing are 'mentalistic' terms (see Skinner, 1971,
for example), and attacks on a range of such terms typically work against
the importance of 'inner processes'. For Watson, the concept of an
'instinct' was still a problem to be dealt with in discussions, because
'Philosophy will never answer any question about the instincts' (1925/1926:
12). The reference to philosophy is important: philosophy was seen at this
time as a kind of 'parent discipline'; thus, references to philosophy were
needed to separate (rhetorically distance) psychological discourse from the
philosophical. So, while philosophy is described as 'never' being able to
'answer any question', psychology is described as fulfilling this function. In
the process, Watson concentrated upon behaviour, and attempted to
remove the 'instinct' in the following way:

> I have in my hand a hardwood stick. If I throw it forward and upward it goes a
> certain distance and drops to the ground. . . . . I retrieve the stick, reshape it
> slightly and make its edges convex. I call it a boomerang. Again I throw
> it upward and outward. Again it goes forward revolving as it goes. Suddenly it
> turns, comes back and gracefully and kindly falls at my feet. It is still a stick, still
> made of the same material, but it has been shaped differently. *Has the
> boomerang an instinct to return to the hand of the thrower?* No? (Watson, 1925/
> 1926: 12, emphasis original)

This extract contains some of the important components of behaviourist
rhetoric. There is nothing inside the stick to have traits or instincts. The use
of the tag question ('No?') stresses the closure (the finality) of Watson's
analogy: the behaviour of the stick when thrown changes only as a result of
external pressure, as the result of 'shaping'. This is an important term for
Watson to use: it allows Watson to claim that the start never determines
the finish. In experimental situations devised by behaviourists, any behaviour
which approximates that required by the experimenter is selectively

reinforced: the rat faces the bar and is given food, then only if it approaches the bar, then only if it touches it with a paw, and so on. Thus, the original behavioural pattern is 'shaped' to that required by the experimenter. The analogy in the extract, then, pivots on this double use of the term: as the shape of the stick is altered, so too is the behaviour of an animal. Development results from external shaping of behaviour (development as shaping). Finally, note that the shaped object only exhibits the shaped behaviour under appropriate circumstances.

Using the shaping term, Watson asks: 'Can we not say, "Man is built of certain materials put together in certain complex ways, and *as a corollary of the way he is put together and of the material out of which he is made – he must act – until learning has reshaped him – as he does act*"?' (Watson, 1925/1926: 14, extract modified, emphasis original). The claim embedded in this question may be used to interpret the following:

> I should like to go one step further tonight and say, 'Give me a dozen healthy infants, well-formed, and my own specified world to bring them up in and I'll guarantee to take any one at random and train him to become any type of specialist I might select – a doctor, lawyer, artist, merchant-chief and, yes, even into beggar-man and thief, regardless of his talents, penchants, abilities, vocations and race of his ancestors.' I am going beyond my facts and I admit it, but so have the advocates of the contrary and they have been doing it for many thousands of years. (Watson, 1925/1926: 10)

The rhetoric here is utopian ('my own specified world'), and Watson notes that he is engaging in speculation ('beyond my facts'; see Myers, 1991b), but the justification Watson uses for including it in the Clark Lecture is that 'advocates of the contrary' have engaged in such speculation for 'many thousands of years'. In the process, Watson is able to assert the importance of environment, training and shaping. Thus, learning is the basic factor in Watson's account of development, and the period in which learning must occur is left unspecified. No critical period is defined and, as a result, future modification will always be possible.[27]

Watson goes on to cite results from observation studies of a variety of 'responses'. He is particularly interested in noting when a response first appears and what causes it to occur. But while there is a sequential assumption grounding such observations, Watson is quick to note many variations in onset. Of one group of responses he concludes: 'At birth or soon thereafter we find nearly all of the so-called neurological signs or reflexes established' (Watson, 1925/1926: 31). This includes breathing, pulse, sucking, swallowing, hunger contractions, smiling, sneezing, erection of the penis and so on, all described in terms of stimulus and response. He also describes a second group, saying:

> Other activities appear at a later stage – such as blinking, reaching, handling, handedness, crawling, standing, sitting up, walking, running, jumping. In the great majority of these later activities it is difficult to say how much of the act as a whole is due to training or conditioning, A considerable part is unquestionably due to the growth changes in structure, and the rest is due to training and conditioning. (Watson, 1925/1926: 31–32)

That some part of the developmental 'process' is innate ('growth changes in structure'), is not questioned – it is undermined. The process of undermining the importance of innate changes is undertaken through the 'difficulty' of discerning the extent of 'training or conditioning' (such difficulties typically require further experimental work). Here Watson constructs a dichotomy in which 'growth changes' are contrasted (only) with conditioning changes. Again, the environment is the important factor: handedness, for example, is discussed (1925/1926: 27–29) as being a habit which begins to develop *in utero*. So, for each of the abilities he describes, Watson emphasises learning first and foremost.

In keeping with the account he has developed, Watson concludes his article by proposing that the Jamesian notion of a 'stream of consciousness' (to be discussed in Chapter 8) should be replaced by an 'activity stream' (of which he gives a diagram, 1925/1926: 35):

> Most of you are familiar with William James' classic chapter on the stream of consciousness. We have all loved that chapter. Today it seems as much out of touch with modern psychology as the stage coach would be on New York's Fifth Avenue. The stage coach was picturesque but it has given place to a more effective means of transportation. Tonight I want to give you something in place of James' classical contribution; less picturesque but more adequate to the facts. (Watson, 1925/1926: 33)

This technique of discrediting an idea by labelling and associating it with something 'old' will be familiar from Chapter 3. Here (in front of an audience at Clark University), the discrediting claim (the Jamesian account is 'out of touch' and factually inadequate) is mitigated by elevating the text by James as a 'classical' and well-loved contribution. At the same time the rhetoric is used to assert the 'more adequate' view: that unlearned movements are quickly organised into stable habits, and to understand this process detailed observations must be made. This, according to Watson, indicates: '. . . the fundamental point of view of the behaviorist – viz. that in order to understand man you have to understand the life history of his activities' (Watson, 1925/1926: 34). In Watson's case, the stage is set for further experimental work, in a discipline described as being different from philosophy.

The lexicon of behaviourism involves an emphasis on the role of the history of the individual. It is not positing a critical period of history, as was the case with Freud and Klein. Rather, an examination of reinforcement history would allow for the 'prediction and control of behavior' (Watson, 1913: 158); influencing the immediate environment, and therefore the recent history, causes behaviour to change. Such a promissory note was taken up and issued again by B.F. Skinner (even as late as 1985).

*Skinner*

Skinner (1904–1990) was influenced by Watson but was more dedicated to pursuing the 'empty organism' metaphor (hence the term 'radical behaviorism'); his work was popularised in *Beyond Freedom and Dignity* (1971) and Skinner's (dis)utopian novel *Walden Two* (1948/1976). Like Watson, Skinner used a great deal of anti-mentalistic rhetoric, along with claims of being purely descriptive (and not at all philosophical or speculative; see Chapter 1). Again, the discussion here will be restricted largely to a single article).

In an essay in *Science*, 'The phylogeny and ontogeny of behavior' (1966), Skinner begins by stating that Watson went 'beyond his facts', but defended him by saying that Watson never took the position that an 'animal comes to the laboratory as a *tabula rasa*' (Skinner, 1966: 1205; the animal as a blank sheet was a popular target for attack). Skinner then goes on to pose the question, 'What does it mean to say that behavior is inherited?' He acknowledges the role of genetic traits, noting that some 'kind of inheritance is implied by such concepts as "racial memory" or "death instinct" but a sharper specification is needed' (1966: 1205; psychoanalysis is the target here). Such a sharper specification will, Skinner claims, result from behaviourism. By posing the initial question in such a form, Skinner has already restricted the discussion to what behaviour (not thoughts or unconscious memory) is exhibited within a limited context; only the external and observable is to be considered. Skinner's style consistently uses the term 'behavior' (often a general term),[28] yet the rhetoric emphasises the ways in which behaviour may be broken down into smaller, and smaller sections: he examines the 'identifiable unit' of a given behaviour (1966: 1206). Elsewhere he proposes: 'Consider the act of drinking a glass of water. This is not likely to be an important bit of behavior in anyone's life, but it supplies a convenient example' (1953: 31–32): the act may be subdivided. Behaviourist rhetoric invokes metaphors of divisibility, in which all behaviour may be sectioned; taken to pieces, without becoming unintelligible within a behaviourist text. The term 'shaping' is part of this network of rhetoric: it involves directing the effort of the experimenter (or therapist, in behavioural therapies) toward changing small sections ('bits') of behaviour in order to attain the required (general/larger) behaviour.

Skinner performs two rhetorical shifts which need close examination. First his use of the term 'ontogeny'. In much of the material examined in this chapter 'ontogeny' has been shown to have been used to characterise the development of the individual. The term 'development' has, in turn, been used to signify changes which occur within an organism as a result of internal maturation. This is not the case in Skinner's essay:

> The provenance of learned behavior has been thoroughly analyzed. Certain kinds of events function as 'reinforcers', and, when such an event follows a response, similar responses are more likely to occur. This is operant conditioning. By manipulating the ways in which reinforcing consequences are contingent upon behavior, we generate complex forms of response and bring them under the control of subtle features of the environment. What we may call the ontogeny of behavior is thus traced to contingencies of reinforcement. (Skinner, 1966: 1206)

In this account Skinner uses the term 'ontogeny' to refer to changes in an organism's behaviour which result from events external to the individual. Such events make up a history of reinforcement; a history consisting of a linear progression of events, fixed by changes over time. The term 'stage', for example, does not appear in Skinner's text. He assumes a linear, and not a sequential, model of development. Such an assumption makes reference to the age of the organism irrelevant. On this account, ontogenetic behaviour originates in the behaviour of the individual; phylogenetic behaviour is a class indicated by behaviour across individuals of the same species.

The basis of the second rhetorical shift is perhaps the more difficult. Throughout the article Skinner poses a parallel between ontogenetic and phylogenetic 'contingencies': he maintains that experiments which demonstrate ontogenetic development involve essentially the same mechanisms at the phylogenetic level. Here is one of his illustrations:

> Ontogenic [sic] contingencies remain ineffective until a response has occurred. In a familiar experimental arrangement, the rat must press the lever at least once 'for other reasons' before it presses it 'for food'. There is a similar limitation in phylogenic contingencies. An animal must emit a cry at least once for other reasons before it can be selected as a warning because of the advantages to the species. It follows that the entire repertoire of an individual or species must exist prior to ontogenic or phylogenic selection, but only in the form of minimal units. Both phylogenic and ontogenic contingencies 'shape' complex forms of behavior from relatively undifferentiated material. (Skinner, 1966: 1206)

Questions, then, of how phylogenetic factors influence development, are matters of the behavioural history of a species. Behaviours are transmitted through the genes of the successful individuals that have exhibited the behaviour. What is inherited is the increased likelihood of giving a certain response in a particular circumstance, and Skinner gives examples concerning bees and the African honey guide. Phylogenetic development is described by Skinner as modelled on ontogenetic mechanisms which involve the linear progression of a reinforcement history. That, in turn, is dependent on environmental contingencies: the behaviourist account of development is one in which the (empty) individual is controlled by external variables. This (rhetorically) sets the stage for a child to be (almost endlessly; see Skinner, 1971: 203) reshaped by the world; at the same time, it leaves some 'shaped' people in charge of setting the reinforcement schedule (perhaps to avoid 'lethal cultural mutation'; Skinner, 1971: 178).

**Piaget**

Within Anglo-American developmental psychology one of the most influential theorists is Jean Piaget (1896–1980). An interdisciplinary thinker and logician, he began publishing a series of books and articles on cognitive development in the 1920s and 1930s, but did not become popular in America (for a variety of reasons) until the early 1960s (Heatherington and Parke, 1986: 338–339; Cairns and Ornstein, 1979: 499).

Piaget's model may be classified as a sequential model insofar as it depicts development as a progression through a series of stages, therefore progress is a function of some biological programme within the child.[29] Unlike Freud's sequence, Piaget's has it that the child can only proceed from one stage to the next, allowing some differences in the age of onset, in the pattern Piaget describes. And the term 'description' is very important in any theoretical consideration of Piaget's work: logical structures, and the symbolism involved, are used to describe the structures purported to exist within the child's mind.[30] As one of Piaget's translators puts it: 'logic may be applied as a theoretical tool in the description of the mental structures that govern ordinary reasoning . . .' (Parsons, Introduction to Inhelder and Piaget, 1958: viii). However, Piaget's use of the theoretical tool of logic has also been applied, through the use of metaphor (Gigerenzer and Murray, 1987), such that the tool becomes identical to the processes of reasoning:

> If we are to explain the transition from the concrete thought of the child to the formal thought of the adolescent, we must first describe the development of propositional logic, which the child at the concrete level (stage II: from 7–8 to 11–12) cannot yet handle. (Inhelder and Piaget, 1958: 1)

Here, too, is an emphasis on 'transition': in this case, from one form of logical system (the 'concrete'), to a 'formal', 'propositional' logic (development as changes in logical systems): this is sequential development at its most strict.

Thus, Piaget is part of the psychological tradition which assumes that mental tests may be carried out which will reflect some aspect of the underlying, internal structure (an assumption criticised by Vygotsky). Piaget's view of language was similar to, and influenced by, the Freudian view: the language the child used was regarded as a set of 'symptoms' through which reasoning processes could be observed (synecdoche). Language was not regarded as an essential tool in the process of development, as we shall later see it was for Vygotsky (see pp. 77–81), but an indicator of the logical processes within. Heatherington and Parke contrast the behaviourist linear model with the Piagetian sequential one by saying that: 'In learning theory, development was explained as a function of learning, whereas Piaget argued that learning was a function of development' (Heatherington and Parke, 1986: 364). That is, learning is something which can only occur within the bounds and limits of a particular mental system:

> The child does not build systems. His spontaneous thinking may be more or less systematic . . . but it is the observer who sees the system from the outside, while the child is not aware of it since he never thinks about his own thought. (Inhelder and Piaget, 1958: 339)

The child is unaware of its own system of thought and is unreflexive;

the system of logic governs the process of development. And again: 'at the level of the third period . . . the beginnings of formal thought allow the discovery of some complete combinatoric systems for a small number of elements' (Piaget and Inhelder, 1975: 214). Here the important term is 'allow'; the child's thinking is restricted by its logical system until such time as it has developed into the next system. Moreover, explanations of the child's thought processes are to be found within the logic of a given system, and not, for example, in the child's history (as with Freud and Klein) or as a result of environmental contingencies (as with Watson and Skinner).

*The Language and Thought of the Child* (Piaget, 1926/1959) shows an early formulation of way the Piagetian child was constructed. I want to focus on a set of three questions which appear in the second chapter of the book:

> The questions we have to answer may therefore be stated as follows: 1 What are the types of conversation between children? 2 Are the types contemporaneous, or do they represent different stages of development? 3 If they constitute stages, what is their genesis? Are they derived from ego-centric language? If so, what is the process of evolution by which a child passes from ego-centric language to the higher types of conversation? (Piaget, 1926/1959: 53)

These questions are closely related and they lead the reader along a particular path excluding several alternatives along the way ('we *have* to answer'). By the time the last (unnumbered) question has been reached, several crucial assumptions have been made: (1) conversations between children may be divided into various types; (2) these types are either contemporaneous *or* they represent a developmental sequence; (3) the process of evolution is one in which a child passes from one stage to the next. The final question (presented as a kind of tacit extension – or enthymeme)[31] suggests (with the rhetoric of evolution; see Beer, 1983; Costall, 1985; Gross, 1990) that ego-centric speech is a basic or low form of conversation and that higher types of conversation exist. The task for Piaget, then, in this particular chapter, was to devise a taxonomy of conversations in order to describe the development of logical thinking. Ego-centric speech, defined as language not directed in a social manner ('repetition', 'monologue' and 'collective monologue') was an early type in this taxonomy. The child begins by being discursively isolated, despite the production of many words: 'we may say that the adult thinks socially, even when he is alone, and the child under 7 thinks ego-centrically, even in the society of others' (1926/1959: 40).

These questions may be regarded as a miniature of the way Piaget's discourse was structured. Children indicate the stage of development in which they are situated through the way they talk (in the same way as the child's conversation gives an 'insight' into the unconscious for psychoanalysis). Once this assumption (rejected by Vygotsky) has been made, a number of methodological consequences arise which affect the way in which Piaget's experiments proceeded; the child developed alone, its language a symptom, not a tool which enabled development. Another consequence was that it made sense for Piaget to calculate a 'coefficient of ego-centrism' which involved dividing the child's total number of spontaneous socialised sentences (that is, not in response to questions put by an adult) by the number of ego-centric sentences. This coefficient was described in the following way:

> Now in Lev and Pie [two experimental subjects aged 6½], who represent fairly different types, the coefficients of ego-centrism are very close (0.47 and 0.43). Can we infer from this that the average coefficient between 4 and 7 will be 0.45 or somewhere near? The calculation was made on the sum total of the remarks made by our 20 subjects (boys and girls differing in race and upbringing). The same procedure was adopted as before of taking successive sections of 100 sentences each. These 100 consecutive sentences are thus no longer the successive remarks of one child, but the general conversation in a given room where there are always three or four children talking together. There is therefore every chance that the calculation will yield objectively valid results. Now the average coefficient of ego-centrism which was reached in this way was of 0.45 + or − 0.05, representing the proportion of the ego-centric categories to the total language minus answers. As the average age of the children is 6, this is an interesting confirmation of the conclusions of the last chapter. (Piaget, 1926/ 1959: 51–52)

By the end of this description there are ten times the number of subjects than the original sample; each child is assumed to represent a different personality type. The sample of 100 sentences was recorded and the resulting coefficient (0.45) lies mid-way between 0.47 and 0.43, the coefficients for the original two 'fairly different types'. Furthermore, this is taken as 'objectively valid'. The persuasive force of the way this result is presented lies in the likelihood that it could have been otherwise. Each claim is given to suggest mutually reinforcing findings.[32] The final result is the existence of ego-centric language.

As with psychoanalytic and behaviourist rhetoric, once a psychological object (in this case, ego-centric speech, and *therefore* thought) is identified and labelled, the rhetorical consequences are the expansion and 'clearer' description of such objects. In Piagetian rhetoric, then, the existence of the object requires further investigation. The Piagetian child requires monitoring in order to discern which 'stage' in the sequence the child has 'reached'; and the child reaches the next stage through internal changes: the lexicon describes a particular sort of object. In this way, questions concerning methods for 'accelerating' such 'growth' could be (and perhaps must be) 'dismissed . . . as "la question américaine"' (Bruner, 1983: 141).

## Vygotsky

The work of the Russian psychologist Lev Vygotsky (1896–1934) is becoming increasingly important almost half a century after his death (Wertsch, 1985).[33] Translations of his work began to circulate privately in the late 1950s with the first edition of *Thought and Language* (published in Russian in 1934) being published in 1962 (Bruner, 1986: 72). To date there are only two main sources for his work on developmental psychology (Vygotsky, 1934/1986, 1978). In this section I shall focus on a chapter from *Mind in Society: The development of higher psychological processes* (a collection of essays published in English, 1978).

Vygotsky's texts contain many references to other psychological texts (see later discussion). The references to the work of Freud and Piaget are particularly important (for example 1934/1986: 24) in that criticisms are made of both writers.[34] Vygotsky's critique (esp. 1934/1986: 12–57) of Piaget, for example, focuses on Piaget's conception of 'ego-centric' language in order to assert a fundamental difference between their descriptions. For example, Vygotsky undertook a series of experiments to frustrate children in their attempts to play; he constructed situations in which they should draw pictures and did not provide the necessary equipment: the ratio of ego-centric speech doubled. This, according to Vygotsky, indicates something about the function of the language of the child. It is the use of the term 'function' which illustrates the essential difference here: Vygotsky argues that language plays an important role in development (language as developmental goad). Piaget, on the other hand, assumes language to be a reflection of inner processes. Vygotsky, then, asks why ego-centric speech reduces at around 'school age' (expecting a functional answer), whereas Piaget, according to Vygotsky, 'believes that ego-centric speech simply dies off' (Vygotsky, 1934/1986: 32). In this attack, Vygotsky claims that speech is not subject to some kind of separable, time-dependent process. This is the important difference between the two writers: for Vygotsky, learning 'to direct one's own mental processes with the aid of words or signs is an integral part of [for example] the process of concept formation' (1934/1986: 108).

The rhetoric of Vygotsky's critique should not suggest that his own account is purely linear. Indeed, Vygotsky uses many sequential metaphors:

> The development of the processes that eventually result in concept formation begins in earliest childhood, but the intellectual functions that in a specific combination form the psychological basis of the process of concept formation ripen, take shape, and develop only at puberty. Before that age, we find certain intellectual formations that perform functions similar to those of the genuine concepts to come. With regard to their composition, structure, and operation, these functional equivalents of concepts stand in the same relation to true concepts as the embryo to the fully formed organism. To equate the two is to ignore the lengthy developmental process between the earliest and the final stages. (Vygotsky, 1934/1986: 106)

The attack on the Piagetian account is specific to the role of language in the developmental process, and is not an attack on claiming that other (or all) developmental processes do not 'ripen' and 'die off': other aspects of the child's development (in this case, 'concepts') are held to 'take shape', from being 'embryonic' to 'eventually' resulting in the 'fully formed organism' after 'the lengthy developmental process' required. Nevertheless, Vygotsky insists that: 'Real concepts are impossible without words, and thinking in concepts does not exist beyond verbal thinking.' Thus,

Vygotsky's account emphasises the role played by language in development:

> Initially speech follows action, is provoked by and dominated by activity. At a later stage, however, when speech is moved to the starting point of an activity, a new relation between word and action emerges. Now speech guides, determines, and dominates the course of action; the planning function of speech comes into being in addition to the already existing function of language to reflect the external world. Just as a mold gives shape to a substance, words can shape an activity into a structure. However, that structure may be changed or reshaped when children learn to use language in ways that allow them to go beyond previous experiences when planning future action. (Vygotsky, 1978: 28)

Here, the role of the 'word' is described (through metaphor) as being a 'mold'. The emphasis is on an inherent flexibility; one able to 'shape' (not in the behaviourist sense) activity to the point where it becomes 'a structure'. But such a structure is itself flexible: the child is 'allowed' (in this context, 'able') to 'change or reshape' their use of language in order to 'go beyond previous experience'. Such inherent flexibility entails the potential for the 'future' to become detached from the past (previous experience) insofar as the child is able to increase its language abilities. It also promotes the role of the child as an active agent (rather than, say, the role of the environment in the behaviourist account).

This emphasis on the function of language may be taken to stem from the assumption that 'human behaviour differs qualitatively from animal behaviour' (Vygotsky, 1978: 60, discussed below). It also gives an insight into the title of the chapter I shall now examine: 'Interaction between learning and development' (1978: 79–91).

Vygotsky opens the chapter by stating that the relationship in the title is 'the most unclear of all the basic issues' in theories of development. It will be useful here to attend to the way in which Vygotsky formulates the 'errors' of previous theories. He indicates 'three major theoretical positions': 'The first centers on the assumption that processes of child development are independent of learning' (Vygotsky, 1978: 79). Here the culprits are Piaget and Binet, who assume that mental functions that have not matured are not aided by instruction; thus, 'learning trails behind development' (Vygotsky, 1978: 80). 'The second major theoretical position is that learning *is* development' (Vygotsky, 1978: 80, emphasis original). The culprit here is James, although Vygotsky alludes to a 'group of theories'. Watson, for example, is criticised earlier in the collection of essays (1978: 58).[35] James is characterised as having 'reduced the learning process to habit formation'. For the second group, then, learning and development 'occur simultaneously'. 'The third theoretical position . . . attempts to overcome the extremes of the other two by simply combining them. A clear example of this approach is Koffka's theory' (Vygotsky, 1978: 81). Such a view, according to Vygotsky, has several novel components, one of which is that learning and development are 'mutually independent and interactive'.

Vygotsky then announces that he rejects all three positions (a good rhetorical tactic) and identifies an aspect of a child's situation not normally taken into account. Koffka, for example, 'does not see the specifically new elements that school learning introduces' (Vygotsky, 1978: 84). It is in order to discuss this novel element that Vygotsky introduces the 'zone of proximal development', which leads to a discussion of 'two developmental levels':

> The first level can be called the *actual developmental level*, that is, the level of development of a child's mental functions that has been established as a result of certain already *completed* developmental cycles. When we determine a child's mental age by using tests, we are almost always dealing with actual mental development. In studies of children's mental development it is generally assumed that only those things that children can do are indicative of mental abilities. (Vygotsky, 1978: 85, emphasis original)

The last claim is an assumption which Vygotsky rejects. He goes on to use an example in which he talks to two children of the same 'mental age' (the term is Binet's), and engages with them in the solution of a problem. If only one of them can solve the problem, Vygotsky asks, are they the same age? No; they differ according to the zone of proximal development which is: 'the distance between the actual developmental level as determined by independent problem solving and the level of potential development as determined through problem solving under adult guidance or in collaboration with more capable peers' (Vygotsky, 1978: 86).

Vygotsky's conception of development is generally much more dynamic (1978: 61) than the theories reviewed thus far, and so he is interested in 'functions that have not yet matured but are in the process of maturation, functions that will mature tomorrow but are currently in an embryonic state. These functions could be termed the "buds" or "flowers" of development rather than the "fruits" of development' (1978: 86). The zone of proximal development is a product of being a language user. Thus, according to Vygotsky, primates do not have one. Further: 'human learning presupposes a specific social nature and a process by which children grow into the intellectual life of those around them' (Vygotsky, 1978: 88).

So the Vygotskian account of development is one which stresses social interaction through language; the process of learning 'creates the zone of proximal development', and development 'lags behind the learning process' (1978: 90). The 'practical implications' are discussed by Vygotsky (citing Burt, for example), in terms of teaching methods: both teacher and child have an active role in the course of development (1978: 116–119). As Bruner notes, the learning situation Vygotsky describes fits 'the Oxford tutorial system or the discussion methods of the elite academy far better than it fits the ordinary common school' (1986: 142). Thus, Vygotsky's rhetoric involves both linear and sequential terms (see the quotation on p. 57) but, at least in the development of language, the immediate social environment plays a rhetorically important role: the stage is set for bringing about changes in education policy: 'children should be taught written language, not just the writing of letters' (1978: 119).

## Merleau-Ponty

The term 'existentialism' has frequently been used to describe the work of Sartre (see also Chapter 5), de Beauvoir, and Merleau-Ponty (for example Wahl, 1946/1990; Cooper, 1990). Amongst others, these writers cite texts by psychoanalytic authors such as Freud and Klein, as well as Watson (Sartre, 1943/1966: 311), and Binet (Sartre, 1940/1972: 90). So there is an overlap with some of the texts examined here. Moreover, there is a small literature which attempts to reconcile existentialist and behaviourist accounts (for example Kvale and Grenness, 1967; Day, 1969; Giorgi, 1975; McDowell, 1975; Slife and Barnard, 1988; Woolfolk and Sass, 1988; and essays in Wann, 1964). Recently, Costall has labelled Merleau-Ponty as one of the 'radical critics of traditional perception theory' (1991: 11). Thus, while the influence of existentialist texts may have been marginal, their existence in the psychological archive has provided a rhetorical counterfoil in 'mainstream' psychology (see also Broadbent, 1973; Bruner, 1983; Manicas, 1987; Billig, 1991).[36] In this section I shall examine an essay by Merleau-Ponty, 'The child's relations with others' (1960/1964).

Merleau-Ponty's argument (1960/1964, hereafter by page number) was originally presented as a lecture series held in the Sorbonne. He begins by reviewing previous lecture material concerning 'certain aspects of the child's relation with nature – for example, the child's perception' (97). This is important in the present context because a discussion of the way children 'perceive' may, on some accounts, be taken as more 'fundamental', or 'basic'. However, in outlining his lecture series on 'the child's relations with others', Merleau-Ponty dismisses such a possible account in the following manner: 'I do not at all believe that the question of the relations with others is a secondary and more particular problem, more strictly confined to affectivity than the problem with which we occupied ourselves last year' (97–98). That is, the existentialist account to be developed in this text argues against alternative conceptions which treat 'the problem of relations with others as secondary and subordinate' (98), as would the Piagetian account with its emphasis of 'ego-centric' speech. By placing this argument at the beginning of the text, Merleau-Ponty begins to shift the focus of attention (of the reader/listener) away from accounts which concentrate on the 'development' of processes within the child. This rhetorical manoeuvre is given as an unmitigated statement in the text:

> In speaking of the child's perception or of causal relations as grasped by the child, what struck us was the fact that, in the case of the child's perception, it is not a matter of a simple reflection of external phenomena within the child or of a simple sorting of data resulting from the activity of the senses. It seemed to us be a question of an actual 'informing' [Gestaltung] of experience in the child. (98)

In this account, 'facts' about 'perception . . . struck us': 'it is not' just 'simple reflection'. That is, an alternative account is being attacked and dismissed. This style of argument will be examined in more detail in Chapter 8, when the discussion will turn to a consideration of ways in which a reader may be 'enrolled' in a text. But it is important to briefly examine such a manoeuvre here, as it allows Merleau-Ponty to attempt a major shift in which metaphors are relevant to the topic of development (development as social interaction).

In the extract, the status of the term 'we' is ambiguous: we who attended the lecture series last time, we the author of the text, or we who have taken such arguments seriously. However, such an ambiguity does not render the text difficult to interpret: alternative (and unfortunately uncited, of which more in a moment) accounts miss out important aspects of the phenomenon which is under discussion. That is, accounts which treat 'relations with others' as somehow superimposed on more basic processes (of which the Piagetian account is an example, and may be the intended object of the attack)[37] are, according to Merleau-Ponty, seriously flawed (hence the strong terms: *'fact'*, 'it *is* not a matter'). Only when the reader is presented with the candidate replacement ('informing') is the rhetoric given in a mitigated manner ('It *seemed* to us'). In the process, the child is construed as an active agent, and an agent for whom the role of the 'other' is of primary importance (see also, Cooper, 1990: 116–124; Barnes, 1992).

Following this construction, a review is given again of material previously covered, but instead of reviewing material on 'perception', the text shifts to the 'imagination'.[38] Again, earlier accounts of this object are also attacked:

> What classical academic psychology calls 'functions of cognition' – intelligence, perception, imagination, etc. – when more closely examined, lead us back to an activity that is prior to cognition properly so called, a function of organizing experiences that imposes on certain totalities the configuration and the kind of equilibrium that are possible under the corporeal and social conditions of the child himself. (99)

It is the material (corporeal) and social conditions which are held to be 'prior'; thus the 'classical academic' account should not 'lead us' to first emphasise the importance of cognitive 'functions'. Instead, work should focus on the 'imagination' which 'is an emotional conduct' (98). But the important rhetorical shift is that: the 'functions of understanding' (99) are not to be regarded as 'beneath' (98) that of 'affectivity itself' (99). Rather, there must be a 'simple subordination' of understanding to emotional conduct (affectivity). Thus, Merleau-Ponty emphasises the social environment ('the learning of a structure of conduct'; 99). Such a manoeuvre involves regarding the 'use of language' (99) as a 'tool or instrument', because it entails that language-use is also 'a kind of *habituation*' (99, emphasis original). Language is the tool of habit, and it is used in a primarily social manner. Unlike some of the accounts reviewed earlier in this chapter which suggested that language could be regarded as a symptom of internal processes reflecting purely intellectual development, Merleau-Ponty emphasises the social situation: 'To learn to speak is to learn to play a series of roles, to assume a series of conducts or linguistic gestures' (109). It is this concentration on the 'lived' which sets this account apart.

This rhetorical shift allows the discussion to turn toward wide social concerns. It also provides an example of one author (Merleau-Ponty) using the discourse of previous texts (Frenkel-Brunswik, Klein, de Beauvoir) in order to construct a new rhetoric. As such, it will provide material for the next section.

Merleau-Ponty describes 'psychological rigidity' by first citing an essay by Frenkel-Brunswik. This essay, and the experiments it reports, investigates 'rigidity': 'a notion that originated in psychoanalysis, although it is far from being an orthodox Freudian conception' (101). Indeed, 'psychoanalytic' investigations of racist 'attitudes' (such as Murphy et al., 1931/1937; Fromm, 1942/1960; Adorno et al., 1950/1969; and essays in Swanson et al., 1952) were important in Anglo-American research into social and personality accounts around this time.[39] The important aspect of Frenkel-Brunswik's work, in Merleau-Ponty's account, is the (Freudian) 'reaction formation':

> The principle of this formation is well known: If the individual is very aggressive he conceals his aggression under an acquired veil of politeness, and often the most apparently polite people are, at bottom, the most aggressive. . . . More often than not, such persons are traditionalists. (101)

Following Frenkel-Brunswik, rigidity is described as an aspect of personality. At the same time, the identification of a 'type' of person ('traditionalists'), and the description of a 'principle', removes (through the use of a short summary of previous texts) the psychoanalytic (especially Freudian) emphasis on personal history. Instead, the discussion is in terms of general personality types at the widest range:

> Of course, nobody denies that each of these differences is considered to be an absolute difference, found in nations, excluding any appearance of transition, degree, or change. Mrs Frenkel-Brunswik thinks that these subjects have acquired this attitude [rigidity] in their initial relations with the family, inasmuch as these relations are also their first relations to values and to the world. (102)

Freud's interest in 'accident and constitution' has all but disappeared; the replacement is the 'corporeal' reality of 'attitudes' and 'principles' which ('of course') affect nations in a universal manner ('excluding change' etc.). Thus, Merleau-Ponty offers a palimpsest which rewrites other accounts of development.

The next reference is to Klein: again the emphasis is on using psychoanalytic rhetoric to discuss social relations at the societal level:

> As Melanie Klein has said, two images (the 'good mother' and the 'bad mother'), instead of being united in relation to the same person, are arranged by the child with the former prominent and the latter completely concealed from himself. When questioned, the child overtly recognizes only the favourable image, and this is what, according to Melanie Klein, defines ambivalence. (102)

Merleau-Ponty constructs a similarity between the works of Klein and Frenkel-Brunswik: both have identified a mechanism which influences

perception (social, rather than cognitive). Moreover, Klein 'has established a profound distinction between ambivalence of this kind and
ambiguity' (103), in which the first relates only to the child's perceptual
processes, while the latter is a 'phenomenon of maturity, which has nothing
pathological about it'. Thus, 'in rigid subjects', the development of
ambivalence does not 'mature' into 'ambiguity'. This is what Merleau-
Ponty takes from Klein's texts in order to explain personalities, 'attitudes'
and, therefore, social divisions. Moreover, the 'authoritarian' families, in
which 'rigid' children are 'found', are 'socially marginal'.

By giving descriptions of previous texts in this manner, Merleau-Ponty is
then able to relate his discussion to de Beauvoir's analysis of the
'mechanisms' in 'the phenomenon of the "battle of the sexes" ' (103).[40]
Here the 'mask' (101) of rigidity, becomes a 'masquerade' between the
sexes, maintained by 'a sort of tacit agreement', in which 'men and women
are at the same time accomplices and enemies' (104). In this way, Merleau-
Ponty's text presents a unified account of previous work, and, at the end of
his introductory remarks, the point of arrival is a reference to a member of
his own 'school' (Wahl, 1946/1990). The stage is set for a long discussion
of the 'ego in the eyes of the other' (153; see also Sartre, 1943/1966); or, as
the end of the introduction has it:

> It remains for us to see how the type of personality and of interpersonal relations
> designated by the term 'psychological rigidity' express themselves in the
> anonymous functions of external perception. Let us now turn to . . . a mode of
> relation to self and others, and perception in its own right' (104)

The remainder of the text is given in existentialist terms (see also Chapter
5). By emphasising social 'mechanisms', personality 'types' and the role of
language as a kind of 'habit' gained from both, Merleau-Ponty is able to
discuss the process of perceptual development in exactly those terms. The
child, in this case, is one for which the 'primacy of perception' is directly
affected by the perception of the 'other', beginning with the 'alienating'
affects of encountering a mirror (see also Lacan, 1975/1988). Further, the
role of the 'other' is complex in this account because the other becomes
internalised (through 'habituation'): the child's speech becomes a 'plural'
(148) conversation, and 'conducts of duplicity . . . emerge' according to
the age of the child. Thus, Merleau-Ponty presents a structural, or
universal, account of development, through a sequence of approximate
stages, stressing the importance of the 'other' within that ahistorical
sequence. Unlike the Piagetian account (in which such existentialist terms
are completely out of place), Merleau-Ponty discusses development as
being a product of social interaction – emphasising the perceptual rather
than the discursive (unlike Vygotsky).

**The conceptual child**

This chapter has so far examined the presuppositions incorporated into a
variety of schools of thought concerning development: the differences in

the conception of the child have been the most obvious finding. Indeed, the developmental psychologist I showed an earlier draft of this chapter to was surprised at the extent of the differences between these various accounts of development. However, at a high enough level of abstraction it is also possible to emphasise a number of potential similarities. In this section, then, an account will be given of the conceptual child developed by each system of presuppositions covered in the chapter.

If a 'conceptual child' were to be constructed using each of the theories covered here, it would be a confusing (if not wildly inconsistent) entity. Suppose that, with Freud, Watson and Skinner, the child's personal history was regarded as important; that, with Klein and Piaget, the child's personal history was always ordered through the (genetic) imposition of a set of 'stages'; and that, with Merleau-Ponty and Vygotsky, the child's perceptive and discursive relationships with other people were crucial. It would then be possible to construct a system of presuppositions in which the rhetoric of each of these writers was regarded as consistent: a metaphor of the child as determined stages of contingent consequences.

Alternatively, the theorists may be connected (at the 'abstract' level) in a different way. Suppose, with Watson, Skinner and Merleau-Ponty (and Sartre, for that matter), that the environment in which the child is engaged is the crucial factor of theoretical interest; that, with Piaget, Freud and Klein, a sequence of stages is important to the development of the child, but that such a sequence both determines later thought and comes to a virtual stop after some age; that, with Vygotsky and Freud (again), conversation (and, in Freud's case, action) involving other people (rather than Piagetian ego-centric speech) is the deciding factor in determining the speed (or pace) of development. Again, it would be possible to construct a metaphor of development with such a configuration of previous theorists: the child as a product of environment and conversation. Moreover, it remains possible to connect previous accounts in other ways, stressing in each case the abstract connection between various texts. Indeed, the analysis of the text by Merleau-Ponty showed some of the potential of incorporating some aspects of another writer's work (at the expense of other aspects): the construction of a new rhetoric remains possible, so long as the intention is not to adhere too closely to the texts of the earlier writer.

However, in adjusting such permutations, it is difficult to maintain all of the presuppositions and metaphors incorporated into earlier texts. Of course, this does not prevent new discourses concerning development being written, but in the process of dealing with the previous texts, new accounts, such as the one constructed by Merleau-Ponty (or Skinner, 1971; or Watson, 1917), construct new discursive forms. This could also be seen in the work of Klein, who claims to have followed the path originally described by Freud; yet in Klein's texts new-rhetorical forms (metaphors/descriptions) 'over-write' the earlier text. Perhaps, then, new texts (including the present one) will almost always do this.

## Conclusions

Each text considered in the present chapter was shown to posit different abstract entities, all of which were products of assumptions often given in metaphorical terms. The present text was constructed in order to show that the accounts considered are at odds with each other; that the assumptions made, and the metaphors used, each construct a different account of how 'development' might be described and defined. The rhetoric used in each case was shown to work against the description of a single unified account, and the networks of assumptions made in each text help to create discourses in which some rhetorical shifts seem more obvious than others. It is only when such discourses are examined in detail that the amount of rhetorical work involved becomes clear, and it is only when a range of discourses are compared that the extent of the differences between texts becomes obvious. There are further conclusions which need to be drawn out of this material, but an extended conclusion will be kept for Chapter 9.

The huge variety of terms covered here makes it difficult to promote some of them as literal descriptions and others as metaphorical. With frequent use, a single set of terms may be treated as a literal description (but combinations of some terms will involve an inconsistent set of presuppositions). From a behaviourist perspective, for example, one would not recognise Klein's discussion of 'splitting' the mother's breast, or the existence of 'positions' to which someone may 'regress,' as being anything more than a metaphorical way of describing behavioural differences. Knowing which discourse to privilege becomes more difficult as more discourses are applied to the same object; there is no 'natural' set of terms with which to undermine all others – maintaining one set of descriptive terms is a rhetorical achievement. The tactic in the present chapter, then, has been to suspend all of the terms applied to development as metaphorical. Indeed, the very distinction between the literal and the metaphorical requires further discussion – one that will be given in Chapter 6. But, for the moment, the present argument will be extended by a further case-study: on theories of emotion.

## Notes

1. This is not a novel claim: for a variety of such discussions (and orientations), see, for example, Pepper (1942), Gellner (1985), Leary (1990b), Bazerman (1988), Coan (1979), Hillner (1985), Holton (1981), Kimble (1984), Koch (1981), McGovern et al. (1991), Mitroff (1974), Sampson (1977, 1991), Secord (1986), Manicas (1987), Shotter (1975), Staats (1983), Weimer (1979), Kimmel (1991), Myers (1990a) and Jordanova (1989), Soyland (1994a). The literature on values and presuppositions in science (and in psychology) is now fairly large. For a longer account, and a larger set of references, see Soyland (1994c).

2. Or, in Latour's (1988: 1–17) terms, to attempt to open the 'black box' of development. If development is not an 'object' (or 'process') which has achieved a degree of rhetorical closure, it is at least an area in which competing theories attempt to render alternatives redundant.

3. Such a characterisation is sometimes given, and will be discussed in Chapter 7. The 'nature/nurture' dichotomy is sometimes used in psychology in something approaching the 'either/or' form (where 75 percent or 90 percent of either is taken as excluding the priority of the alternative). For an early account of the 'nurture' perspective, see Mead (1928/1943: 9–18); she describes her work on 'adolescence' as being in opposition to the work of G. Stanley Hall (1844–1924), and the 'American psychologist' generally. Hall could easily be described as having invented the category of 'adolescence'. For an early account of the 'nature' perspective, see Galton (1869). Later, Spearman described Galton as 'the most original of British psychologists' (1923: 3; see also O'Connor, 1988: 123–126). While it is possible to characterise Galton as on the nature side of the debate, the connection with the term 'genetic' came later. Again, the 'genetic' side of the debate on intelligence is discussed in Chapter 7. For an account of the history of the debate in England (1869–1939), see Rose (1985: 62–89) and Hearnshaw (1964), and of the debate in the United States (1890–1930), see Chapman (1988). More recently, arguments have been given for a third component to this characterisation: 'developmental noise', which cannot be accounted for *either* by the content of genes *or* environmental factors (see, for example, Lewontin (1991: 27)).

4. Such changes pose a small dilemma. Several recent texts do examine the philosophical and historical basis of developmental accounts. See, for example, Walkerdine (1988), Sinha (1988, 1989), Richards and Light (1986), Bradley (1989), Costall (1985, 1991) and essays in Russell (1988). But the question is whether or not to regard such texts as part of the specialist literature on 'development', or part of the wider debate on the importance of 'development' for 'psychology' (more generally construed). In the present context, the latter option has been taken. (Reflexively: this is the safer option.)

5. This marginalisation of developmental psychology may be regarded as partially accounting for the popularity of the 'after Watson' account of the history of Anglo-American psychology discussed in Chapter 1 (Note 16). But it is probably only part of some larger story – yet to be described. The use of the 'after Watson' (or, 'rise of behaviourism') account of the history of psychology is one possible direction for future research.

6. Such an image would accord well with the rhetoric of psychology at the end of the nineteenth century, which was itself merely a sub-section of the quest for unity in the sciences generally (see also Leary, 1987, 1990a). Each area of psychology was to lay down its brick in the 'cathedral of knowledge', and the result would be a complete understanding of humans and animals (the measured and time-dependent connotation is intentional). In reviewing such a conception, Sigmund Koch (1981; also discussed in relation to Vygotsky in Kozulin, 1986) has concluded it to be a myth unsustained by a century of psychological investigation. Further, many of the theories to be discussed have been regarded as competitors rather than dealing with separable areas of inquiry. Bruner (1986: 136), for example, discusses Freud, Piaget and Vygotsky as being 'titans' suggesting a clash of opposing views. Debates on the status of 'psychological knowledge claims' are ongoing (and there is little reason to think this situation will change; see Soyland, 1994e).

7. The definition of 'psychology' was discussed in Chapter 1 (esp. Note 16). Before the work of Wundt, the definition of 'psychology' had been regarded as problematic (e.g. Ash, 1982; Rose, 1985; Koch and Leary, 1985; Danziger, 1990: 336; Smith, 1988; Richards, 1989). Smith presents an argument, from the perspective of the historian, which raises many relevant questions for scholars in this area; see Danziger (1991).

8. Cairns and Ornstein (1979: 461) point out that the German scientific community of the 1860s onwards used a single word to cover both phylogenetic and ontogenetic issues: *Entwicklungsgeschichte*. On this large topic, see Gould (1977) and Costall (1985). Costall's argument, for example, attempts to undermine the importance of Darwin's theory of evolution to theories of development (unfortunately, Costall does not discuss Foucault's characterisation of developmental accounts). For a collection of papers resulting from a conference on 'The Biopsychology of Development', see Tobach et al. (1971). This collection includes various accounts from a range of writers on this issue. In the present context, the English definitions will be the most important. Conventionally, 'phylogenesis' refers to the evolutionary development of a plant or animal type; 'ontogenesis' refers to the development

of an individual (*OED*). The rhetorical importance of such a distinction will be discussed later in the chapter, with particular reference to Skinner.

9. The use of the term 'symptoms' here will be a recurring feature of this rhetoric: the 'symptoms' are taken as indicating changes in (internal) mental processes, in much the same way as a medical doctor will discuss 'symptoms' as indicating changes in the 'physical' aspects of the patient. Later, it will be shown that Vygotsky describes Freud and Piaget as making a similar assumption (which Vygotsky then rejects).

10. It is also true that some have claimed to have 'outgrown' these theories (Bruner, 1986: 148). However, Bruner does not go on to supply a replacement account. Various accounts are on offer (e.g. Vasta, 1992), but, again, the solutions describe alternatives which attempt to reduce the importance of rivals (see Soyland, 1994e).

11. Freud's 'stage' theory was examined by Lacan (see Forrester, 1990a: e.g. 118–119). For a more general discussion and critique of stage theories (esp. in relation to accounts of 'depiction'), see Costall (1991).

12. For parts of Lacan's account of Freud's essays on sexuality, see Lacan (1973/1979: 176ff; 1975/1988: 113ff).

13. 'Seduction' is an important term in psychoanalysis, with a complicated history: see Forrester (1990a: 62–89).

14. For accounts of the history of such discourse, see Rose (1985), and Kevles (1985).

15. Such rhetoric has been examined in the (largely hostile) account of psychoanalysis by Gellner (1985). The rhetorical tension created by Freud between 'investigation' and the 'resistance' to psychoanalysis will be examined in Chapter 8.

16. For a longer discussion of time in relation to Freud's work (esp. in relation to *The Interpretation of Dreams*, and revisions Freud made after the publication of that work), see Forrester (1990a: 90–96).

17. Again, this functions as a promissory note: when the biological processes are understood, then the 'essence' will be explained.

18. Ideally, this point should lead on to a discussion of the impact of the anthropological literature on theories of development, but such a topic is beyond the scope of the present chapter. For accounts of such work, see Cole and Bruner (1971/1974), Cole (1975/1977), Scribner (1977) and essays in Bruner (1974). These studies depend, in part, on the work of Vygotsky (discussed later in this chapter). For an account of later psychoanalytic work which attempted to promote a 'new anthropological type', see Adorno et al. (1950/1969). This work will be mentioned again in relation to Merleau-Ponty later in the chapter. For another post-Freudian account which attempted to relate psychoanalytic terms to anthropological issues, see Fromm (1942/1960: esp. 1–18); Fromm (1942/1960: 51) cites work by Mead, for example.

19. For various accounts of what such 'understanding' entails, see Gellner (1985), Forrester (1980, 1990a), and essays in Meltzer (1988).

20. The rhetorical construction of this paper, delivered to the International Congress of Psychoanalysis in 1951, also raises issues concerning the ways Klein could account for her relationship to Freud's writings, the views of Anna Freud, and the ways in which Klein describes her own work as an original development. A discussion of this topic should be a direction for future research. For a connected paper, on the relationship between Lacan and Freud's writings, see Eaton and Soyland (1994).

21. 'Transference' is an important topic in the psychoanalytic literature – some scholars even maintain that psychoanalysis *is* transference. See, for example, Forrester (1980, 1990a), Gellner (1985) and Frosh (1989). The psychoanalytic process is discussed more generally by Foucault (1954/1976: 30–42). Brooks (1991) reviews 'transference' in relation to literary criticism. In a discussion of 'schizophrenia', Clare (1976/1980: 215–218) notes that, while Freud did not attempt 'to analyse a psychotically ill patient' (because of problems relating to the process of transference), Klein did make such an attempt: Klein's 'system holds that schizophrenia is a regression to an infantile stage of personality development. The small child, according to Mrs Klein, is capable of forming intense transferences, both positive and negative' (Clare, 1976/1980: 217).

22. Two versions of the story may be given as: (a) never eradicated and therefore liable to

be revived; or (b) liable to be revived and therefore never eradicated. Is there a difference between the two versions? In (a), 'never eradicated' is being stated as the fact from which Klein draws her conclusion: it is the same form as the one above in which it was held that transference 'operates throughout life'. Sentences of this form serve to locate an entity, the existence of which is then reinforced by successive observations. In (b), the components have been reversed; thus, the 'revivable' anxieties are used to justify the claim that they were never eradicated. Such a reversal appears to weaken the persuasive force: the observation of successive appearances has already been described as a 'revival' and therefore anticipates the explanation given in the second component of the sentence. Thus, the causal account being given begins to look empty: the use of the term 'therefore' makes it appear as if some deductive work is being performed, but the central claim is merely being restated. Now, a philosopher of an essentialist disposition might go on here to claim that Klein presents the reader with a version of Molière's *virtus dormitiva* which is empirically vacuous. This is not the point I want to make. Instead, what is being examined is the way Klein attempts to persuade by positing the existence of something which serves to explain later observations; the question is one of rhetorical construction, not empirical truth: this will be useful as the discussion of the text proceeds.

23. As Freud has it: 'suppose that Rome is not a human habitation but a psychical entity with a similarly long and copious past – an entity, that is to say, in which nothing that has come into existence will have passed away and all the earlier phases of development continue to exist alongside the latest one' (1930/1961: 70). Such a developmental metaphor would not, for example, be incorporated into the Piagetian account of stages. This view of development also has implications for Freud's neurological theories: see Forrester (1980), Harrington (1987: 235–247) and Hebb (1949: 245–250).

24. There have been several historical studies of Watson, and of behaviourism. See, for example, Cohen (1979), O'Donnell (1979), L.D. Smith (1990a, 1990b), Buckley (1989) and Leary (1990a).

25. The consequences of this methodological shift have recently been described by Bazerman (1988) as being embedded in the rhetorical construction of the experimental article in psychology – this is discussed further in Chapter 8.

26. This rhetorical manoeuvre, in which a previous psychological concept (description) is given a negative gloss, was examined in Chapter 3 in relation to debates in neuropsychology.

27. But it may also be 'required'. Skinner, for example, argues for a 'technology of behavior' by claiming that in 'trying to solve the terrifying problems that face us in the world today. . . . We play from strength, and our strength is science and technology' (1971: 9); moreover, the technology of behaviourism is 'possibly the only way to solve our problems' (1971: 30): cf. Skinner's rhetoric of anti-rhetoric examined in Chapter 1.

28. While Skinner consistently uses 'behavior', other behaviourist writers prefer (in the behaviourist sense: spend time) using the plural term, 'behaviors'. Two authors cited by Skinner (1966: 1205) argue that

> Here we have animals, after having been conditioned to a specific learned response, gradually drifting into behaviors that are entirely different from those which were conditioned. Moreover, it can easily be seen that these particular behaviors to which the animals drift are clear-cut examples of instinctive behaviors . . .' (Breland and Breland, 1961: 683)

For later examples of the use of 'behaviors', see Baldwin and Baldwin (1978) and Renner and Rosenzweig (1986). These writers employ lists of 'behaviors', each item being described as a small unit or bit (as in Skinner's text).

29. For longer discussions, see Cohen (1983), Boden (1982), Heatherington and Parke (1986) and essays in Russell (1988) – including an essay in which Hopkins compares, and draws similarities between, Piaget and Klein.

30. I use the term 'mind' because Piaget does not claim that such structures exist as part of the neuronal structure.

31. Haack defines an 'enthymeme' as 'an argument with a suppressed premise' (1978: 245). The similarity here is that the final question in the extract is without number: to be answered,

but not as a separate issue, because a concern with evolution is part of Piaget's rhetoric. Thus, it functions here as a kind of 'of course' clause. (Reflexively: this may seem a strong interpretation. Turner argues: 'Style . . . is more easily recognized than analysed . . .' [1973: 23]. I can only suggest that this is the main connotation of Piaget's questioning.)

32. This experimental verification of Piaget's original finding is not given in any more detail than I have listed. The ('objective') verification is not at issue here; rather, the task is to show how such a verification was constructed.

33. For longer discussions of Vygotsky's work, and its relation to other developmental theories, see Bradley (1989), Wertsch (1985), Walkerdine (1988) and Sinha (1988, 1989).

34. For example, Vygotsky takes issue with both Freud and Piaget in that both 'made the unconscious character of autistic thought a starting point for their theories. Ego-centric thought is also viewed as not fully conscious. It occupies an intermediate position between the conscious reasoning of adults and unconscious dream activity (1934/1986: 24). For an account of the relationship between Piaget and Vygotsky, see Piaget's entry in *A History of Psychology in Autobiography*; for further points, see Soyland, 1993).

35. Unfortunately, Vygotsky does not cite a particular text by Watson in this case. However, he cites and criticises Watson's *From the Standpoint of a Behaviorist* elsewhere (e.g. Vygotsky, 1934/1986: 84–89).

36. The connections between existentialist texts and those of psychiatry is rather more obvious, particularly through the work of R.D. Laing (e.g. 1960/1965). Nevertheless, the interconnection between psychology and existentialism remains, largely, an area for future research (but see essays in Howells, 1992).

37. This is likely as Merleau-Ponty attacks a view of 'egocentrism' later in the essay:

> Since the primordial me is virtual or latent, egocentrism is not at all the attitude of a *me* that expressly grasps itself (as the term 'egocentrism' might lead us to believe). Rather, it is the attitude of a *me* which is unaware of itself and lives as easily in others as it does in itself – but which, being unaware of theirs in their own separateness as well, in truth is no more conscious of them than of itself. (Merleau-Ponty, 1960/1964: 119, emphasis original).

This extract will also indicate the absence of psychoanalytic terms; this will be important in the following discussion.

38. The subject of the imagination was a significant one for existential psychology. Sartre (who was in personal contact with Merleau-Ponty; see conversations between Sartre and de Beauvoir in de Beauvoir, 1981/1984) wrote at length on the topic (see Sartre, 1940/1972). For evidence that Sartre was influenced by Merleau-Ponty's texts, see Sartre's essay 'What is writing?' (1948/1990), and his essay after the death of Merleau-Ponty (Sartre, 1964/1965). For recent accounts of existentialist writing, see Cooper (1990) and essays in Howells (1992).

39. Frenkel-Brunswik appeared as the second author of *The Authoritarian Personality* (Adorno et al., 1950/1969). Merleau-Ponty does not refer to this text, although there is another citing of Frenkel-Brunswik and Sanford, dated 1945. Sanford was the fourth listed author of Adorno et al. (1950/1969). The importance of *The Authoritarian Personality* in Anglo-American psychology should be noted. Merleau-Ponty's account was, then, not as marginal as it may first appear, insofar as there existed a common archive of research findings.

40. The reference cited here (by the translator) is de Beauvoir's *The Second Sex*.

# 5

# Accounting for Emotion: Metaphor as System

Ah, reason, seriousness, mastery over the affects, the whole somber thing called reflection, all these prerogatives and showpieces of man: how dearly they have been bought!

(Nietzsche, 1887/1969, II, sec. 3)

I decried the habit of drawing heavy conceptual boundaries between thought, action, and emotion as 'regions' of the mind, then later being forced to construct conceptual bridges to connect what should never have been put asunder.

(Bruner, 1986: 106)

The affective is not like a special density which would escape an intellectual accounting.

(Lacan, 1975/1988: 57)

Metaphors for the realm of emotion are frequent in the psychological literature, no less than in everyday discourse. Emotion is perhaps inconceivable without metaphor: a previous lexicon is needed, even to understand the most personal feelings. In common parlance, for example, metaphors of emotion often rely upon an understanding of the body: in fear a person 'goes to pieces'; becomes 'faint-hearted', 'spineless', 'lily-livered'; has 'one's heart in one's mouth'; the experience is 'hair-raising', and so on (see also Averill, 1990). Other metaphors rely on a form of spatial separation: often a division is postulated between the emotions and thought, or reason. The emotions are regarded as a kind of 'beast within', capable of the over-riding the 'higher' faculties of judgement, with the risk that emotions or passions may 'penetrate the world of reason' (Foucault, 1961/1971: 89) and lead to madness. Such a view may be fundamental to our culture. Indeed, as Smith argues: 'The Victorian language of "loss of control", which was both political and personal, conveyed the sense that the suspension of a higher power released the innate activity of a lower power' (1992: 41–42). And in doing so, the potential for insanity was always possible: 'The Victorians tended to elide differences between dreaming, emotions, drunkenness, epilepsy, and insanity, since each of these states involved a loss of control . . . the prescriptive and moralistic language considered appropriate for discussing the regulation of emotion or drinking was carried over without remark into writing on insanity and nervous diseases' (Smith, 1992: 45; see also Soyland, 1994d). So, in some descriptions of the class of psychological objects labelled 'the emotions', there is an element of danger, of release; a lack of mastery. But alternative metaphors are possible, and will be explored here as a kind of theoretical reaction.

The present chapter follows on from Chapter 4: it provides a theoretical extension by examining ways in which rhetoric concerning psychological objects may be used to form networks or systems of presuppositions and assumptions; and it provides some discussion of 'the emotions' as related to theories of 'development'. Once certain assumptions are made about the way in which the emotions relate to other elements of the psychological complex, the remainder of the discursive field is already structured: affect becomes the legitimation of reason (Freud, 1916–1917/1963; see Chapter 8), or affect becomes prior to (because faster than) judgement (Zajonc, 1980), or emotion becomes relative to cultural context (Harré, 1986), or emotion becomes the consequence of perception (Darwin, 1872/1890), or emotional reaction becomes the consequence of behaviour (rather than thought; James, 1884). Each of these descriptions complicates, or undermines, the other. However, rather than provide a detailed account of the texts which are examined in the present chapter, shortened discussions are given in order to examine basic metaphorical and conceptual differences.

Whilst changes in a living organism were shown in Chapter 4 to have been described in a variety of accounts of development, accounts of 'emotion' are at least as complicated. Moreover, accounts of research on the emotions have successively noted a lack of sustained investigation. Ribot began his account by stating that the 'psychology of states of feeling, it is generally recognised, is still in a confused and backward condition' (1897: v). More recently, Lazarus claimed: 'After being in the doghouse for many decades, written off as an unscientific concept . . . the study of emotion in both social and biological sciences has had a sudden and dramatic change of fortune' (1991: 819). Despite such characterisations, the emotions are often defined separately from other psychological objects, such as 'reasoning'. Henle suggested that:

> It may be that a strong attitude toward, or emotional involvement with, particular material is in part responsible for the difficulty which many unsophisticated [experimental] subjects experience in distinguishing between drawing a conclusion that is logically valid and one that is believed to be correct.' (1962/1968: 104)

Thus, research into 'reasoning' becomes complicated by 'motivational influences' which 'so often impair thinking' and the 'ability to make distinctions' (Henle, 1962/1968: 103–104). Further, the emotions are not only the subject of psychological description, but form the basis of many fictional and also legalistic accounts of human behaviour. For example, a fairly recent dictionary of law defines 'provocation' as:

> The goading of a person into losing his self control. Where, on a charge of murder, there is evidence on which the jury can find that the person charged was

provoked, *whether by things done or things said or by both together*, to lose his self control, the question whether the provocation was enough to make a reasonable man do as he did must be determined by the jury . . . (see Homicide Act, 1957, s3).' (Ivamy, 1988: 368, italics original)

The 'self' is kept under 'control', on this account, unless verbal or physical action 'goads' a 'reasonable' person into performing a criminal act, such as murder; an antagonism is held to exist between the emotions and reason: even a reasonable person may temporarily lose self-control, and perform an action which calls for legalistic (and perhaps psychological) scrutiny. However, whilst such an account maintains a tacit account of the emotions, it is not the only alternative available within the psychological literature. Describing 'emotion', a dictionary of psychology argues that 'probably no other term in psychology shares its nondefinability with its frequency of use' (Reber, 1985: 234). Thus, rather than consider the question 'What is an emotion?' (James, 1884), the present chapter asks: what descriptions have been applied to the term?

An account of emotion must do many things, not the least of which is persuade the reader that the account is plausible.[1] Historically, descriptions of emotions have often been highly complex[2] and, perhaps unlike questions concerning accounts of development or of the localisation of memories, the reader can be assumed to have a range of their own accounting practices concerning the topic of the theory. This makes the rhetorical problems concerned with developing an account of emotion much more complicated: metaphors must be constructed which persuade the reader that the account is plausible, if not convincing. So the main focus of the argument in the present chapter is to consider how this is done. Once this aspect of the argument is covered, a problem will still remain: each account may be considered persuasive, and yet the accounts are in serious conflict with each other (see also Gilbert and Mulkay, 1984). As with the argument in the chapter on development, this conflict of theories will be used to undermine the rhetoric of objectivity and common sense.

In this chapter four very different accounts of emotion will be contrasted. These are the Instinct Account as explicated by Darwin (1872), the Behavioural Account developed in the James-Lange theory (James, 1884, 1890/1950; Lange, 1885/1967), the Learning Account expounded by Harré (1986) using anthropological data, and the Choice Account put forward by Sartre in his *The Emotions: outline of a theory* (1939/1990). The following example, taken from Sartre, is used to introduce the differences between the four.

Assume a woman has just told a man that she is in love with him. On hearing this the man claps his hands in delight because (a) the instinct or instincts related to love act as a pump to 'fill him with delight' (Instinct); (b) the man feels delight, under the circumstances, as a result of clapping his hands (Behavioural); (c) that is the appropriate gesture within the man's time and culture (Learning); or (d) the man, subconsciously, decides to act in that way in order to maintain a position of power

(Choice). From this example it may be seen that the second explanation is an inversion of the first, and that there is a relation between the third and fourth accounts. A more detailed explication of each of these accounts will be given shortly.


### The thesis of metaphors of emotion

Part of the burden of this chapter is to undermine the conception of metaphor as merely an explanatory device. Here the 'merely explanatory' view is to be contrasted with a 'constitutive' conception of metaphor. The problem with the view of metaphor as merely explanatory is that it suggests a writer has a non-metaphoric conception of a phenomenon, and is only using a metaphor in a pedagogic manner.[3] Katherine Wilkes argues this case in relation to Freud's works:

> There were and are of course solid reasons for [Freud's use of, especially anthropomorphic, metaphors], primarily heuristic ones: few would have understood what he [Freud] was saying without these helpful metaphors, and it is therefore unsurprising that they are found in greatest abundance in his more popularising works (when writing for professional colleagues, there was less need for the crutch of metaphorical terminology). (Wilkes, 1988: 78)[4]

The argument of the present chapter does not claim that metaphors do not have pedagogic functions. Indeed, if metaphors did not have this function they would, I suggest, have virtually no rhetorical force whatsoever. Were that to be the case, we could safely return to a view of metaphor as merely decorative, the province of poetry.

It will be useful here to delineate these three different accounts of metaphor along a continuum. Metaphor would be of the least interest to conceptions of science in the 'merely decorative' account. This view has it that all metaphorical statements can be directly and completely translated into 'literal' language (for a critique of this account see Black, 1962; Ricoeur, 1978; Hesse, 1980; Cooper, 1986). The 'merely explanatory' account increases the importance of metaphors for conceptions of science because it holds that one requires a metaphor to communicate at least some views to one's readers. Thus Freud, for example, is purported to have a new 'literal' conception of a phenomenon in his head, but was unable to communicate such an understanding of that phenomenon, and be understood, without employing a metaphor. To borrow a distinction from the philosophy of logic (Bradley and Swartz, 1979),[5] the 'merely explanatory' account has it that a researcher arrives at a new proposition concerning a phenomenon, embeds the proposition in a sentence, communicates the sentence to others where it is understood in terms of the original proposition. This could be regarded as the 'standard model of communication' – one which has been heavily criticised (for example Eco, 1979/1981).

The 'constitutive metaphor' account is at the extreme of the continuum being outlined, and has the most profound (but not profane) consequences for conceptions of science. In part, it gains some of its impetus from the work of Mary Hesse (for example 1980; see also Arbib and Hesse, 1986) who has defended the thesis that 'all language is metaphorical'. A discussion of this more general thesis will be given in Chapter 6, and need not be of concern for the moment. The more restricted view of metaphor as it will be developed here, in terms of theories of emotion, suggests that (influential) metaphors of emotion shape the way emotions are discussed: the presuppositions entailed by a metaphor are used to develop an account of emotion which then begins to exclude other (rival) accounts.

There is one danger in discussing the constitutive view which needs to be avoided at the outset. Max Black (1962) suggested that if the metaphor 'man is a wolf' is employed, the people who use it would (a) see men as increasingly vulpine, and (b) see wolves as increasingly human. This is fine so far as it goes, in fact something very similar will be argued here; but what needs to be avoided is that idea that there was some original, 'undistorted', theory-neutral vision of what 'men' and 'wolves' actually were. As will be argued in the next chapter, this plays on reading the term 'literal' as meaning 'actual'. The alternative conception adopted here is that 'literal' only refers to 'previous usage', and 'metaphorical' refers to 'current' (new/proposed) usage.[6] Having given this account of metaphor in the abstract, I now turn to the specifics of a variety of theories of emotion.

All the theories of emotion to be discussed have been influential in twentieth-century psychology. Of these, the Sartrean account has been the least discussed, but recent accounts of emotion as 'putting on a show' (Averill, 1990), and reference to the work of Robert Soloman (e.g. 1976), have shifted it further from the archive to the spotlight with a collection of empirical studies being reported (for example essays in Lutz and Abu-Lughod, 1990). I will label each of these theories as 'general types' for convenience; each one is being tagged to a particular name (for example Darwin, James-Lange, Sartre); and each one is, as usual, largely discussed in terms of a few 'representative texts'.

## The instinct account

The instinct account is probably the most common and the one most ingrained into Western languages – it can be seen to some extent in the legal definition cited earlier. It was certainly not new when it the subject of Darwin's *The Expression of the Emotions in Man and Animals* (1872/1890), but the publication date of that work is at the limit of the time period set for the modern discipline of Psychology (see Smith, 1988, for an argument on this point). Darwin wrote this book after publishing *On the Origin of the Species* in 1859, after 12 years of research. In the Introduction to the book he rejects a number of earlier texts on emotion as being unhelpful, thus rhetorically clearing a space for his own construction. Whilst not wanting to claim that the text was *sui generis* (which it was not; see Desmond and Moore, 1991), the publication of the book may be regarded as marking a turn in accounting for emotion; one that is still referred to in current theoretical accounts.

Darwin's account maintains that the emotions, of both human and animal varieties, are indications of some underlying process. The key term in Darwin's text is 'expression': the visible sign of the emotion affecting the creature may vary to some extent (Darwin allows some cultural differences, for humans at least), but there are basic types of emotion discernible through the correct interpretation of that sign. To facilitate the argument, Darwin's text includes several plates depicting the electrical stimulation of the face of a man, each time giving a caption to guide the reader in regarding the expression as a token of a particular type (rage, depression, happiness and so on). But, the central thesis of the book is that 'most of our expressive actions are innate or instinctive' (1872/1890: 377); 'only a few expressive movements . . . are learnt by each individual; that is, were consciously and voluntarily performed during the early years of life for some definite object, or in imitation of others, and then became habitual' (1872/1890: 373). The result of such an account is that the emotions exist within each individual and are expressed – that is, forced out of the body – in appropriate circumstances. Further, the role of inheritance was emphasised to the extent that Darwin said 'I have endeavoured to show in considerable detail that all the chief expressions exhibited by man are the same throughout the world' (1872/1890: 381). This account then allows Darwin to speculate on the possibility of all humans having 'descended from a single patent-stock', thus extending to the emotions the account he had generated in *On the Origin of the Species*. Such an essentialist account bound the discussion of emotions to the explanatory power of the theory of evolution and, in the process, reaffirmed the emotions as expressive of some innate inner state of being; the emotions-as-expression metaphor benefited from the success of Darwin's more general theory of evolution through natural selection.

### The behavioural account

The James-Lange theory of emotion gains its title from the work of William James (1842–1910), notably the article 'What is an emotion?' which appeared in the journal *Mind* in 1884, and the independent work of the Danish physiologist, Carl Lange (1834–1900), who argued for a similar position on the basis of different data in his paper (1885/1967). When James rewrote this material as a chapter for his two-volume work *The Principles of Psychology* (1890/1950; see also Chapter 8), he incorporated Lange's work to support the argument being developed. All three pieces were collected by Knight Dunlap for a volume in which the editor claimed that:

> this theory of the emotions has not only become so strongly entrenched in

scientific thought that it is practically assumed today as the basis for the study of the emotional life, but has also led to the development of the hypothesis of reaction or response as the basis for all mental life. (Dunlap, 1922/1967: 5)

Thus, with behaviourism waiting in the wings, I turn to an exposition of the chapter by James.

James begins his chapter on 'The emotions' (1890/1950, Vol. 2: 442–485, hereafter by page number) by giving several long quotations from authors who describe the physiological signs of different emotions: grief (using Lange), fear (using Darwin) and hatred (Mantegazza). He then complains that one could continue to give such physiological accounts without achieving much of substance because of the number of variations existing between people:

> The result of all this flux is that the merely descriptive literature of the emotions is one of the most tedious parts of psychology. And not only is it tedious, but you feel that its subdivisions are to a great extent either fictitious or unimportant, and that its pretences to accuracy are a sham. (448)

Further, he complains that such descriptions 'give nowhere a central view, or a deductive or generative principle'. James then offers to give his more central viewpoint, or theoretical characterisation. He begins by stating that 'the general causes of the emotions are indubitably physiological' (449): this is an important step, the very claim to this not being dubious indicates a basic premise of the argument; while other writers may regard physiology as being a consequence of events in perception or thought, James regards physiology as a cause. As a result, the basic tenet of the argument is assumed from the beginning. To reinforce this, James cites the work of Lange, and his own article from *Mind*, before giving his general account of the causes of the emotions. The account involves postulating two different causal sequences. The first 'common-sense' account is that 'mental perception of some fact excites the mental affections called the emotions, and that this latter state of mind gives rise to the bodily expression' (449): such a description best fits the account from Darwin. This first account is to be contrasted with the one developed by James: 'the bodily changes follow directly the perception of the exciting fact and . . . our feelings of the same changes as they occur *is* the emotion' (449, emphasis original). He then says that such a 'hypothesis is pretty sure to meet with disbelief' (450), but he defends it by taking the following argumentative steps:

1  objects do excite bodily changes;
2  bodily changes are felt;
3  emotions do not exist without bodily changes.

With each step, the reader is drawn further into the argument: emotions become primarily an aspect of the body. James goes on to claim that: 'If such a theory is true then each emotion is the resultant of a sum of elements, and each element is caused by a physiological process of a sort already known' (453). The terms suggest a level of scientific plausibility: sums, elements and known physiological processes; each signals that James seriously intends to counter the reader's purported disbelief. James claims that his theory allows 'causal' questions to be asked, rather than questions of classification (the subject of his tedium): 'We step from a superficial to a deep order of enquiry' (454). It is this claim to be giving a more substantial or significant contribution which sets James's chapter apart from other contemporary work on the emotions, but, in the process, several radical steps have been taken; steps which realign the accepted metaphors of emotion. It is only through the use of an intricate number of assumptions that reaction-as-emotion begins to become persuasive: the network entangles the reader in a new construction.

B.F. Skinner (see also Chapter 4) turned to the topic of the emotions on several occasions; for example, his book *About Behaviorism* contains a chapter-length discussion on 'The inner world of motivation and emotion' (1974: 148–166). In each case, his behaviourist account was drawn in relation to the behaviour-as-emotion metaphor constructed by James. But the account from Skinner is an important addition insofar as he offers ways of translating common-sense (or even intentional) terms into behaviourist rhetoric and, as a result, reduces further the roles given to the 'inner world'. According to Skinner's account, James maintained that 'we do not run away because we are afraid but are afraid because we run away' (1971: 18), thus promoting the reversal of the causal story outlined earlier. The translations Skinner gives extend such a reversal but they do so in terms which remove the role of the agent almost completely. For example:

> Consider a young man whose world has suddenly changed. He has graduated from college and is going to work, let us say, or has been drafted into the armed services. Most of the behaviour he has acquired up to this point proves useless in his new environment. The behaviour he actually exhibits can be described, and the description translated as follows: he lacks assurance or feels insecure or is unsure of himself (*his behaviour is weak and inappropriate*); he is dissatisfied or discouraged (*he is seldom reinforced, and as a result his behaviour undergoes extinction*); he is frustrated (*extinction is accompanied by emotional responses*); he feels uneasy or anxious (*his behaviour frequently has unavoidable aversive consequences which have emotional effects*); there is nothing he wants to do or enjoys doing well, he had no feelings of craftsmanship, no sense of leading a purposeful life, no sense of accomplishment (*he is rarely reinforced for doing anything*) . . . (Skinner, 1971: 144)

This form of double description continues through to the point at which the young man has an 'identity crisis', and in each case the behaviourist translation concentrates on observable differences. Skinner then points out that: 'the italicized paraphrases are too brief to be precise, but they suggest the possibility of an alternative account, which alone suggests effective action' (1971: 145). This rhetoric of practical application was in keeping with the major tenets of behaviourism but, in the process, the emotions were reformulated as inner states which were the consequence of observable behavioural action – an element in keeping with the James-Lange account. Using this form of account, the importance of subjective feelings could be removed from any explanation of individual behaviour; the metaphor of emotion-as-behavioural consequence reasserted the explanatory power of the empty-organism metaphor discussed in Chapter 4; the organism could, on this account, thus be 'reprogrammed' to the point at which problematic emotional behaviour could be altered or completely revised.

**The learning account**

The suggestion that emotions may be learned, and therefore be dependent upon contingent socio-cultural circumstances, may be regarded as a subversion of the metaphors of emotion as expression, and emotion as behavioural consequence. This is the third metaphor to be discussed: emotions as learned cultural products. According to this account, emotions are 'reproduced in individuals in the form of embodied experience': this account privileges learning because to 'learn how, when, where and by whom emotions ought to be enacted is to learn a set of body techniques including facial expressions, postures, and gestures' (Lutz and Abu-Lughod, 1990: 12). Thus, the metaphor of emotion as learning removes discussion of naturally occurring essences, as in the case of expression, and removes discussion of behaviours which lead to emotional states, as in the case of the James-Lange account. This is also an account which emphasises the role of language (linguistic or otherwise), and I will return to this issue shortly (especially in relation to Sartre).

According to this account, emotions may be regarded as a form of socially sanctioned display; they are discursive and bodily acts performed in reaction to particular circumstances (for example, Averill, 1990, 1993). According to Harré, 'it is a mistake to suppose that there are native (or "natural") emotions, found amongst all human beings. Nativism is just another example of the ethnocentrism of much current psychological research'; thus, 'the very idea of an emotion as a response suffered by a passive participant in some emotive event is itself part of the social strategies by which emotions . . . are used by people in certain inter-actions' (1986: 111). Thus the emotions, and explanations of emotional behaviour, become, on this account, the consequence of a given and variable socio-cultural context. 'Nativism' is an approach, of which Darwin's account would be one example, which is dismissed here on methodological grounds as a mistake. In the process, the account Harré and others are proposing requires further research into variations between cultures, each being used to undermine the accounts which emphasise common elements of emotional behaviour, between cultures or even between species.

**The choice account**

The suggestion that the emotion may be a matter for (possibly pre-conscious) choice is related to the last section, in that learning and social factors are involved, but it puts further emphasis on individual action rather than socio-cultural influence; hence my use of the term 'choice'. The proposal, in a sense, is that an individual enacts a particular emotional state in order to maintain a particular power hierarchy; that emotions are chosen so that an individual's aims are furthered. The main text analysed in this section will be *The Emotions: outline of a theory* (Sartre, 1939/1990), but examples will also be taken from Sartre's other works, so it will be appropriate briefly to place the *Emotions* within his corpus.[7]

References to the emotions are frequent in Sartre's writings particularly because he gave a philosophical account of the relations between the self and the Other (a term always written with a capital in French discussions of the issues involved).[8] The *Emotions* is a fairly early work, written after *The Transcendence of the Ego* (1937/1957) but before he produced *Being and Nothingness* (1943/1966; the text frequently taken as a major statement of existentialist philosophy; see Cohen-Solal, 1985). Sartre built on this early account in further discussions of the emotions and the relationship with other people in an attempt to elucidate the constructions of self, contingency, being-in-the-world, and sadomasochistic relationships (1943/1966: 471–558). While the work of his later career added political dimensions which complicate such discussions, much of the original position remains intact and was often reasserted (for example in de Beauvoir, 1981/1984). This general position was also highly influential for texts such as Soloman (1976) and others that were discussed in the previous section.

The Sartrean account describes emotion as a 'magical transformation' of the world; emotions are purposive rather than reactive. This metaphor carries claims concerning what things ought to be discussed when describing emotions. I will review a little of the detail of the theory to make this clearer. Sartre complains that the 'peripheric' theory (the label he uses for the Jamesian account) does not seek to explain the 'general and essential structures of human reality' (194). Further, in an attack on anatomical studies carried out by Sherrington, Sartre claims that facts about 'physiological disturbances' (204) do not account for the 'organised character of emotion' (205). This is what Sartre purports to do in an account which 'must evidentially have recourse to consciousness' (215). Thus, 'emotion is a certain way of apprehending the world' (224).

The Sartrean account of the mind is one in which there exist two 'planes', unreflective and reflective; the first of these involves no level of self-awareness. In an emotional state, consciousness is unreflective: 'in emotion it is the body which, directed by consciousness, changes its relations with the world in order that the world may change its qualities. If emotion is a joke, it is a joke we believe in' (230). The way the world appears is altered by emotion; the world is transformed in a way desired by the agent. In describing emotions as transformations, Sartre's account plays on ways of seeing (see also discussions of 'the look', in 1943/1966).

It may be asked what role language (in the broadest sense of the term) plays in such an account given that emotional displays are read by the

Other as signifying some internal state. Here a brief diversion into Sartre's discussion of 'love, language and masochism' is relevant; it gives an account of love in terms of the role played by the Other, and the suggestion that 'love is in essence the project of making oneself be loved'; and further that 'love is the demand to be loved' (1943/1966: 488). The argument was that 'Language is therefore not distinct from the recognition of the Other's existence' (1943/1966: 486). The subject then, at least in terms of emotional relationships with other people, coincides with language: 'I *am* language' (1943/1966: 485), and the aim is to communicate a complicated level of desirability to the other person thus forming a kind of binding emotional attachment.

The Sartrean account may be regarded as important for the metaphors covered in the previous section is the following way. First, writers such as Lutz and Abu-Lughod note that: 'If earlier scholars who rejected the notion that emotion was sensation preferred the notions of emotion as judgment (Soloman, 1976), their view has since been supplemented by the insight that judgments might better be viewed as socially contested evaluations of the world phrased in an emotional idiom and evident in everyday speech' (1990: 11). I take the term 'judgment' here as being the discursive equivalent of choice, and that Sartre has been important in promoting such an account of emotion. Thus there is a fairly discernible connection between the choice account and the one described earlier as the learning account. Each privileges language and social context in order to undermine more essentialist accounts, or accounts which reduce the role of the active social agent.

## Conclusions

Extending the chapter on development, the present material has been used to suggest that metaphors are basic to the understanding of the emotions. Each of the theories covered may be regarded as competing with each other for persuasive effect, and attempts at rhetorical resolution are unlikely to be achieved without the rejection of fundamental aspects of each theory. The James-Lange account, for example, is a full inversion of the instinct account from Darwin: Darwin's theory depends upon the metaphor of 'expression', the sign being an indication of some underlying reality within the organism; for James and Lange, on the other hand, the expression is the emotion itself, and not a sign. The other two accounts – learning and choice – offer more radical constructions insofar as they largely ignore physiological material and concentrate on human situation and cultural context: the emotional 'act' as a function of power, belief and social practice.

If it is the case that everyday conceptions of emotion are impossible without some recourse to metaphorical description, then the accounts rehearsed in this chapter at least show the variety of possible conceptions on offer. The collection here is by no means exhaustive, and yet the number of alternatives on offer canvass possibilities which either reduce or increase the role of the emotional agent; from expression to choice, these various accounts vary between essentialist descriptions to accounts which emphasis individual or socio-cultural factors of importance. Again, in accordance with the conclusions of Chapter 4, the variety of theories considered here could be used to undermine any particular account. But the working psychologist or philosopher should not see these accounts as requiring a kind of crucial experiment that will decide on the validity of any particular instance. Rather, these accounts involve assumptions that are fundamentally antagonistic and not reconcilable to some basic, quantifiable situation. Networks of assumptions are simply not divisible by some common denominator.

I began the present discussion by suggesting that the metaphors of emotion covered would be at odds with each other, and that each account was an indicator of networks of assumptions which were, at the very least, divergent in important ways. Towards the beginning of the chapter, I also gave an outline of more theoretical material on metaphor: the last three chapters of case-studies – giving complementary discussions of neuro-psychology, childhood development and theories of emotion – now require a larger discussion of the theory of metaphor. To undertake such a task I will need to turn once again from the literature of psychology to that of philosophy, but the argument that follows is only undertaken because it is important to the analysis of science, and psychology in particular. It is only through a discussion of the role of metaphor, and the relation between language and truth, that novel forms of psychological description can be analysed and understood in relation to the practices of science.

## Notes

1. The range of accounts of emotion in various texts is very wide ranging, and some emotional experiences would only seem to be describable by employing a small paragraph rather than a single word such as 'anger' or a phrase such as 'flights of passion'. As an example, consider the following from the memoirs of Dimitri Shostakovich:

> There are plenty of diversions in a communal kitchen. Some like to spit into the neighbour's pot. Others limit spitting to teapots. It calls for certain skills, after all. You have to wait for the person to leave the kitchen, rush over to the teapot, pull off the cover, and cough up lots of sputum. It's important not to scald yourself. There is the element of risk. The person might come back any second. If he catches you, he'll punch you in the face. (1979: 68)

Here is a complex description of a combination of delight of defilement, achievement, risk and possibly revenge; anticipation (of being caught, of waiting for the moment, and of the enjoyment of spitting) and anxiety (of being seen, punched or scalded). The rhetorical power of such a description depends on the reader being given enough information to be able to imagine the circumstances, and possibly identify with the agent. A further passage from Shostakovich will illustrate a possible recognition of this problem: 'Tragedies in hindsight look like farces. When you describe your fear to someone else, it seems ridiculous. That's human nature' (1979: 72). While this passage relies on the assumption of a distinction between emotions and descriptions, which some may find unacceptable, it shows that, under some circumstances, a description may fail as a result of its construction – as a problem worthy of further consideration through rhetorical analysis.

2. The variety of emotions, the speed of their occurrence, and the range of things described as 'causing' them is also worth noting in this context. Consider the following excerpt from August Strindberg's diary (dated 15 April 1908):

> I ate dinner; cautiously and without aquavit. When I got up and opened the window a whole army of *White Flags* was waving to me (out on Gaardet). Then I understood, was so moved that I began to weep. Went to my desk and opened this diary. At that moment there came a scent of roses which threw me into ecstasy. (Strindberg, quoted in Meyer, 1985: 502, emphasis original)

Aquavit is a strong Scandinavian spirit similar to vodka; the spelling of the name varies between Scandinavian countries. In terms of rhetoric, the crucial aspect of such descriptions is that they must communicate the variety of experiences in an intelligible manner. It is a difference of degree rather than of kind for theories of emotion to be able to do the same. (The examples in this note and the previous one were chosen to avoid the general tendency in studies of 'science and literature' to rely solely on the 'great books' tradition.)

3. For a brief critique of this view as presented by Averill (1990), see Soyland (1991b). Averill gives an account of six metaphors of emotion where his own view – strategically placed as number six – is given not as replacing the other five, but in order to cover aspects of the phenomena not already included by the others. Again, this employs a split between metaphors on the one hand, and the 'raw data' or observation on the other. As noted in Chapter 1, the claim to tolerate a pluralistic set of accounts has a considerable rhetorical force – at least in the contexts considered here (the aim is not to develop a taxonomy of rhetorical 'forms', in any Platonic sense). The problem with Averill's claim to plurality, as the remainder of the present chapter will attempt to show, is that it depends for its force on an unacceptable account of metaphor.

4. The rhetoric in the passage from Wilkes is worth examining briefly. Freud had 'solid reasons' for needing the 'crutch of metaphorical terminology', especially when writing for a popular readership. However, when writing for professional colleagues, this was less necessary. This has the tone of reassurance, but seems to suggest that single terms in Freud's terminology were unrelated to metaphor. However, the reader could fruitfully reflect on whether the terms 'transference', 'unconscious', 'superego' and so on, do indeed *not* depend on a metaphorical use of language. The extent to which they have passed into common usage, and become literal, is a function of the rhetorical success of Freud's works (but not only those works; for a socio-historical account of the rise of psychoanalysis, see Gellner, 1985).

5. On this distinction see Bradley and Swartz (1979), and similar discussions in Grayling (1982) and Haack (1978).

6. This is cheating a little. It assumes the validity of an argument only developed in the next chapter of this text. Little depends on it in the context of this chapter. However, the next chapter will benefit (read: be more persuasive) from the prior discussion of case-studies.

7. A reader may consider the Sartrean view of emotion to be novel, and peculiar to the twentieth century. The other accounts of emotion would seem to have a more obviously longer history. One quick example from the 'great books' of English Literature should quickly dismiss such a view. In Defoe's *Robinson Crusoe* there is the following passage from the introductory section:

> . . . I have often observed, how incongruous and irrational the common temper of mankind is, especially in youth, to that reason which ought to guide them in such cases [as Crusoe's], viz. that they are not ashamed to sin, and yet are shamed to repent; not ashamed of the action for which they ought justly to be esteemed fools, but ashamed of the returning, which can only make them be esteemed wise men. (1719/1965: 38)

Such an account incorporates a view of what someone ought to feel with the perception of others, and that the 'irrational' temper 'especially in youth' is overcome with age. It also suggests the view common to the times (and continued at least up until the Second Book of Hume's *Treatise*, II, X, 'Of curiosity, or love of the truth' [1739/1972: 184–189]) of a distinction between reason (which ought to guide one towards the truth) and passion (which here overcomes the reasons not to act). It is this distinction which Sartre may be said to have undermined. And yet it is not too much of a leap to suggest that, in the quotation, what is being alluded to is a feeling of personal power which 'especially in youth' overrides what 'ought to guide them'. Robinson Crusoe, as a result, did not return home to York because he would 'be laughed at among neighbours, and be ashamed to see, not my father and mother only, but even everybody else' (1719/1965: 38).

8. For a more recent discussion of the role of the Other and its importance for psychology, see Sampson (1993).

# 6

# The Theory of Metaphor:
# The Extension of Discourse

> If, then, we loosen up our ideas of truth and falsity we shall see that statements, when assessed in relation to the facts, are not so very different after all from pieces of advice, warnings, verdicts, and so on.
>
> (Austin, 1956/1979: 251)

> It is the advent of truth into the world. . . . To be communicable, it must become picture or sensible object. We must learn the language of facts. The most wonderful inspirations die with their subject, if he has no hand to paint them to the senses.
>
> (Emerson, 1881: 139)

> But as the metaphor gains more and more ground, accommodates more and more in itself, it invites the onlooker to rest in it, to anticipate a pleasure to which restless reflection perhaps would lead one by a long detour.
>
> (Kierkegaard, 1841/1989: 103–104)

This chapter offers some discussion of the distinction between metaphorical and literal discourse. In doing so, some discussion is made of the status of true statements. Such a discussion touches on many vexed questions about which much has been written. Thus entering the arena at all may simply be a mistake, but some account should be given of what theoretical questions are at stake. In essence, the same strategy used in Chapter 1 against the distinction between philosophy and rhetoric (where it was claimed that the distinction could be undermined as itself being rhetorical) will be used against the distinction between literal and metaphorical discourse: the second pair of terms only gains its rhetorical power as a dichotomy, through the use of a metaphor. This argument is not new: in making it, the chapter relies on arguments developed largely by Heidegger, Derrida and Rorty. The novelty rests in the offer of a simple (possibly simplistic) solution to the rhetorical problems which may be used against the manoeuvre of dissolving the distinction. The suggestion is that employing metaphors in science is inescapable and that, over time, some metaphors may be regarded as a literally true through habitual use. Thus, metaphors provide a way of extending discursive practice.

First a note on terminology: 'metaphorical discourse' will be used here to cover all the finer distinctions between analogy, metonymy, synecdoche and metaphor. This attempt to collapse a variety of terms into a single category has been made for three reasons. First, the term 'discourse' is employed in order to signal that it is *language use* which is being discussed, rather than a more abstract account of language in (linguistic) isolation.[1] Second, 'metaphor' (or 'metaphorical') is used as an umbrella term incorporating the finer distinctions (of analogy, metonymy, synecdoche and so on) in order to simplify the discussion. The questions of interest here do not concern teasing out the differences between different kinds of non-literal tropes. What is at issue is the relationship between the literal and the non-literal. This is to employ 'metaphor' in a broad manner, one which preserves something of Aristotle's definition: 'giving the thing a name that belongs to something else' (*Poetics*, 1457b: 6–9; see also Ricoeur, 1978: 13; Cooper, 1986: 13).

The theoretical literature on 'metaphor' is large and varied. The object here will be to concentrate on a sub-set of this literature; to discuss texts related to describing 'metaphor' as 'constitutive' and 'pragmatic' (rather than 'definitive'). Within the literature on regarding metaphorical discourse as constitutive, the importance of Nietzsche's writings is frequently stressed: by Heidegger, Derrida, Foucault, Ricoeur, Rorty and Cooper, for example (see later discussion). Thus, Nietzsche's work will be used as a starting point for the present discussion. Early in his career, he asked:

> What then is truth? A mobile army of metaphors, metonymies, and anthropo-morphisms: in short, a sum of human relations which have been poetically and rhetorically intensified, transferred and imbellished, and which, after long usage, seem to a people fixed, canonical and binding. Truths are illusions which we have forgotten are illusions; they are metaphors that have become worn out and drained of sensuous force . . . (Nietzsche, 1873/1979: 84)

Such attacks on 'truth' and 'certainty' 'were frequent in Nietzsche's works (Kaufmann, 1974; Derrida, 1978/1979; Nehamas, 1985; Schrift, 1990).[2] It is this connection between metaphor and truth which needs to be explored; the possibility that by effacing the metaphorical origins of a statement we can arrive at a 'truth'. Cooper labels this the 'primacy of metaphor' thesis, according to which 'it is metaphor which provides the possibility of literal talk and therefore of literal truth' (1986: 258). Cooper argues that this thesis is 'not coherent. People can only forget that a use was metaphorical if at some time they had been aware that it was this. But they could only have this awareness if they were able to distinguish metaphorical from literal usage' (1986: 262). In reply, it should be said that we can readily identify statements as 'literal' – keeping the distinction is an option I will favour at the end of the chapter – but, nevertheless, some (perhaps most) literal statements may be shown to have had a metaphorical origin. Take, for example, 'mental illness': a description applied literally but one which had an historical starting point when a resemblance was forged between physical sickness and mental incapacity (see Sarbin, 1990; Soyland 1994a). This transition from metaphorical to literal description was a result, not of amnesia, but a change in discursive practice. In the last three chapters I tried to suggest that a similar process was at work in discussions of memory, development and emotion; that there has been an ongoing process of elevating particular metaphorical descriptions and using them as sets of literal categories.

## Enrolling Heidegger

In order to discuss the status of metaphorical discourse some issues must be raised concerning the traditional converse: literally true statements. However, there is a danger in this discussion in that the points at issue will remain obscure. Indeed, texts by Heidegger are sometimes described within the Anglo-American philosophical literature, for example, as being interested in questions which are 'too deep' and, therefore, too obscure to be understood. But the following points are worth making in a discussion of the processes of language use.

The use of the English language (and probably all languages) involves the constant employment of the copula 'is' and its functional equivalents, and it has been a subject in discussion of formal logic (at least) since Aristotle, in terms of a basic component of general statement forms (Kneale and Kneale, 1962/1984: 61–67). Sentences from the most mundane ('the train is late') to the most technical in science ('$E = mc^2$', where 'equals' is a functional equivalent of 'is') all rely on the status of the copula being taken for granted. However, it becomes problematic in the present discussion because, while few people would wish to populate their ontology with (Platonic) forms of late trains, this is exactly what is expected of sentences from science: not only is it expected that sentences of the 'A is B' form have practical consequences (as in the case of the late train), but in science (and in philosophy) those practical consequences are expected to remain stable for all time. Indeed, the sentences of science are sometimes admired because they are thought to be proven true (and thus have some ontological status) and may be devoid of practical consequences.[3]

These points touch on topics discussed by Heidegger, and I shall examine arguments from Heidegger written quite late in his career (the period after 1930 is considered to be late Heidegger), after his so-called 'turn' against metaphysics (Roberts, 1988: 255–257), against the 'quest for certainty' (Rorty, 1991b: 29), but before Heidegger produced his first study of Nietzsche (in 1950; Heidegger, 1961/1991; see Schrift, 1990: 20–21). The 'late Heidegger' has been very influential (Spivak, 1976) on Derrida's critiques of philosophical discourse (for example 1967/1976, 1972/1982, to be reviewed in section 4), and Rorty's recent studies (for example 1989, 1991a, 1991b) and, therefore, relevant to the present theoretical framework. Roberts, for example, characterises Heidegger's critique of 'modern philosophy' as one 'in which philosophers are rulers: they speak the truth of the community's structure, and in speaking it they bind the community to its truth' (1988: 262–263).

Heidegger (1949: 319–351, hereafter by page number) gives an account of the 'essence of truth' by first attacking its 'conventional conception'; that the 'True is the Real' (321). In order to do this, he focuses upon language: 'it is not the *thing* that is right but the *proposition*' (322). Thus the conventional conception relies on a 'correspondence' between what is said, and '*objective* truth' (323): 'objective truth always implies conformity of the object in question with the essential or "rational" idea of it. The impression is given – wrongly – that this definition of the essence of truth is independent of the explanation of the essential nature of all that is "is". . .' (324). Heidegger then contrasts this conception by claiming that: 'we take it as equally self-evident that truth has an opposite and that there is such a thing as untruth' (325).

Now, because Heidegger has used the conventional emphasis on a difference between true states of affairs (about the world), and descriptions of such true states (propositions), he is then able to claim that a proposition is incorrect when it fails to conform with the world: 'untruth can be understood as a failure to agree' (325). In this way, he is able to concentrate on ways in which 'agreement' between 'statement and thing' is achieved (326). To do this, Heidegger examines the relationship between propositions and things, and claims (again in accordance with the conventional account) that the proposition *must* give an 'approximate' description of the thing (327); the description must be approximate because a description can never be a perfect copy of the object it describes without the proposition being of exactly the same form as the object it describes: 'No statement can do that' (the sentence is not the helix, for example; 327). Thus, the statement must be 'representative' of the object. Once Heidegger has introduced the terms 'representation' and 'agreement', he is able to discuss a conception of 'movement'. This spatial metaphor will be important for the remainder of the chapter, and will be given in some detail.

The description which represents a state of affairs is a discursive one: 'The representative statement has its say about the thing represented, stating it to be *such as* it is. This "such as" applies to the representation and what it represents' (327). So, not only must a description represent a state of affairs in the world, it must also be given in a form which represents the statement itself as an adequate representation. This is why the term 'agreement' is important: speakers of a language must negotiate an agreement concerning which particular statement is worthy of the task of 'representing the world'. In Heidegger's terms, this involves:

> . . . letting something take up a position opposite to us, as an object. The thing so opposed must, such being its position, come across the open towards us and at the same time stand fast in itself as the thing and manifest itself as a constant. (328)

The 'object' in this extract is the statement: it must appear to various speakers as a 'constant' which stands fast. When a term is being used, it must appear to be stable and not a matter for negotiation (which would render the object unstable). But, at the same time, each of the terms used must have been negotiated at some time, in order to be allowed ('letting something') to take up the position of 'being constant'. Thus, giving a statement in a form which at least appears 'constant' may nevertheless be subject to continued negotiation (in a scientific controversy, for example). This was shown earlier: the majority of the statements examined in the case-studies appeared to indicate constant descriptions, but such statements were either re-negotiated over time (Chapter 3), or may be open to re-negotiation once a variety of descriptions of the 'same' psychological object are contrasted (Chapters 4 and 5; see also Latour, 1987).[4] Cooper gives an account of Heidegger in the following way:

> . . . 'the clock is broken' can only be a true (or false) assertion if the clock can be referred to as a clock; and it can only be referred to as this because we have let it disclose itself in a certain way. The same object would be not be a clock for primitive tribesmen whose 'concern' does not encompass time-telling. . . . The 'same' objects can disclose themselves to us as clocks, collections of molecules, works of art and much else. To describe, in each case, what is disclosed is to depict a complex network of behaviour, attitudes, interpersonal relations, and much more, within which the objects take their place. (Cooper, 1986: 252–254)

Heidegger's argument, then, discusses this process of negotiation (of letting) in spatial terms: 'This manifestation of the thing [here the discursive representation] in making a move towards us is accomplished in the open, within the realm of the Overt, the overt character of which is not initially created by the representation but is only entered into and taken over each time as an area of relationships' (328). That is, the process of making a description appear constant (or 'overt') is a discursive ('human'; 331) accomplishment. Further, such an accomplishment 'initially' involves 'moving' the status of the representation from being 'negotiable' to being 'constant' (overt or 'in the open'). A process that may be referred to, perhaps, as idealisation. To put this into Nietzsche's terms: first the representation is metaphorical, then the temporary status of the metaphor is changed (it dies), until the status of the representation is upgraded to being classed as a member of the class of 'truths'. What disappears in this process is the social, practical circumstances in which the original meaning was forged (on this disappearance rests the standard image of science). Or, according to Heidegger: 'What is thus, and solely in this narrow sense, made manifest was experienced in the early stages of Western thought as "that which is present" and has long been termed "that which is" ' (328). Therefore, when a representation is held to be satisfactory, it will be classified as truth: 'Directing itself in this way the statement is right (true). And what is thus stated is rightness (truth)' (329).

The present interpretation will avoid describing language as something capable of 'directing itself': it will be assumed that language cannot perform functions without the aid of writers (speakers) and readers (listeners); language is not an agent. Rather, language will be held to become discourse whenever it is employed by agents capable of using language. As Heidegger puts it elsewhere: discourse 'has the task of making manifest in its work the existent, and of preserving it as such'; thus, even 'the essential word, if it is to be understood and so become a possession in common [for a number of speakers], must make itself ordinary' (1936/1949: 298–299). Therefore, a representation is 'directed' by an agent to perform a function, and one of the functions discourse may be used to perform is giving a 'truthful' (constant, common and essential) description. Such an interpretation of Heidegger's argument may be supported insofar as Heidegger gives an account of behaviour:

> The statement derives its rightness from the overtness of behaviour, for it is only through this that anything manifest can become the criterion for the approximation implicit in the representative statement. Overt behaviour must apply this criterion to itself. Which means: it must be for a start something of a criterion for all representation. This is implicit in the overtness of behaviour. But if rightness (truth) of statement is only made possible by the overt behaviour, then it follows that the thing that makes rightness possible in the first place must have a more original claim to be regarded as the essence of truth. (1949: 329)

In this way, Heidegger introduces an element of human choice into deciding which discursive representations are to be classified as 'true'; by emphasising the role of negotiation in this process, he renders the process (of labelling something as 'true') as one which is always open to further negotiation. Moreover, he attacks accounts which may suggest that 'true' statements unproblematically remain 'true' statements. Instead, he emphasises the amount of rhetorical work involved: 'letting be' does not 'refer to indifference and neglect, but to the opposite of them. To let something be is in fact to have something to do with it' (333); to allow something to maintain a particular status 'means participating in' (333) the process. Truths are those things which we decide to leave alone. Thus, maintaining the status of a description is an active and ongoing process; it always requires rhetorical work.

In the remainder of the essay, Heidegger goes on to argue that there are limits to the extent to which choice is involved in the process just described; he does not 'licence' the process of negotiation to the point where discourse is not at all constrained by 'reality' (334). Nor does the present argument entail such a conclusion. However, the object here is to use Heidegger's argument as an interim; to proceed to an account of metaphor (rather than of 'truth').

### Towards an account metaphor

In Chapter 1 an attempt was made to undermine the distinction between philosophy and rhetoric. I used that argument to justify the inclusion in my analysis of any piece of discourse which aimed to persuade, rather than attempt to present an analysis of what might otherwise be considered the 'central ideas' of one position. The case-studies presented accounts of various debates in psychology in an attempt to show how certain rhetorical devices function. In part, a number of scientific metaphors were examined, as were the functions they perform in different texts. These discussions relied on a distinction between literal and metaphorical language. In order to be consistent with the argument in Chapter 1, the literal/metaphorical distinction now needs to be further undermined; or, rather, it needs to be shown that such a distinction does not rely on the 'essentialist' or metaphysical foundations which were originally rejected from the outset. Undermining this distinction should then block a possible reflexive counter-argument. The argument in Chapter 1 and the one about to be presented are related insofar as the Venn diagram used to explain the distinction between philosophy and rhetoric may again be invoked to describe the literal/metaphorical distinction. Here it will be argued that the literal is a sub-class of the metaphorical: there is no distinction between metaphor and 'mere metaphor'. Making this argument will cause some problems; the solution will be that the use of the literal/metaphorical distinction *can* be maintained so long as the essentialist consequences can be blocked (or undermined).

David Cooper (1986) reviews and then briefly discusses some of Jacques Derrida's conclusions concerning metaphor. Derrida's arguments will be reviewed in some detail in the next section; but here it is necessary to fill in a little background. Cooper begins by suggesting that there has existed in the literature on metaphor a 'dim sense that the entire discussion is 'rooted . . . in [a] dangerously misleading metaphor' (1986: 23). Thus, paraphrasing Derrida, he suggests that: 'Any attempt to define metaphor in traditional philosophical terms is doomed to fail, since these are themselves irredeemably metaphorical' (1986: 24). Cooper points out that previous attempts to get out of the problem of all terms being, in some sense, metaphorical has been, following Hegel, to distinguish between metaphorical terms and those 'taken up into' (past tense: *aufgehoben*; the present tense, *aufheben*, 'to raise up into', is also used in the philosophical literature) discourse; between live and dead metaphors. In the last section, this spatial metaphor was shown to have been exploited by Heidegger in order to undermine what has been characterised as a kind of grand 'metaphysical programme' in the history of philosophy. It may also be shown to have been employed by anti-metaphysicalist philosophers more recently. For example, the distinction between the metaphorical and the literal, and the denial of the metaphysical importance of that distinction, has been used by Richard Rorty (for example 1989, 1991b), in an attack on regarding metaphors as the bearers of truth-value:

> This is because it is a sentence which one cannot confirm or disconfirm, argue for or against. One can only savor it or spit it out. But that is not to say that it may not, in time, become a truth-value candidate . . . [through habitual use]. It will thereby have ceased to be a metaphor – or, if you like, it will have become what most sentences in our language are, a dead metaphor (Rorty, 1989: 18)

Thus, it may be suggested, at least from this extract, that Rorty continues to use exactly the terminology which he would most like to undermine and stop using (on this issue generally, see Nehamas, 1982). There may be no way around this; even a philosopher who writes against foundationalist assumptions must maintain many of the terms which are part of the earlier tradition.

Cooper (1986) argues that Derrida's critique goes much further than simply pointing to a source of dissatisfaction concerning the definition of metaphor. This time the point arises from a remark of Heidegger's: 'the metaphorical exists only within metaphysics' (in Cooper, 1986: 25). Cooper rehearses two reasons for this claim:

1   Metaphors 'standardly transfer expression from the sensible [here: that related to the senses] to the non-sensible' [here: that related to the 'realm of thinking'].
2   The 'notion of transfer – and therefore of metaphor – requires a distinction between the physical vehicles of meanings and certain non-physical entities – the meanings themselves' (Cooper, 1986: 25).

It is the second assumption which needs to be examined closely, and to do this I shall turn to Derrida's 'White mythology' (1972/1982).

## Derrida on philosophical discourse

Following (at least) the later works of Nietzsche and Heidegger, Derrida's rhetorical style undermines attempts to classify and summarise one of his texts (see later discussion). The purpose of such a style may be to 'tympanize philosophy' (1972/1982: x); to criticise and publicly ridicule philosophical discourse. Indeed, some philosophers (for example Rorty, 1989, 1991b) praise Derrida for fulfilling such a role (see later discussion). Nevertheless, the construction of the present text requires a form of exposition.

In 'White mythology' Derrida (1972/1982: 209–271; hereafter by page number) provides a discussion of 'Metaphor *in* the text of philosophy' (209), in which 'metaphor seems to involve the usage of philosophical language in its entirety' (209). Such a proposal might be regarded as requiring a very long (book-length) discussion; but Derrida notes that it is in his own interest to subvert such a requirement, to promise more than he can give, *and* that such a tactic is self-exemplifying: Derrida's own subversion is an example of what he claims all philosophical writing to have depended upon. That is, philosophical discourse depends upon the artifice (the conceit) of suggesting that its terms are 'literal' and not 'metaphorical': without such an artifice, philosophical discourse could (at least) not continue in the form it has typically been given.[5]

To this (rhetorical) end, Derrida employs a variety of metaphors taken from the philosophical literature; each one suggests that philosophy 'reveals' some kind of universal structure inherent in the object in question. And, in each case, the philosopher who has characterised the process of philosophical discourse in such a manner is attacked. Thus, discourse which is 'interminably explicative' (213) is described as having 'erased within itself the fabulous scene that has produced it' (213), because 'metaphor has always been defined as the trope of resemblance; not simply as the resemblance between a signifier [text] and a signified [object] but as the resemblance between two signs, one of which designates the other' (215, see also Aristotle, *Poetics*). The 'scene' being referred to is one in which choices were made concerning the way in which a particular (in this case, philosophical) text was constructed. Here, as in the argument from Heidegger, what is being attacked is the attempt to remove the role of the writer (speaker, and, by extension, the reader/listener) in having negotiated a relation between statement and object and, *at the same time*, having negotiated a relationship between one statement and another. Thus, metaphor:

> ... implies a continuist presupposition: the history of a metaphor appears essentially not as a displacement with breaks [or] separations without origin, but rather as progressive erosion, a regular semantic loss, an uninterrupted exhausting of the primitive meaning. ... Not that the enterprise of the authors [philosophers] cited is entirely covered by this presupposition, but, rather, the enterprise recurs to it every time it gives the metaphorical point of view the upper hand. (215)

For present purposes, this extract may be related to comments given in Chapter 3 in which Lashley and Patricia Churchland attempted to degrade particular research endeavours by labelling them as merely metaphorical: the extract from Derrida can be used to suggest that, once such a manoeuvre has been attempted, an author will then attempt to return to discussing an object in a way that is not 'eroded'; that returns the discussion to one which has not suffered a 'regular semantic loss', one that gets at the 'primitive meaning'. The possibility of such a process needs to be denied.

According to Derrida, giving an account of metaphor will always involve further metaphors because the account would rely on 'philosophy's unique thesis'; that there is some 'essence rigorously independent of that which transports it' (229); that meanings can be separated from words, such that meanings are contained *in* words. In giving this description there is a reliance on metaphors based on physical action, spatial metaphors of containment. This is one of Derrida's main points: that in defining metaphor one will always implicate more metaphors: 'The recourse to a metaphor in order to give the "idea" of metaphor: this is what prohibits definition' (253). In particular, there is a tendency to privilege physical terms: metaphors *transport* meaning, the name is *given* to another. This can be seen later in the essay when Derrida is attacking Aristotle's description of some statements being obscure:

> The appeal to the criteria of clarity and obscurity would suffice to confirm what we stated above: this entire philosophical delimitation of metaphor already lends itself to being constructed and worked by 'metaphors'. How could a piece of knowledge be properly clear or obscure? (252)

Here Derrida is suggesting that the terms 'clear' and 'obscure' rely on metaphors involving light (from the sun) and looking (see also Ricoeur, 1978: 289). Again, there is an emphasis on metaphor being implicated in its own definition. Derrida also claims that: 'Each time that a rhetoric defines metaphor, not only is *a* [particular] philosophy implied, but also a conceptual network in which philosophy *itself* has been constituted' (230, emphasis original); that metaphor 'is less in the philosophical text . . . than the philosophical text is within metaphor' (258). Thus, a 'literal' definition of metaphor is impossible. Further, any definition will invite physical processes.

Derrida's (1972/1982) text attempts to maintain two antagonistic claims at the same time. First, that the philosophical literature has (past tense) been engaged in a practice of taking 'metaphorical' terms and giving them in a 'literal' manner; that 'explicative discourse' (213) has rendered the process of negotiating the status of a particular description as unproblematic. Not to perform such a function, according to Derrida, involved removing 'light' (here: truth) from the words employed (230–244). In this way, Derrida's text may be regarded as self-exemplifying. His text does not provide access to some non-sensible realm of meaning. However, there is a second claim in the text which may be used to characterise Derrida as a 'reformer' of philosophical discourse: this involves the antagonistic sugges- tion that Derrida is *only* engaging (present tense) in such a practice in 'White mythology'; that is, he implies that it may be possible to do otherwise. Thus, the rhetoric employed in the text is used to suggest that past philosophical practice has involved 'taking terms up' from 'metaphori- cal' discourse to 'literal' discourse (*aufgehoben*; past tense), and that the text of 'White mythology' engages in the same practice (*aufheben*; present tense). The constant rhetorical play on this difference is, in turn, used to suggest that Derrida may possibly be able to avoid such a practice. That possibility is (and will be) denied in the present book. Having discussed the content of 'White mythology', I turn to a brief account of its rhetorical style. This is not to suggest that style is separate from argument, but that style is worth further comment.

Derrida's style of writing may be regarded as a form of philosophical argument in addition to the content of what he appears to be claiming:[6] the sheer difficulty of reading a text such as 'White mythology' may be regarded as part of an argument concerning interpretation, understanding and the stability of discourse. The following one and a half sentences will serve as an example:

> . . . if woman is truth, she at least knows that there is no truth, that truth has no place here and that no one has a place for truth. And she is woman precisely because she does not believe in truth itself, because she does not believe in what she is, in what she is believed to be, in what she is not (Derrida, 1978/1979: 53)

This passage is not being quoted with irony to suggest that this is the sort of writing which makes Continental philosophy deserve a bad name.[7] Rather, it is being used to show that, in order to understand such an extract, a large amount of background knowledge of the philosophical literature is needed (in this case, a reading of Nietzsche); but, more than that, the reader needs to have followed the particular way the terms from such a literature are being interpreted (in this case, to suggest that Nietzsche uses 'woman' in order to give an account of 'truth'). Derrida's texts are certainly not unusual in this respect, and the psychological debates covered in the case-studies presented here also often require a high degree of technical, discursive facility (Broadbent, 1973: ix, makes a related point). But what is unusual about Derrida's texts is the way they employ the terms of a previous author; that the authors are 'transfigured, beaten into fascinating new shapes' (Rorty, 1991b: 120). So, if it is possible to interpret Derrida as saying *anything at all*, it can only be on the basis of adopting (for however long) the terms of argument in the way he uses them in a particular text. Thus, it is because of the ability of a (some) reader(s) for reconstructing a text as difficult as one of Derrida's, and for giving an interpretation to such a text, that *the terms themselves* cannot be grounded in a foundation tied to a non-discursive world.[8] Or, in Rorty's terms, the discourse in which Derrida's arguments are couched is a 'disposable ladder-language, one which can be forgotten once it has been *aufgehoben*' (1991b: 125). That this may be the case has also been suggested (rather more simply), in the context of research in psychology, by Gergen et al. (1986) into the hermeneutics of personality descriptions, where, again, it was shown that readers of texts have a large facility for coping with meaning and meaning-change. The main point here is that if meaning-change is (potentially) so fluid, then the literal/metaphorical distinction becomes difficult to maintain. This point will be returned to in the next section. Before that, some points relating to Derrida's anti-metaphysical project.[9]

Rorty (1991b: 119–128) summarises and expands a debate on the methodological status of Derrida's arguments in his essay, 'Is Derrida a transcendental philosopher?' The details of his replies to other authors are largely irrelevant here; however, in his characterisation of that debate, Rorty puts forward a dichotomy of ways of reading Derrida's texts which, for the purposes of the present argument, needs to be denied. In what follows, this denial is based on claiming that there is a major inconsistency in Rorty's text; or, as Rorty may prefer it, I shall be 'playing off' parts of his text against each other to make his 'language-game look bad' (Rorty, 1991b: 126). Although the present critique is technical, it is also ideological insofar as it attempts to resist the 'political conservatism' (Rorty, 1991b: 120) which Rorty identifies as a consequence of his version of pragmatism.

Largely, Rorty's account is based on the observation that, as he sees it, some authors take Derrida's texts too seriously; that such authors read Derrida 'to get ammunition, and a strategy, for the struggle to bring about social change' (1991b: 120). Rorty contrasts such an approach with his own, in which Derrida is regarded as 'a private writer'; a writer with an audience of readers who 'share his background, who find the same rather esoteric things as funny or beautiful or as moving as he does' (1991b: 120).

Philosophy, then, on Rorty's account, is a rather marginal form of enquiry associated, using a 'public–private split' (1991b: 127), with personal development; that is, personal development associated with 'one's own private, autonomous, philosophical language' (1991b: 127). So, reading Derrida's texts in the way Rorty prefers would suggest that the account given in this section (and, quite likely, the section on Heidegger) is misguided because the 'result of genuinely original thought, on [his] view, is not so much to refute or subvert our previous beliefs as to help us forget them by giving us a substitute for them'; he takes 'refutation to be a mark of unoriginality', and values 'Derrida's originality too much to praise him in those terms' (1991b: 121).

The bulk of Rorty's text is taken up with an attack on those authors who suggest that Derrida's arguments are rigorous, and who, consequently, suggest that Derrida's arguments show something more connected with the non-discursive world than with philosophical discursive practice. In the process, Rorty argues that Derrida is certainly not a 'transcendental philosopher', and makes explicit what he regards as the dangers of suggesting that Derrida is making metaphysical claims. Although Rorty does concede, at the end of the argument, that Derrida did 'use words like "rigorous" a lot' (1991b: 128) in his early texts (that is, before 1987), and that Derrida has made some transcendental claims, he goes on to suggest that such things should merely be regarded as a 'false start' (1991b: 128).

The manoeuvre in the present text is to deny the public-metaphysical versus private-ironist dichotomy by giving a third alternative; one in keeping with the present analysis both of Derrida's texts, and of the literal versus metaphorical distinction. Such a manoeuvre involves attacking Rorty's own textual devices.

The main argument of the present chapter is that a structural account of meaning-change can (and must) be given to account for the textual developments examined in the previous case-studies. Using (largely Continental) arguments concerning the general way meaning may be changed, it is suggested that the psychological texts examined in the present book exemplify a process of metaphorical discourse being 'taken up into' (*aufheben*) literal discourse through changes in the rhetorical form of particular sentences. This process was discussed as one which is fairly widespread; that there is often a slide between giving a metaphorical and a literal description. Further, it has been argued in the present section that Derrida's texts both identify (in terms of argument content) and exemplify (at least in terms of his own style) this process of meaning change. In Rorty's (1991b) argument, the present account is one which takes Derrida 'too seriously' and, therefore, is 'transcendental' and 'bad'. Thus, Rorty's (I suggest, 'meta-rigorous') inference needs to be undermined: this will be done in two stages.

First, although the present book has a structural conclusion, there is no need to suggest that the conclusion is 'transcendental': no claims are being made concerning meaning-change in other 'possible worlds', and certainly none are being made about the way meaning-change *must* occur. However claims *are* being made about the structure of meaning-change in the past, and those claims might possibly be maintained in the future (that is, they may have some predictive value), but nothing has been said here to suggest that the process of meaning-change discussed throughout the book might be 'transcultural' (that is, applied to Asiatic or African texts concerning psychology). So, while the language used to describe meaning-change is structural and, therefore, given the tradition of philosophical discourse concerned with structural claims, such a conclusion may be regarded as 'metaphysical' (in some sense of the term), there is no reason to suppose that such conclusions (including those some people take from Derrida's texts) are also 'transcendental' (in the Kantian sense of the term; see Roberts, 1988: 10–51).

Second, at one point in Rorty's argument he states: 'On my view, it is precisely *Aufhebung* that Derrida is so good at' (1991b: 126). This is consistent with the present argument; indeed, it was exactly the point of the remarks above related to Derrida's style of writing: that the style of Derrida's texts exemplifies the very process which, I suggested, in the 'serious' reading given above, Derrida identifies and uses to 'refute or subvert our previous beliefs' (Rorty, 1991b: 121). So, while Rorty may regard 'refutation to be a mark of unoriginality' (1991b: 121), and something which Rorty may hope to avoid, it is suggested that Rorty's text is *not self-exemplifying* because, as the quotation at the beginning of this paragraph shows, he too takes 'serious results' from Derrida's texts and uses such results to refute others. That is, Rorty engages in the same discursive practices which he criticises others for performing.

The two points just made may now be put together. The concern that Rorty expresses regarding a tendency (which Rorty identifies) to read Derrida as if he were a transcendental philosopher is shared by the present author. But, if the present argument is persuasive, there seem to be no good reasons for the dichotomy of ways of reading Derrida's texts which Rorty proposes: a discussion of Derrida's texts, in which an interest in identifying discursive processes is used 'in the struggle to bring about social change' (Rorty, 1991b: 120), *ought* to be possible without that discussion being used to invoke transcendental consequences. But, at the same time, there also seem to be no good reasons for marginalising Derrida's texts (and philosophical literature in general) to a realm of purely personal development. That manoeuvre, I suggest, along with its politically conservative consequences, ought to be resisted.

## Reconciling Black and Wittgenstein

In the examination of texts of theoretical psychology which I have discussed in this book, I limited myself to a discussion of the function of metaphor; that is, what metaphor does rather than what it really means.

This methodological position was adopted to avoid entering into a discussion of whether a given text is right or wrong about its object of enquiry. But as my discussion of metaphor shows, the use of the term 'metaphor' as a term to be contrasted with 'literal' enters once more into a metaphysical debate; it relies on a distinction between 'words' and 'meanings'. Thus, a reflexive treatment of my book has the potential to undermine the methodology employed. To avoid such a possibility, I want to develop a remark from Wittgenstein:

> Here one might speak of a 'primary' and a 'secondary' sense of a word. It is only if the word has a primary sense for you that you use it in the secondary one. . . . The secondary sense is not a 'metaphorical' sense. If I say 'For me the vowel *e* is yellow' I do not mean: 'yellow' in a metaphorical sense, – for I could not express what I want to say in any other way than by means of the idea 'yellow'. (Wittgenstein, 1958/1968: 216, II xi)

Here Wittgenstein uses the term 'metaphorical' in a way which was rejected by Max Black (1962): Wittgenstein is suggesting (assuming) that metaphor is the mere re-description of some literal description. So the sentence in question would be a metaphor, according to Wittgenstein, only if it were possible to translate it into a literal sentence. Black labelled this idea the 'substitution view' because a substitution of the literal for the metaphorical would communicate the same meaning. Black argues that:

> This account treats the metaphorical expression (let us call it 'M') as a substitution for some other literal expression ('L' say) which would have expressed the same meaning, had it been used instead. On this view, the meaning of M, in its metaphorical occurrence, is just the literal meaning of L. The metaphorical use of an expression consists, on this view, of the use of that expression in other than its proper and normal sense, in some context that allows the improper or abnormal sense to be detected and appropriately transformed. (Black, 1962: 31)

So, to adopt the substitution view is to hold that understanding 'a metaphor is like deciphering a code or unravelling a riddle'. Black goes on to argue for an 'interaction view' of metaphor by claiming, in part, that metaphors function by activating a 'system of associated implications' (1962: 44). Thus, a metaphor 'selects, emphasises, suppresses, and organises features' (1962: 45) of what is being described metaphorically (and the terms in the quotation are themselves metaphorical; see above discussion). This is labelled the 'interaction view' because, Black argues, the associated implications also work the other way, such that to say 'man is like a wolf' is to say something about both men and wolves (see also Hesse, 1980). This is to suggest that, when a metaphor is being used, a complicated system of implications is involved which could not be produced by using a simple substitution of some literal statement: meaning is being extended in a way that cannot be easily captured by literal re-description (for an argument against Black, see Cooper, 1986: 144–152).

According to Black's argument, then, Wittgenstein uses the term 'metaphorical' is a way that does not do justice to the way in which metaphor works in practice. Yet there remains something very useful (pragmatically) in the way Wittgenstein attempts to replace 'metaphorical sense' with 'secondary sense'. In order to say that two terms may 'interact', some understanding must be had of the ways in which those terms normally refer. I assume this to be consistent with both Wittgenstein's and Black's position. Thus, any interaction may be said to involve a secondary use of the terms involved: to say 'memory is holographic' (an example from Chapter 3) involves an understanding of the primary (in Black's case 'literal') use of these terms, and their interaction is such that a number of implications may be drawn about both 'memory' and 'hologram'. So, I suggest, Wittgenstein's use of the term 'secondary' and Black's use of the term 'metaphor' are functionally equivalent: what Wittgenstein does not like about the term 'metaphor' is exactly what Black denies a metaphor involves.

### The thesis of metaphor as extension of discourse

In a moment I will come back to a discussion of the number of metaphysical claims I may or may not be making. But first, a review of where this argument has taken us: I borrowed Nietzsche's suggestion that truths are a collection of worn out metaphors; this suggested that maintaining something as true is a matter of discursive practice. I used Heidegger to argue that investing a proposition with truth is a social act, one which must hide its social origin – holding them at a distance – in order not to be undermined; it is a social act to maintain that some propositions contain true meanings. I then used Derrida to argue that attempts to define metaphor will always implicate further metaphors; arriving at a 'literal' definition of metaphor is not possible. This was the 'serious' conclusion I took from Derrida and I then defended such an act with reference to Rorty. Now, this conclusion about metaphors is important because it suggests that metaphor will always be involved in the creations of new meanings; that in describing something new we will always be 'raising things up' into a realm of literal discourse. So, while the literal/metaphorical distinction seems to depend on, and sustain, a distinction between words and meanings – and thus re-enter a metaphysical debate some would prefer to bring to an end – maintaining the use of such a distinction seems to be useful.

What is being proposed is a functional account of metaphor: the use of the term 'metaphor' should be maintained as a way of distinguishing between primary and secondary uses of any particular term under discussion. On this definition, a term is metaphorical only insofar as it entails a different, primary (logically prior) sense of the term. So to say, for example, that 'memory is holographic' (or 'human behaviour is like a boomerang', or 'emotions are a physical reaction') is to make a metaphorical statement because it involves an understanding of a primary use of the terms 'memory', 'hologram', 'behaviour' and 'physical reaction'. In order for the phrase 'memory is holographic' to be used in a text, some understanding of the primary senses of the terms involved must be given. To say, then, that a term is being used metaphorically is only to say that the use of the term has been extended beyond its primary use. It is not, on my account, to define it as opposed to a literal use; 'primary' (although it may be regarded as a metaphor) is not to be taken as a metaphor for 'literal'. Rather, it is to say something about the practicalities of using a term in a novel way: if it were regarded as useful to use a term in a new way, some explanation must be given of the way the term was previously used: that is my only claim. The distinction I end up with is between 'old' (previous) and 'new' (contemporary) or 'primary' and 'secondary'. That will avoid maintaining a distinction between 'discourse' being in the head and 'meanings' being in the world. It provides a functional account of metaphor, involving not the extension of meaning, but the extension of use: to use a metaphor is to do something with words (see Austin, 1962/1975).

At the beginning of the present chapter, it was hinted that the simple solution offered here concerning the distinction between literal and metaphorical discourse may be overly simplistic. In conclusion, then, such a possibility needs to be answered with a counter-argument. By giving a possible resolution of apparent inconsistencies between Wittgenstein's and Black's views of metaphor, it was suggested that the literal/metaphorical dichotomy could be maintained. However, such a view of metaphor would entail a change in (some characterisations of) its 'ontological status'. So, it was argued that the distinction should be maintained insofar as it is useful as a way of differentiating past usage from present usage. But in using the distinction in this way, emphasis was given to historical change, and not to a realm of (ontologically) literal versus metaphorical discourse. It was claimed that the distinction should be maintained because without it discussions of changes in the use of a term would become increasingly difficult. This argument was used to justify the way the term 'metaphor' has been used throughout the book.

The possibility that such an account of metaphor is overly simplistic may be derived from remaining doubts about the ontological status of metaphorical discourse. It was stated in Chapter 1 that the present book was only a discussion of rhetoric, and the implication of such a claim is that a discussion of ontological concerns is to be avoided. However, in order to counteract claims that the present account is 'simplistic', some issues concerning ontology need to be raised.

The legacy from Heidegger, expanded by Derrida and promoted by Rorty,[10] is a growing reluctance to discuss ontological issues. Such a tendency may be fostered in philosophy if it is regarded as an essentially destructive (or deconstructive) enterprise, but it would seem to become enormously self-defeating if applied to science: because science (along with many forms of creative writing) is essentially concerned with attempts to find out about the universe and the place of humankind within the universe; it can only be a constructive enterprise. Further, the possibility of developing a constructive enterprise, without the production of ontological claims, must, at the very least, see the production of a Gordian Knot, and one quite likely not to bring with it the desire to see it untied. This may even be seen in the work of Derrida where, for all its discursive difficulty, a new ontology seems to emerge regardless of the efforts to avoid the metaphysical projects he (and Heidegger) criticise. However, in Derrida's case, supposing his efforts have been successful, the ontology only consists of 'sign' and 'play'. This leaves open the question of whether Derrida's ontology can be one sensibly employed in science studies (on this connection see Ashmore, 1989).

The account of metaphor described in this chapter implies the following view of the process of meaning-change. Following Rorty (1989), words have been regarded throughout this book as discursive tools with context-dependent functions: a scientist-writer uses such tools to describe an object of enquiry. Some of these tools are going to be new to the discursive context; in that case they are best described as metaphors. When the tool is no longer new, it is best described as literal. In labelling the tool-word in such a way, no claims are being made concerning the possibility that 'literal' descriptions have an ontological superiority over 'metaphorical' ones. At that level, the present discussion has avoided making claims about which descriptions are 'true' and which are 'false'. However, a constructive (and therefore, in some sense, ontological) claim is being made here: the view of meaning-change described is the most plausible one available, and the one which provides the 'best fit' for the historical material covered in the case-studies. If this description is persuasive, it still remains the case that it needs to be made persuasive in other contexts: that, in the final analysis, must be the characteristic which studies of science (including studies of scientific rhetoric) share with science itself.

## Notes

1. For a ('classic') paper in which such a distinction between 'language' and 'discourse' was developed, see Ricoeur (1971: 530). For an account of some of the more recent uses of the term, see Kendall and Soyland (1994).

2. Accounts in Nietzsche's writing of the relationships between language, metaphor and truth may be found throughout his corpus. See Nehamas (1985: 42–73) for a discussion of 'untruth as a condition of life'. Derrida (1978/1979) gives a discussion of Nietzsche's use of the term 'women' in order to describe 'truth'.

3. A good example of this comes from the the mathematician, Euler (1956), whose proof, that the seven bridges of Koenigsberg could not each be crossed without re-crossing one of them, was admired because of its lack of practical application.

4. In Chapter 3, a variety of writers were shown to have re-negotiated the status of earlier claims through the suggestion that such earlier claims were 'old', and therefore not to be taken seriously. It also showed that writers such as Lashley and Churchland had attempted to undermine some descriptions by claiming that such descriptions were 'merely metaphors'. In Chapter 4, Klein was shown to have re-negotiated Freud's account of the role of inheritance in 'development'; Watson and Skinner to have re-negotiated the role of 'mental entities' in

behaviour and therefore in 'development'; Vygotsky to have re-negotiated the function and importance of Piaget's account of 'egocentric' in development; and Merleau-Ponty to have re-negotiated the relevance of earlier writers.

5. On philosophical literature, see also Ree (1987). On sociological literature, see Woolgar (1983, 1988b) and Ashmore (1989). By the way, Derrida's text can be pretty difficult to read, but it rewards attention – it reminds me of a passage from Lewis Carroll's book on logic: 'When you come to any passage that you don't understand, *read it again*: if you still don't understand it, *read it again*: if you fail, even after *three* readings, very likely your brain is getting a little tired. In that case, put the book away, and take to other occupations, the next day, when you come to it fresh, you will very likely find that it is *quite* easy' (1896/1977: 52, emphasis original).

6. This is an obvious claim to make about Derrida's texts given that he has devoted many words to the analysis of philosophical writing styles (e.g. 1967/1976, 1978/1979). Derrida (1983) makes a lot of his strategic use of form explicit in a discussion of 'content' and 'performance structure'. For an analysis of Derrida's arguments related to Nietzsche's style of writing, see Schrift (1990: 97–113). But I do not want to suggest here that Derrida is performing a novel act: *all* of the texts examined in this book are rhetorical in *both* form and content. Derrida's forms are merely more obvious in their construction; but even the most scientific text (see Bazerman, 1988 and Gross, 1990, on the double helix) involve the use of rhetoric: publications without rhetoric are simply impossible.

7. For an analysis of the use of irony in this way in an academic text, in the context of a debate between groups of linguists and cognitive scientists, see Myers (1991b).

8. This, I suggest, may be one of the reasons for Derrida employing such a style of writing. But it is not the only one, and an analysis of the professionalization of the literary critic (hinted at by Bazerman, 1988: 18–53) or philosopher would be an interesting project for future research. (Reflexively: the tone here is deliberately ironic.)

9. Anyone unfamiliar with the sorts of anti-metaphysical claims Derrida has made could consider the following:

> The ontico-ontological [sic] and its ground (*Grund*) in the 'transcendence of [Heidegger' s conception of] Dasein' are not absolutely originary [sic]. Différance [sic] by itself would be more 'originary', but one would no longer be able to call it 'origin' or 'ground', those notions belonging essentially to the history of onto-theology [sic], to the system functioning as the effacing of difference. (Derrida, 1967/1976: 23, one citation omitted)

The passage was the first to be used, in the text quoted, to introduce Derrida's concept of 'différance' [sic]. Anyone who reads this passage and finds it difficult to interpret will better understand the point made above concerning the level of background necessary for reading such a text. Harold Pinter has one of his characters (a professional philosopher) make a similar point: 'You wouldn't understand my works. You wouldn't have the faintest idea what they were about. You wouldn't appreciate the points of reference. [. . .] It's nothing to do with intelligence. It's a way of being able to look at the world' (Pinter, 1965/1978: 77).

10. For an account of the form of philosophy promoted by Rorty (not given by Rorty himself), see Nehamas (1982). But it should be remembered that there is a social connection between these two authors (see Nehamas, 1985: ix), and the account by Nehamas, though a critique, is highly sympathetic. A further defence of Rorty's views of philosophy will be found in Kolenda (1991). For a less sympathetic account of Rorty's version of philosophy, and one related to Rorty's reading of Nietzsche, see Conway (1991).

# PART II   RHETORIC

# 7

# The Rhetoric of Validity in the IQ Debate[1]

First of all, there is an observation that everyone must have made: a man's historical sense and knowledge can be very limited, his horizon as narrow as that of a dweller in the Alps . . .

(Nietzsche, 1874/1983: 63)

Nature does not like to be observed, and likes that we should be her fools and playmates.

(Emerson, 1881: 174)

Few elements of psychological technology have attracted as much critical attention as the intelligence test and the concept of IQ with which it is associated.

(Rose, 1985: 112)

**A case-study of the IQ debate**

This chapter presents a case-study of the rhetoric used in the IQ debate by focusing largely on texts by Cyril Burt and Hans Eysenck. This area has been important in the formation of the discipline of psychology, and is one in which the social consequences are potentially large; at stake are the processes of education, and attempts to change the course of development of children. The chapter does not present an account of the sociological consequences of the rhetoric employed in this area,[2] although accounts of such consequences do feature in the texts presented by the psychologists involved (for example, Burt, 1969; Jensen, 1969; Kamin, 1974; Brand, 1979; Hearnshaw, 1979; Eysenck versus Kamin, 1981; Joynson, 1989). Instead, the present account will examine a rhetorical continuity; one that appears to be sustained despite changes in experimental practice. That is, the rhetoric within this debate will be examined in terms of persuasive force: both sides will be shown to engage in persuading the reader of the 'validity' (or lack of validity) of a given description. However, on either side of the debate claims are made to having access to the 'facts', whereas the claims of an opponent are described as merely the product of argument: they attempt to minimise the role which rhetoric plays in sustaining a given position. Some of the rhetorical strategies I will consider in this chapter include the offering of exact numbers used to describe a psychological object, the assumption of an overview of a field which suggests that any remaining questions will shortly be answered, the evocation of scientific consensus in an attempt to dismiss alternatives, resistance to the personalization of criticisms and so on. The task is not to give a taxonomy of the rhetoric used in this debate – there seems little point in mapping out debates in science as if they only consisted of a repeated series of rhetorical manoeuvres – but to call attention to the amount of rhetorical work involved in the 'useful illusion' that 'the results of science depend not on argument but on nature herself' (Gross, 1990: 32).

The main focus of attention will be on texts by Sir Cyril Burt (1883–1971). He began publishing in the psychological literature early this century in journals such as the *Eugenics Review* (Burt, 1912). Although the term 'eugenics' hardly features in Burt's later publications, the importance of this 'movement' on texts such as Burt's (and, for example, Eysenck's) has been frequently stressed (see Kamin, 1974; Hearnshaw, 1979). For example, Kevles (1985: 83–84) connects Burt with other eugenicist authors such as Galton and Pearson, as well as Spearman (for example 1923), who is described (in more mitigated terms) as 'a eugenics sympathiser' (Kevles, 1985: 334). Such writers form an important part of the background to the texts Burt produced: at least initially, Burt was explicit in his preference for eugenic ideals, and the very topics he chose to examine and construct (the backward, the gifted) reveal a continuation of those interests.

The remainder of the chapter is divided into two sections. First, an account of the work of Cyril Burt will be given to show some of the ways in which he structured arguments in some of his papers. In the second section I shall examine the relation between Burt's rhetoric and that found in more recent discussions of intelligence. The suggestion is that the forms of argument are largely the same, despite changes in the data to which the arguments refer.

### Historical background

Cyril Burt began work in British psychology when the investigation of 'intelligence' was central to the existence of the discipline of psychology (see Rose, 1985; Chapman, 1988). Hearnshaw's (1979) account suggests that Burt may be considered as the first professional psychologist to be appointed outside a university in Britain (to the London County Council in 1913), and the first to be knighted (in 1946). Burt was appointed to the Chair of Psychology at University College, London, in 1932 after the retirement of C.E. Spearman (1863–1945). His work followed that of Spearman's in that both were largely concerned with the psychology of individual differences, using the methodology of mental testing and the statistical analysis of the results.[3] Both were, in turn, influenced by the earlier work of Binet.[4]

Spearman (1923: 1–32) presents an 'origin' of his own work, citing Binet as having promoted an 'epoch-making' advance in the measurement of 'intelligence' (1923: 7). Spearman's promotion of a 'factor' account of intelligence (two factors in 1923; one in 1927) was one on which Burt performed later work. The factors were given as '*s*' (specific ability) and '*g*' (general ability). The investigation of such factors was intended to secure 'principles of cognition' for the human mind. Spearman sometimes employed a form of utopian rhetoric to describe the consequences of understanding intelligence:

> After this fashion, all enters into unison. Faculties, life, tests, and world-views, so too practice and theory, nature and artifice, philosophy and common-sense, all, so to speak, dance fatally to one and the same psychological tune. (Spearman, 1923: 355)

The 'unison' conceit (from musical theory) was extended throughout the text, beginning with the 'internal discord . . . in modern psychology' (1923: 23). Thus, the final 'Summary and outlook' provided a totalising 'tune' and the promise of the 'foundations of psychology' (1923: 355). For both Spearman and Burt, such a promise could only be fulfilled through the application of statistical and mathematical theories. The use of such technical discourse involved 'theorems', given in the form of algebraic equations; hence the importance of assigning numbers to the results gleaned from the 'tests' employed.

Spearman went on to promote a single factor account: 'The view is put forward that this *g*, far from being confined to some small set of abilities whose intercorrelations have actually been measured and drawn up in some particular table, may enter into all abilities whatsoever' (1927: 76). Burt went on to promote his own accounts of the number of 'factors' involved in the particular processes of intelligence, but there was always a continued emphasis on the validity of some unified, general and innate account of various abilities; that emphasis continues in some of the more recent accounts (see later discussion).

Burt worked on delineating and ranking levels of ability and intelligence with particular interest in those placed at either extreme of the 'normal distribution curve'. He published books such as *Mental and Scholastic Tests* (1921), *The Young Delinquent* (1925), *The Subnormal Mind* (1935), *The Backward Child* (1937), *The Factors of the Mind* (1940), and *The Gifted Child* (published posthumously, 1975). He was also the author or co-author of several hundred articles (for a complete bibliography, see Hearnshaw, 1979). Burt was involved in the development of the Mensa Society for the intellectually able, and was its president from 1959 almost until the end of his life (Hearnshaw, 1979) and was an early member of the Eugenics Education Society (Kevles, 1985: 83).

Within all this activity, the concept of intelligence holds an important place. It was defined by Burt as innate, general, cognitive ability (Burt,

1955); or, sometimes, 'innate, all-round, intellectual efficiency' (Burt, 1937/1961: 11). From the beginning, the assumption was that inheritance played a crucial role: 'Burt no doubt had an initial bias towards heredity stemming from the intellectual climate in which he had been brought up. At no stage in his career did he display a shadow of a doubt on what was very early a central article of his faith' (Hearnshaw, 1979: 57; see also Kevles, 1985). This can be seen early on, for example, in Burt's 1912 article in the *Eugenics Review*:

> Among individuals, mental capacities are inherited. Of this the evidence is conclusive. General mental efficiency (that is, 'intelligence' or 'ability') and its absence are undoubtedly inherited both in extreme and moderate degrees. Special mental capacities are probably inherited also, the several qualities being transmitted in relative independence on one another. The intensity of mental inheritance appears to closely resemble that of physical inheritance both in man and other animals; and, so far as mental capacity rather than mental content is concerned, far outweigh the intensity of environmental influences. The fact of mental inheritance, therefore, can no longer be contested, and its importance can scarcely be over-estimated. (Burt, 1912: 183)

The distinction given between 'capacities' and 'contents' was used to 'discriminate between . . . properties of the mind' (Burt, 1912: 170), and entailed describing the mind in terms of properties derived through inheritance versus those of contingent content: the content was variable, the capacities with which to deal with such content were not. In describing such an account, Burt employs little rhetorical mitigation: 'capacities *are* inherited', 'the evidence *is* conclusive'. When a mitigating term is employed (for example 'probably') it is only used to refer to the status of 'special' capacities, but these are also 'transmitted' through mechanisms of inheritance. The final sentence of the extract will be the focus of attention: the claim that the 'fact of mental inheritance' could no longer be 'contested'. Were it the case that such rhetoric became regarded as completely persuasive, such a claim would be regarded as 'valid'. Further, the acceptance of such a claim has 'importance' which 'can scarcely be over-estimated'. This rhetorical urgency is continued in many more recent publications.

On the environmentalist side of the debate, authors such as Kamin (for example 1974) have used the biography of Burt produced by Hearnshaw (1979) to support claims that Burt's work was fraudulent.[5] On the hereditarian side of the debate, authors such Jensen (for example 1969) have used Burt's research conclusions to support their own arguments for changes in social and educational policy (Chapman, 1988). Joynson (1989) has attempted to combat the charges of fraud against Burt by arguing that authors such as Hearnshaw (1979) made such claims unjustly, or at least that the case remains undecided. This reaction has, in turn, produced calls (for example Phillips, 1992) for an enquiry to be held by the professional body of psychologists in the United Kingdom (the British Psychological Society). The debate on Burt is still in progress. Thus, there are a variety of social, professional and political interests explicitly involved in a consideration of the debates on Burt, and on the status of IQ generally.[6] This chapter does not attempt to canvass an argument for one side or the other. Such a position would go against the symmetrical methodology employed here (see Chapter 2; see also Mulkay, 1985). However, while the present approach does not involve a consideration of the empirical validity of claims made in the IQ debate, that does not mean that the present study is ideologically neutral.

### 'Sketch of the skeleton of the mind'

The title for this section comes from a presidential address Burt made to the 91st meeting of the British Association for the Advancement of Science (Burt, 1923). In that address, Burt intended to give an overview of psychology and not a scientific report on new results. He concluded:

> It may be that I am too optimistic, and that my views are premature. But it is my personal conviction that the main outlines of our human nature are now approximately known, and that the whole territory of individual psychology has, by one worker or another, been completely covered in the large. We have viewed the whole continent from above by rapid aerial flights towards different quarters. It remains to link up and to co-ordinate the numerous reconnoitring pioneers; then to descend, and, by the laborious method of exploring feature by feature, to correct our maps in definite detail. Once its broad principles have been determined, it is from the close and microscopic detection of minutiae, of tiny items and small but telling indications, that every science is built up. This must be the individual psychology in the near future. . . . Here rather than in grand discovery must future progress lie. (Burt, 1923: 239)

The new continent exists, a basic map has been made, and all that remains is to fill in the details of that map. Or, to put it more simply: we know the basics, the details will follow. The validity of this account begins by resting on 'personal conviction'; however the developmental nature of 'progress' implied here suggests that 'every science' undergoes a sequence of stages until it is 'built up'. Further, the approach of the next stage lies 'in the *near* future'. Hence the use of 'must' in the final sentence of the extract: the future must entail no further need for 'grand discovery'.

Burt's account assumes a particular view of psychology, one which relates psychology to the biological rather than the social sciences. It assumes that there is such a thing as 'human nature' and that the investigation of the individual will result in the understanding of the group. That is, the rhetoric of such an extract assumes that the technical terms it contains (human nature, individual psychology, science and discovery) all have referents in a non-discursive world; that there is such a thing as the way 'every science is built up,' and that such a process is undertaken first by examining the 'whole territory', and then through the detection of 'minutiae'. So, Burt's rhetoric helps to construct a particular view of science, and it does so by relating sets of terms which entail a network of philosophical presuppositions and assumptions. Human nature is assumed to be inherited, fixed and little affected by environmental or social circumstance; the statistical analysis of test results will result in the discovery of the components of that nature, and some centralised, single faculty 'intelligence' underlies a variety of abilities.

Such rhetoric also promotes Burt's position as 'grand discoverer' whose views now only need the 'microscopic' correction of people working on the 'minutiae' of individual differences.[7] This is one of the periodic claims made concerning the end of a science, with only the details to follow; what is required is the mere refinement of experimental techniques, and the filling in of remaining minor questions. The novel thing about this announcement is that it was made shortly after the Psychological Section of the British Association was inaugurated; that with this added legitimation of the discipline, it could be announced that little theoretical work remained.

Later in the present chapter there will be a discussion of the more recent debate on IQ, through an examination of a published debate between Hans Eysenck and Leon Kamin. It will be useful here to introduce that discourse briefly because the rhetoric involved is fairly similar. To give a little of the flavour of Eysenck's work, I'll quote the end of a chapter of his entitled 'Is intelligence inherited?', in which we find the following conclusion:

> We conclude, therefore, that a simple model giving heritability of something like 80 per cent for IQ is both realistic and defensible. Errors of measurement are, of course, always present in scientific studies and make absolute accuracy impossible. But it seems unlikely that the heritability of intelligence in modern Western countries would be lower than 70 per cent or higher than 85 per cent. (Eysenck versus Kamin, 1981: 52)

Again we are being told that it is merely a matter for science to refine the techniques and reduce the errors; the general parameters are known and, although 'absolute accuracy is impossible', essentially the facts are there (but see also Lewontin, 1991: 29). This assumption of the existence of the psychological object under discussion is important: it is only with this step that rhetoric may be used to herald the bright future to come; and the implication that only details remain posits the ground from which detailed figures must emerge.

Eysenck goes on to make two points under the heading 'How many genes are involved?' Here is the second one:

> Another method is to look at the relationship between the degree of inbreeding depression and the inbreeding coefficient, which tells us the degree of consanguinity between parents. These and other methods lead us to postulate that roughly 50 genes are involved in the determination of differences in intelligence; this is a rough and ready estimate, but not one likely to be too far out. (Eysenck versus Kamin, 1981: 66)

Once more we have psychology being positioned in relation to the biological sciences: genetics is responsible for finding the number of genes involved, and psychology finds the components which these genes control and which go to make up the innate level of intelligence. Eysenck claims that this estimate is 'rough and ready', but also that it is 'not too far out'. That is, by noting a margin of error he implies a degree of accuracy; that what remains to be done involves the reduction of that margin, but further theoretical work is unnecessary. Here is another example from Burt:

> Probably all the more important broad group factors have now been approximately identified. But there is still room for research on their precise specification and nature, and still more on the various sub-factors into which each of them may be sub-divided. However, from the standpoint of the educationist, the most urgent problem, calling for experimental study, is the influence of heredity, or rather of genetic constitution. Every measurable ability is the product of a genetic potentiality interacting with certain post-natal and environmental conditions. . . . Lastly, I should repeat that the list I have here brought forward is by no means final or complete; it is rather to be regarded as a working basis for current practice and a provisional scheme for future research. (Burt, 1949: 199)

Although there is still a little room for research to complete the specific detail of the picture, Burt is able to get on with the rhetorical task of advising the educationist, for as psychology builds on the foundation of biology, so education builds on the findings of psychology: the promissory notes Burt issued (and which are largely re-issued by Eysenck), are assumed in such rhetoric to be fulfilled soon, and it is on the basis of that assumption that Burt went on to offer advice on the educational debate, in a large number of publications (for example Burt, 1969; see Hearnshaw for further details). Again, the emphasis on details to be gained in the future, and on the 'approximately identified' important components, solidifies the object under discussion.

**The repetition of numbers**

Another specific rhetorical strategy, involving the repetition of numbers, which the author then claims to refer to stable objects, may be accounted as follows: if the numbers are the same then it is assumed that the object, in this case the level of inheritance between parents and siblings, must also be the same. Consider the following two extracts from a 1949 paper of Burt's:

> The strength of a person's memory (in the sense of sheer retentiveness) appears to be largely innate. 'Some minds', says James, 'are like wax under a seal – no impression is wiped out; others are like jelly, vibrating to touch, but keeping no permanent marks'. Using estimated factor-measurements, Miss Pelling and I found that the correlation between the memories of siblings amounted to 0.37 and between those of parents and children to 0.28. It is difficult to see how environmental influences, such as training or imitation, could explain such resemblances; we must, therefore, attribute the correlations mainly to heredity. (Burt, 1949: 179)

The interest here is in the numbers: later in the same paper, Burt states:

> [The] inheritance of special ability and special disability in arithmetic was studied by Mr E.T. Hewlett, who found correlations of 0.37 between siblings and 0.28 between parents and children. (Burt, 1949: 186)

Here the same two numbers relating to correlations are described as having emerged from two different experimental studies, on two sets of people, of two different psychological 'abilities'. The only major thing in common, then, is held to be the method of testing siblings against each other, and children against their parents. This may be regarded as an ideal of an experimental science: the resulting correlations are exactly the same. But the text does not call attention to this point. Instead, it is left to the reader to draw the conclusion that such correlations are an objective aspect of genetic inheritance: not only is Nature reliable, it is accurate to two decimal places. As a rhetorical strategy, such accuracy involves an element of risk: the level of accuracy may be used by an author from the opposite side of the debate to cast doubt on the whole issue. Such a technique was employed by Leon Kamin (1974) and was rhetorically successful in that the issue of repeated correlation figures was used to bring about the accusations of fraud which followed the publication of Kamin's 1974 book (Joynson, 1989). Kamin, then (not surprisingly) continued to use the issue of the repetition of numbers in his later texts:

> By 1955, Burt had managed to increase his sample of separated twins to 21 pairs [from an original 15]. . . . The correlation was now said to be 0.771, based on a group test of intelligence. . . . By 1958, Burt claimed that his sample of separated twins had been increased to 'over 30'. The correlation was still reported as 0.771. . . . By late 1958, Burt's research associate, Conway, was able to report that the sample of separated twins had increased to 42 pairs. This sudden swelling of the sample size did affect the correlation, but not much. The correlation was now said to be 0.778. When Burt last reported on his separated twins, in 1966, the sample size was said to have increased to 53 pairs. The correlation, almost supernaturally, had returned to the originally reported 0.771.
> (Eysenck versus Kamin, 1981: 100–101)

So, while accuracy and consistency are ideals to be chased after, catching them, or appearing to catch them, can be used by a critic (such as Kamin) as a way of dismissing them altogether. The likelihood of a correlation remaining almost exactly the same despite increases in the sample size is dismissed as 'almost supernatural'. In terms of the history, it was these correlations on separated twins which alerted Kamin to the possibility of fraud and which Kamin first used in his book *The Science and Politics of IQ* (1974). Only later did the story make headlines when, in 1976, *The Sunday Times* made the allegation more explicit. Later, Joynson (1989) took up the issue of repeated numbers, attempting to reduce the level of their importance in the debate on Burt's reputation by attempting to reduce the statistical importance of those repeated numbers for the arguments Burt originally constructed.

The status of Burt's reputation has remained a controversial topic in psychology (see for example Phillips, 1992). Investigations into Burt's conduct were undertaken by Leslie Hearnshaw and resulted in a large biography in 1979 (but not an inquiry called for by members of the British Psychological Society). More recently the issue was again raised by the publication of Robert Joynson's book *The Burt Affair* (1989). When I gave a version of this chapter to a conference held by the British Psychological Society, Professor Joynson was in the audience: he later sent me a letter suggesting that I had taken the Kamin passage quoted above seriously as an indication of Burt's alleged fraud. But I should repeat that the true status of Burt's work is not in question here, and I am only calling attention to the way Kamin made rhetorical use of the statistics in a bid to discredit them. Kamin claimed that the 'kinds of data collected by scientists in the real world simply do not behave with such incredible stability' (Eysenck versus Kamin, 1981: 101). Thus, there was a point at which the stability of a correlation figure could be used as an avenue for criticism.

## More on the present debate

To what extent does the examination of Burt's arguments contribute to an understanding of contemporary debates on the nature of intelligence? The answer to such a question lies in the comparison of rhetorical forms, and I hope to show that a great deal can be gleaned from such an exercise. In undertaking this task I choose to analyse arguments presented by Hans Eysenck and Leon Kamin in a book called *Intelligence: The battle for the mind* (1981). The book was intended to address a general audience who were invited to decide the winner of the debate; to add to this gladiatorial impression, the authors are listed as Eysenck *versus* Kamin to indicate that the book was not co-authored in a conventional way. The book takes the following form: each author was asked to contribute a number of chapters (Eysenck, no. 1–12; Kamin, no. 13–24) presenting their positions. Then, before publication, each was given access to the other's contribution. Each wrote a response to be included in the book as 'rejoinders', without being able to alter the text of their own chapters. As such these rejoinders may yield a great deal of material for the analysis of rhetoric because they provide a controversial debate in a single forum, given equal time. However, the following discussion is limited to those portions of the text which benefit most from a comparison with Burt's arguments.

But first a proviso: it might be suggested that I do Eysenck a disservice by comparing his arguments with those of the much discredited Burt; in other circumstances such a tactic could be employed by someone arguing against Eysenck, and later I will show that Kamin does indeed employ such a device. However, that is not the intention here: the topic under discussion is the way texts are constructed so that they are persuasive; this does not involve making claims about the nature of intelligence or the personal credibility of the various protagonists, and I am not in a position to answer the question of who won the debate.

Eysenck's reply to Kamin is a kind of fireworks display of rhetorical brilliance. He begins by suggesting that Kamin broke the rules of scientific debate insofar as he adopted an adversarial rather than scientific approach (*ad hominem* rather than *ad rem*, p. 158). He labels this 'abusing the opposition's attorney', a move which suggests that Eysenck writes as a representative of the facts of a case in a disinterested manner. He complained that:

> A whole section (Chapter 19) of his contribution is devoted to the alleged vices and follies of H.J. Eysenck; this not only does me too much honour but is also clearly irrelevant. Even if I had often been wrong in the past, a fact I would be the last to deny, this would be quite irrelevant to the force of the facts and arguments with which we are dealing. . . . Although the temptation to answer Kamin's criticisms in detail, pointing out the way in which quotations are wrenched out of context, misinterpreted and generally abused, is almost irresistible, I will not give way to it . . .' (Eysenck versus Kamin, 1981: 157–158)

The use of the term 'honour' implies that the issues involved have little to do with Eysenck's personal contribution; he is merely one of many workers, and it would give him too much credit to be singled out. Notice that, had Eysenck said 'this does me a lot of personal harm' the tone of the reply would switch from calm retort to wounded irritation. At the same time, such a manoeuvre would diminish the authority with which Eysenck writes: science should not be concerned with an author's personal arguments; to engage in such a practice diminishes the status of the debate. Moreover, because Kamin is described as having performed such a role, Eysenck is able to marginalise Kamin's status as a 'scientist'. This sentence is followed by a general mitigating claim: Eysenck concedes ('even if . . .') the possibility (but not the fact) of having been wrong in the past. This both leaves open the question of which parts of his previous arguments he might agree were wrong, and diminishes the force of a critic's words: agreeing with a critic is a good way out of the criticisms. Finally in the extract is the image of Eysenck not 'giving way to the temptation' of answering Kamin in detail. Two things are fulfilled in this way: Eysenck suggests that he *could* answer particular criticisms but simply chooses not to; he also suggests that to do so would be a bad thing. In posing such a rejection, Eysenck presents himself as an impartial scientist worthy of trust; he defends himself by giving a personalised reply (ethos) rather than answering Kamin's points directly (logos).

Such a passage may be contrasted with the following from a more recent volume. In both extracts, published at roughly the same time as the debate with Kamin, the diplomatic tone is removed:

> Even in the field of intelligence, where the importance of genetic factors had been widely accepted, voices began to be raised in criticism, and soon even the strong empirical evidence in favour of the genetic view was unable to stem the flood of criticism that was beginning to submerge it. All this reached its all-time high with the assertion by Kamin and others that there was no evidence at all that any genetic factors were implicated in producing differences in intelligence between people . . . it is difficult not to believe that ideological causes played a large part in this denial; readers of our debate will be able to judge for themselves. (Eysenck, 1982: 46)

Here the importance of genetic 'factors' is described as being 'widely accepted' in Eysenck's own area; moreover, there is a suggestion that while Eysenck has access to empirical evidence, Kamin's views are (merely) ideologically motivated. Thus, Kamin's alternative is marginalised, if not rendered 'invalid'. Later in the same volume Eysenck describes a 'continuum' of views concerning the importance (often described in terms of a percentage in this debate) assigned to environmental and genetic influences of intelligence:

> Few psychologists would be found at the opposite end of this continuum, but . . . many others certainly tend in that direction, although they are possibly less dogmatic and doctrinaire than extreme environmentalists (e.g. Kamin, 1974). (Eysenck, 1982: 251)

Again the rhetoric reduces the significance of 'extreme' environmentalists: only a few psychologists 'would be found' on one end of the continuum (and perhaps more at the other extreme). Whilst in the 1981 text Eysenck started his response to Kamin by listing a large number of points on which the two authors agreed, in the two extracts given above, he turns to characterising Kamin as 'dogmatic', 'doctrinaire' and 'extreme'. This suggests that a single characterisation does not have to be maintained; rather, descriptions perform rhetorical functions in local contexts.

## Analysing the critic

In their rejoinders Eysenck and Kamin also engaged in giving detailed accounts of each other's texts. The strategy in each case is to invalidate a particular argument, and therefore the entirety of the work being presented. Burt also engaged in and excelled at such a rhetorical practice (Hearnshaw, 1979: 288). The first extract in this section is accredited to J. Conway, an author whose non-fictional status has been called into question[8] (for example Hearnshaw, 1979), and doubts about such undermining have also been raised (for example Joynson, 1989). For present purposes, the existence of the author is irrelevant. The passage shows Conway making much of a distinction between 'may' (or 'might') and 'is' (or 'must'):

> The logic of [a given criticism] is again rather puzzling. Dr Halsey apparently is only prepared to admit the partial influence of genetic factors if the proof shows that this conclusion is 'certain'. But in empirical science no proof can ever yield an absolutely certain inference. . . . No doubt a critic can always claim that the opposite conclusion may be true. But why Dr Halsey should transform this into the statement that the opposite conclusion is 'more likely' remains altogether obscure. (Conway, 1958: 182)

The rhetorical possibility of asserting that something 'may be true' is held to be different from asserting that something is 'more likely'. The 'logic' of the critic's reasoning is 'puzzling' insofar as it entails something (a 'proof') which an 'empirical science' cannot attain. Because it is the critic's use of 'logic' which is being attacked, Conway is able to rely on the reader

recognising that the 'transformation' of 'may' to 'is' remains 'obscure'.
Thus, Dr Halsey's[9] critique is rendered invalid. The same point was made
in more detail by Burt later:

> The general style of inference seems to be – 'this, that, or the other condition in
> home or school *might* account for the apparent differences in ability quite as
> satisfactorily as the alleged genetic influences; therefore, they *must* do so.' (Burt,
> 1969: 85, italics original)

This distinction is used by Burt to dismiss alternative possibilities in favour
of his own, and this sort of device can be found throughout Eysenck's
rejoinder to Kamin. On the other side of the debate see, for example,
Lewontin (1991) and Gould (1990: 124–144) for arguments of a similar
form used against biological determinists.

A related form of attack is to claim that the critic has left out important
texts from the literature in question. Conway (1958) continues to attack
Halsey later in the paper:

> Studies of foster children he dismisses quite briefly on the grounds that the
> placement of such children tends to be selective. However, his references suggest
> that he has in mind only those investigations which have been carried out in
> America. In the London inquiries [citations of Burt 1942, 1955] the main
> comparisons related to children of different parentage brought up from early
> infancy in L.C.C. residential institutions: here there could be no question of
> selective placement. But about these researches he is silent.' (Conway, 1958:
> 183)

Conway leaves out the question of the status of the American studies cited
by the critic, and defends two studies by Burt about which 'there could be
no question'. Thus, the critic is accused of being silent about studies which
are inconsistent with the critique. As a result, the validity of one author's
work is maintained in the face of attack. The rejoinders by Eysenck and
Kamin (1981) both engage in the use of such rhetoric. Eysenck leaves open
the following question: 'Kamin must have been familiar with this study;
why did he not mention it?' (Eysenck versus Kamin, 1981: 162). He also
complains that 'Kamin mentions in passing some early studies of reaction
times, but does not discuss more recent work'. The suggestion is that there
is always more material which the critic has not dealt with, and therefore
the criticism should not be taken seriously. This tactic may also be seen at
work in a recent debate ('Does intelligence exist?') between Howe (1990,
and rejoinder) and Nettelbeck (1990):

> In the case of IT [inspection time] Nettelbeck (1987) has concluded that shared
> variance with IQ is at least 25 per cent, an estimate recently confirmed by an
> independent follow-up of available data by Kranzler and Jensen (1989). Howe
> (1989) has disagreed with this conclusion – but to date has not indicated how he
> would contest additional relevant information provided by Stough and Nettel-
> beck (1989). (Nettelbeck, 1990: 496; see original for bibliography)

Again the method involves ignoring the material that the critic has dealt
with and focusing upon the work which the critic has either ignored, not
mentioned, or has not had access to (on this point see Kamin's, 1981,

complaint that Eysenck does not give proper references, or hides important findings in obscure journals). Nettelbeck (1990) was giving a rejoinder to an attack by Howe (1990). His text gives an example of a further form of critique also employed within the IQ debate: the citation of an archive of previous findings:

> Howe implies, but does not state, that cognitive skills can be remarkably domain-specific, without acknowledging that for over 60 years a succession of talented and diligent investigators have found enormous difficulty in demonstrating this.' (Nettelbeck, 1990: 494).

Here 'implication' is a negative characterisation, insofar as Howe is characterised as only implying something; this is reinforced by the allusion to 'over 60 years' of 'diligent' work which has been 'found' to create 'enormous difficulty' for those attempting to 'demonstrate' the validity of such an implication. After quoting Nettelbeck's claim, Howe offers the following:

> 'Well, be that as it may, it is true to say that in recent years a number of investigators have found it almost embarrassingly easy to show that performance levels can be extremely domain-specific, and context-specific as well. Ceci (1990) provides a good review of the evidence. Nettelbeck's position here is like that of someone who claims that a newly-discovered island cannot really exist, because previous explorers have failed to notice it.' (Howe, 1990, see original for bibliography).

The aim here is to give a form of dismissal. Despite earlier difficulties alluded to by Nettelbeck, and apparently conceded by Howe ('be that as it may'), it is claimed that current research has overcome the enormous difficulties with 'almost embarrassing' ease. The suggestion of embarrassment serves to undermine the validity of earlier efforts; overturning earlier research is all too easy, so the detail of the work of the past may simply be passed over. If such a confession is embarrassing, it is not one which Howe finds detrimental to his argument. Howe also employs recent references, not cited by Nettelbeck, in order to back up this plain denial of the validity of the opponent's position. Finally, Nettelbeck is described as someone too respectful of the authority of 'previous exploration'.

## Conclusions

The debate concerning intelligence has been described as a body of land twice in extracts presented in the present chapter. In each case, proponents of different positions have claimed to have found a psychological object worthy of further investigation. The question remains as to whether the debate 'progresses' purely on the basis of the data considered within each text. The alternative 'explored' here suggests that the role of rhetoric may be a 'missing variable' in accounts of debates within psychology. What the participants in a debate do with their arguments is assume the existence of facts as being unproblematically located; that is, the facts are part of the

territory the authors have discovered, and not at all a function of their own
particular positions, or a function of a particular context. The tactic is that
one must call for further methodological refinements to get at these facts
about the world, and not to doubt their existence. Of course, this is a
standard part of the rhetoric of discovery which serves to reinforce public
images of psychology as part of the sciences, one of the endeavours in
which disinterested people merely communicate ahistorical propositions
about the world. But maintaining such an image involves a lot of rhetorical
work; work which is effaced to the extent that it is persuasive: rhetoric
disappears whenever the reader agrees with the claims being made.

The analysis of rhetoric attempts to make more obvious the work
involved in persuasion. But the *tu quoque* arguments which may be used
here point to some of the difficulties in pursuing such an analysis. Giving an
account of what a writer like Eysenck does with words may all too easily be
seen as merely debunking his arguments, or suggesting that there is
something wrong or flawed in a given position, and surely I only manage to
give such an impression through the use of words. The very act of giving
even a symmetrical analysis of rhetoric seems to imply something about
either the topic or the credibility of the protagonists. What, then, is the
role of the analyst of rhetoric? I was sometimes asked which side of the
debate I thought was the correct one. Then there is the issue of Burt's
alleged fraud – how does that affect the analysis? These are serious issues:
but such worries arise, in part, on the basis of some suspicion that there
really are facts to be evaluated in some objective manner; that there is
some rhetoric-free account of intelligence from which to evaluate the
distortions and truths of the debate. Such neutral ground is not to be had,
even though one of the aims of the protagonists in such debates is to
suggest that it has been attained. Similarly, the analyst of rhetoric is bound
to engage in further rhetoric; that is an ongoing component of science
which can not be side-stepped. Whether Burt's work is fraudulent or
exonerated is really beside the point; similarly the aim is not to over-turn
arguments such as Eysenck's. Instead, attention is called to the processes
of persuasion, to the role of both the protagonists and the analyst: having
some account of persuasion could give an understanding of how knowledge
is constituted. With the issuing of such a promissory note on the analysis of
rhetoric, I turn, in the next chapter, further back in history to the work of
James and Freud on the mind; to the networks of claims made about the
heart of the inner realm.

## Notes

1. A version of this chapter was delivered to the 5th Annual British Psychological Society,
History and Philosophy of Psychology Section Conference, 25–27 March 1991. A longer
version was delivered at a seminar for the Cambridge Group for the History of Psychiatry,
Psycho-Analysis and Allied Sciences, 1 May 1991. Many thanks to the audiences at either
meeting.

2. Chapman argues for the significance of the 'intelligence testing movement' thus: 'As the

movement gained support, intelligence testing became common practice in American schools. Today we live with the consequences of that reform' (1988: 170; see also Soyland, 1992). Rose argues: 'Despite the repeated sociological, psychological, genetic and epistemological critiques of the validity of measuring a heritable intelligence quotient with standardised tests, psychometrics constantly extends its remit in education, psychiatry, industry, the criminal justice system, the prison and the army' (1985: 112–113). For another historical account of this area, see Kevles (1985). The literature for and against IQ continues (see later references), but the present chapter is not aimed at closing the debate, or favouring one side by providing a critique; rather, the object is to give an account of the rhetoric used.

3. Burt's personal copy of Spearman (1927 – held in the Lancaster University Library), for example, shows detailed annotation throughout. Spearman (1923) cites Burt's early publications in highly positive terms; e.g.

> Interpretation of pictures in the manner just described has proved to be, not the best of tests, but among the very worst. In one notable instance, on being applied to two groups of children carefully selected as having their intelligence normal and retarded respectively, 74 per cent of the the the former passed successfully and 76 per cent of the latter! In the much more extensive and thoroughly reliable work of Burt [1921], this test is again found to be 'surprisingly poor'. (1923: 125–126)

Burt's name does not appear in the index of Spearman (1923); this is corrected in Spearman (1927); Burt's copy annotates a further missing citation in the Index (with reference to analogy). Spearman's texts are infrequently cited in Burt's later papers. Hearnshaw (1979) gives an account of a personal antagonism between these two researchers. This will be discussed further in the Notes.

4. As were Piaget, Vygotsky and Sartre (see Chapter 4), and Lewis Terman (see Chapman, 1988).

5. Hearnshaw's biography made several basic 'charges': that around 1943 Burt began citing experimental data which did not exist (1979: 91, 141, 230, 314); that Burt published journal articles and book reviews using various pseudonyms (1979: 178, 239–245), and that Burt attempted to rewrite the history of psychological statistics and 'falsely' promote his own account. This last charge relates to the antagonism between Burt and Spearman; Burt continued to discredit Spearman after the death of the latter.

6. For a sociological analysis of the debate on Burt, before and after the publication of Hearnshaw's biography (1979), see Harwood (1977) and Gieryn and Figert (1986). For an account of the status of IQ in the American context, see Napoli (1981) and Chapman (1988; for a review of Chapman, see Soyland, 1992). For an account of IQ in the British context, see Rose (1985), Kevles (1985), Hearnshaw (1979) and Joynson (1989).

7. Woolgar (1976) gives an analysis of the way 'discovery' accounts may be constructed in a discussion of the 'discovery' of pulsars. Schaffer (1989) gives an account of Newton's attempts to protect the 'discovery' of the theory of optics, and the rhetorical and social work involved in getting such a discovery 'replicated'. Collins (1985) argues that 'discoveries' and 'replications' may be analysed in terms of involving similar sorts of processes largely connected with attempts to retrospectively justify actions carried out in the laboratory or field.

8. Burt sometimes published with co-authors named Howard (e.g. Burt and Howard, 1956) and Conway. Both went on to have small publication careers. Conway (1958), for example, received seven citations (not by Burt) between 1960 and 1970. Burt was the editor of the journal in which papers by Howard and Conway appeared. Hearnshaw argues that:

> Of the more than forty 'persons' who contributed reviews, notes and letters [to the *Journal of Statistical Psychology*] during the period of Burt's editorship, well over half are unidentifiable, and judging from the style and content of their contributions, they were pseudonyms for Burt. Howard and Conway were members of a large family of characters invented to save his face and boost his ego. (1979: 243)

However, Joynson (1989) argues that the nonexistence of these authors had not been proven.

9. For an analysis of politeness and irony in academic writing, see Myers (1990b). The article by Halsey appeared in 1958 (in the *British Journal of Sociology*).

# 8

# James and Freud on the Mind: Metaphor and Rhetoric as Enrolment

> None of us can enter into another person's mind; to believe so is fiction.
>
> (Crick, 1980/1992: 30)

> We remain unconscious of the prodigious diversity of all the everyday language-games because the clothing of our language makes everything alike.
>
> (Wittgenstein, 1958/1968: IIxi, 224)

> Thus the *strength* of knowledge does not depend on its degree of truth but on its age, on the degree to which it has been incorporated, on its character as a condition of life.
>
> (Nietzsche, 1887/1974: III, 110)

The purpose of this chapter is to complete the case-studies of the book by applying the conclusions of the previous case-studies to sections of two historical texts from psychology: James' *Principles of Psychology* (1890/1950, hereafter, *Principles*), and Freud's *Introductory Lectures on Psychoanalysis* (1916–1917/1963, hereafter, *Lectures*). These texts were selected for two reasons: they were highly influential (Bruner and Feldman, 1990), and they both come from the period during which the discipline of psychology (and the psychoanalytic movement) was being formed.[1] However, the selection of these two writers (rather than, say, McDougall or Jung)[2] should not be seen in terms of promoting the status of either in terms of 'disciplinary history' (see Chapter 1; see also Fuller, 1991). Both authors had been publishing material for some time before the publication of the two books in question. In Freud's case, the *Lectures* were originally delivered to a wide university audience (at the University of Vienna); he was not just directing his discourse at those people already initiated into his work – far from it, the first lecture is structured as a way of countering the arguments which may have been mounted against his work by members of an intelligent audience who were (almost) completely naive concerning psychoanalysis. In James' case, *Principles* resulted from his teaching of students. While the book ran to 'fourteen hundred continuous pages' (a fact the author says he regretted more than anyone else could; James, 1890/1950: v), it was designed to be read by those beginning to study the topic – provided they skip over some chapters. Thus, *Principles* may be read as both an introduction and, as with Freud's *Lectures*, a summary of the findings otherwise only known to those well-versed in the subject.

For present purposes, these two texts are ideal for mounting a discussion which develops an analytical tool from Actor-Network Theory (Callon, 1986; Latour, 1987): that of 'enrolment'. They will also serve to illustrate material presented earlier in this book in terms of analysing promissory notes, presuppositions, metaphors and rhetoric. Briefly, I will suggest that Freud's rhetoric benefits considerably from his conception of mind; that the description of a mind made up of hidden layers to which ordinary people do not have access serves to encourage the reader to seek further information about those layers, and to be suspicious of things they take for granted about themselves. Freud claims to be able to discern the reasons behind a reader's thoughts and actions; while man is not master of his own house, psychoanalysis holds the key to further understanding. For James, on the other hand, the mind is an ever-changing stream: selecting, modifying and developing. Much the same could be said of the psychology which James professes: a kind of piecemeal striving for the appropriate description, persuading the reader through a series of analogies and approximations. James had argued that 'the best mark of health that a science can show is this unfinished-seeming front' (1890/1950: vii). While Freud claims a kind of privileged access to processes the reader is unable to control, James attempts to combine accounts of brain physiology with introspective descriptions which readers are supposed to recognise from their own experience. In terms of 'reception theory' (for example Holub, 1984; Eco, 1979/1981), I will be treating the works of James and Freud as 'closed texts': constructions which guide the reader towards a given interpretation of their rhetoric, an interpretation which has its greatest effect upon the 'ideal reader' depicted by each author.

First, something needs to be said concerning how important the texts selected for analysis were in the history of psychology. The overview of the history of consciousness by Bruner and Feldman (1990) has already been noted. Another historical account has argued that James' *Principles* 'served as a magnet to draw' Thorndike into graduate work at Harvard (O'Donnell, 1979: 433). But a different way of attempting to give an account of the importance of these texts is to examine psychological texts produced after James and Freud wrote their accounts.

Watson's book *Behaviorism* (1924/1930), and his 'mechanical' conception of human psychology (Buckley, 1989), was the first lengthy statement of a position[3] which went on to influence the downfall of at least some areas of empirical psychology as it was conceived by James (see McGovern et al., 1991, for a recent discussion of the definition of psychology). Yet, in that book, Watson states: 'Nearly every one is familiar with William James' classic chapter on the stream of consciousness' (1924/1930: 137). Watson goes on to subvert the 'stream of consciousness' account, attempting to replace it with a 'stream of activity' account (more suitable to behaviourist texts; discussed in Chapter 4), and he is also scathing in his criticism of James' 'unscientific . . . definition of psychology' (Watson and McDougall, 1928: 15). The passage quoted above, however, defers to the importance of James' text, despite the disagreement.

Within the behaviourist tradition, references to James' description of consciousness soon disappeared, but Skinner continued to refer to the chapter in *Principles* on emotion (for example Skinner, 1953: 160; 1971: 18) in his development of the James-Lange theory. Outside the behaviourist tradition, the references are more frequent (see Boring, 1950; Bruner, 1986: 116), with Boring's book, *The Physical Dimensions of Consciousness* (1933/1963: for example 129), making critical comments on the methods James employed, but nevertheless continuing to cite the importance of the earlier discussion. Later still, Broadbent uses James' discussions of consciousness in a similar way (1973: 21–22). More recently, Bruner's autobiography indicates the importance of James' work in his own development as a theorist (1983), and a recent symposium held by the British Psychological Society to commemorate the continuing importance of James a hundred years after the publication of the *Principles* shows that the trend is continuing.[4] But while such an account suggests the importance of James as a founding figure in the history of psychology, there is little evidence that his particular account of the mind influenced later work. Perhaps, like Lashley, James stands as a figure whose importance is asserted at the same time as the account he produced is down-graded – a position which Freud's continuing importance seems to avoid.

The importance of Freud's texts is more generally held (see Forrester, 1980, for example), and Richards has stated that the 'Freudian vocabulary has probably had a greater impact on psychological language than any other single source in the discipline itself' (Richards, 1991: 214). Watson had attempted to rewrite Freudian terminology into his behaviouristic account (for example Watson, 1916, 1917), and Skinner made use of Freudian terminology in his book *Beyond Freedom and Dignity* (1971). Again, outside behaviourism the citations are more frequent (see Bruner, 1962/1979, 1983, 1986, for example). However, the citations are often fairly general, making it very difficult to claim historical importance for any one of Freud's texts. It may in fact be the case, for example, that Freudian terminology had already become part of the standard vocabulary of the second half of the twentieth century, through some processes whereby technical discourse and everyday discourse interact (Gellner, 1985).

**An overview of two metaphors of the mind**

In the previous case-studies presented here, one of the methods was to give an exposition of a theoretical account by analysing summaries offered by the original author. The account of consciousness developed by James is fairly complicated, so, initially, a summary will also be used in this section.

It is taken from a series of lectures, published in 1899, which were originally given to school teachers:

> Now the immediate fact which psychology, the science of the mind, has to study is also the most general fact. It is the fact that in each of us, when awake (and often when asleep), some kind of consciousness is always going on. There is a stream, a succession of states, or waves, or fields (or of whatever you please to call them), of knowledge, of feeling, of desire, of deliberation, etc., that constantly pass and repass, and that constitute our inner life. The existence of this stream is the primal fact, the nature and origin of it form the essential problem, of our science. (James, 1899/1920: 15)

Consciousness is held to be a 'stream' of successive 'states, or waves, or fields' which 'pass and repass' and constitute 'inner life'. The science of the mind must investigate the problems raised by the existence of this stream; the flow which is 'always going on'. This focus on 'inner life' begins James' chapter on 'The stream of consciousness' and his study of 'the mind from within' (224). For James, the stream of thought was complicated: although it was a 'stream', it also involved some form of ability for controlling the stream, for directing the succession of states. To introduce this, he distinguishes five main points:

> (1) Every thought tends to be part of a personal consciousness. (2) Within each personal consciousness thought is always changing. (3) Within each personal consciousness thought is sensibly continuous. (4) It always appears to deal with objects independent of itself. (5) It is interested in some parts of these objects to the exclusion of others, and welcomes and rejects – *chooses* from them, in a word – all the while. (225)

Whilst noting that his 'chapter is like a painter's first charcoal sketch upon his canvas, in which no niceties appear' (225), he goes on to develop a detailed account of how the mind is to be described. The description of a 'self' which 'owns' thoughts is important, and there is a 'law that all thought tends to assume the form of a personal consciousness' (229). The postulation of an unconscious stream is not made by James (unlike the Freudian account). He does discuss the work of Pierre Janet (1859–1947) on hysterics and anaesthetics (which was also important to Freud), but does so in order to raise the possibility of 'secondary selves'. That is, James does not entertain the idea that some thoughts may arise as a result of some devious inner force. There is no attempt to create the kind of suspicion of motives which Freud uses. Instead, James gives an account of the continuity of thought – hence the stress on the stream metaphor – in which present thoughts are influenced by the 'dying vibrations' (242) of previous thoughts. He rejects descriptions involving 'chains' or 'trains': there is 'no more a break in thought than a joint in bamboo is a break in the wood' (240). He emphasises the role of the mind as an agent which makes various selections: 'the mind chooses to suit itself, and decides what particular sensation shall be held more real and valid than the rest' (286). The question to be addressed in the present chapter is: how does *Principles* get to the point where such descriptions are regarded as persuasive by a reader?

Before coming to such a question, Freud's account of the mind should also be briefly reviewed to draw a contrast with the Jamesian account. Freud's account was largely described in Chapter 4 in reviewing his account of 'development'. He used metaphor to suggest that the mind should be regarded as an ancient city, such as Rome, and built in layers such that the lowest layer affects the structure of the highest:

> . . . suppose that Rome is not a human habitation but a psychical entity with a similarly long and copious past – an entity, that is to say, in which nothing that has once come into existence will have passed away and all the earlier phases of development continue to exist along side the latest one. (Freud, 1930/1961: 70)

This account remained fairly stable across the various texts in which it appeared. The hidden layers of childhood experience affect dreams and (on the Freudian account) much else besides. This is because, essentially:

> . . . [the] mind is not a simple thing; on the contrary, it is a hierarchy of superordinated and subordinated agencies, a labyrinth of impulses striving independently of one another, corresponding with the multiplicity of instincts and of relations with the external world, many of which are antagonistic to one another and incompatible. (Freud, 1917/1955: 141)

The Freudian account will also be given in more detail in the next section. But, for the moment, this 'striving', 'antagonistic' account of the mind as a form of 'hierarchy' will be contrasted with the Jamesian 'stream' of 'choice' and 'selection'.

**Enrolling the reader**

The process of rhetorically enrolling a reader (as contrasted with socially enrolling a reader through, say, economic influence) is one which may be undertaken implicitly or explicitly (or both to varying degrees). The term 'enrolment', as it is used here, is taken from Actor-Network Theory; however, the term is used (it functions) in much the same way as its dictionary definition. If readers become enrolled in a text, they become members of a discursive community; particular assumptions are taken for granted, rules are adopted for continuing a form of enquiry and for using a given lexicon. The extent to which a reader is enrolled in a form of discourse is reflected in what topics are taken seriously, whether it is the content of dreams, introspective accounts of states and feelings, or the statistical correlation of one characteristic with another.

The two key texts to be analysed here are from a time in psychology's history when the process of enrolment was made explicit by the content of what is written. The prose style of psychological texts at the beginning of this century, for example, may be regarded as having a number of common elements. But the journal article, at least, had not been given the highly standardised format which was enforced later (in the 1950s). The term 'enforced' here may seem a little strong at first, but continuing editions of the *American Psychological Association Publication Manual*, and its widespread acceptance,[5] makes the term highly appropriate: journals issue guidelines stating their stylistic requirements and, in psychology, those requirements are either implicitly based on the *APA Publication Manual* (by simply stating the *same* requirements), or stated explicitly by citing the manual as containing the standard format. Authors who then treat such requirements as merely-a-guide, and send a paper which is not in the expected format, are usually corrected (reprimanded) by the journal's editor (and, perhaps, abused by the academics who review the paper).[6]

In the modern journal article, then, the reader is implicitly enrolled in reading the text through being given the expected format: an abstract (not more than 200 words), an introduction (citing the previous studies relevant to the paper in question), a 'methods' section (such that the results may be replicated by others) and so on. Also important, and always listed, are the names of the author(s) and their institutional affiliation(s); however, the process of enrolment in this respect is not *only* related to style: a famous author, and/or a respected institutional affiliation command more attention (Peters and Ceci, 1982),[7] and perhaps help to enrol the reader more quickly.[8] None of this is to suggest that enrolment does not also occur throughout the content of the modern journal article: the content remains an important aspect. However, it is suggested that the task of enrolling a reader is made rhetorically more simple by the use of a stylised format (see also Bazerman, 1988; Myers, 1990a; Gross, 1990).

Away from the journal article, in a book or published lecture, stylistic restrictions are less obvious and thus, it will be argued, the process of enrolment is made more explicit. For example, in the first of six lectures delivered (in 1971) by the psychologist (then Cambridge based, later Oxford Professor), Donald Broadbent, as part of the William James lecture series, is the following discussion. He begins by arguing that, within psychology, there is an 'apparent lack of interest in ideology' and that most psychologists are reluctant 'to talk about broader issues'. He then states that:

> I myself belong to this profession and this generation, and I fully share its values. Accordingly, I will promise my professional colleagues that there will be something for them in these Lectures: there will indeed be tachistoscopes, measurements of reaction time, human beings on line to computers, and free recall of long lists of words. In particular, I think I can promise that every Lecture will contain at least one previously unpublished experiment. Having thus established some degree of respectability, however, I want also to relate what I say about experiments to certain broader issues. (Broadbent, 1973: 5–6)

The lectures were open to the public, and here there is an indication that Broadbent expected to be speaking to (at least) an audience with two components: expert and non-expert. The expert audience is defined in the extract and offered the promise of unpublished (and, therefore, not often well known) experimental data. The author also cites his use of the (then) most technical (or 'hard-nosed') laboratory equipment available for his form of enquiry.[9] Thus, Broadbent holds out the promise of a consideration of 'wide' or general (social) issues; makes explicit his own technical competence; and enrols the expert listener/reader through the offer of unpublished research findings which would be expected to further previously established debates.

In the first of the *Lectures*, Freud may be seen to be attempting to combat a higher level of doubt in his audience than the one faced by James. That is, while James may be regarded as expanding on discussions of psychological topics with a long tradition in philosophy,[10] Freud's text was part of a programme to introduce an entirely new area of discourse: that of psychoanalysis.[11] Gellner (1985: 49–52) has argued that an important component of psychoanalytic discourse is that a person's thinking whilst being initiated (enrolled) into psychoanalytic discourse is split: first, that of a sceptical reader (listener) who places a distance between his beliefs and those of the author (speaker), an aspect shared by both the texts by James and Freud; but, second, the Freudian theory has within it an account of *why* the reader is sceptical. Further, in the Freudian text, the reader's scepticism is confronted with the rewards of a form not envisioned by James. Broadly, Gellner offers a sustained argument to suggest that psychoanalysis constitutes a secularised religion in which the person being enrolled is offered a way of alleviating 'deep' and perhaps only partially realised fears and uncertainties. Yet, at the same time, the offer of salvation contains a threat such that, if the novice does not take up the offer, the rewards will be withheld; more that that, the behaviour of the novice (for example, their attempts to disengage from Freud's interpretations, or to remain sceptical of the benefits and truths of psychoanalysis) is always explained in terms of the theory itself.

Given Gellner's argument, it is then hardly surprising that the first of Freud's *Lectures* is structured as a direct assault on the reader's scepticism. Freud begins by claiming that he expects his reader to be full of doubt; he claims to wish to 'actively warn [the reader] against [entering] into a permanent relationship' with psychoanalysis (1916–1917/1963: 16; hereafter by page number); that 'the hypotheses of psychoanalysis are an insult to the entire world and have earned its dislike' (21); that 'you, Ladies and Gentlemen, naturally cannot understand as yet' aspects of what Freud is saying (22); that 'society' has 'set about diverting attention from [Freud's] whole field of ideas' (23). Thus, psychoanalysis is a dangerous thing, described as something which attacks the 'world' and 'society'; and 'society' has reacted by deliberately 'diverting attention' from psychoanalysis. Two important aspects of such a characterisation need to be drawn out. First, the audience is part of the hostile 'society' which psychoanalysis insults, and yet, because the audience is attending Freud's lectures, they must be distinguished from society in general. Second, Freud continually refers to 'psychoanalysis' rather than to himself: the term 'psychoanalysis' is being used to distinguish a particular 'field of ideas' but, more than that, a particular institution. Both aspects of this rhetoric need to be covered in more detail. To do this, passages from the opening page of the first lecture will be quoted:

> Ladies and Gentlemen, – I cannot tell how much knowledge about psycho-analysis each one of you has already acquired from what you have read or from hearsay. But the wording of my prospectus – 'Elementary Introduction to Psycho-Analysis' – obliges me to treat you as though you knew nothing and stood in need of some preliminary information.
>
> I can, however, assume this much – that you know that psycho-analysis is a procedure for the medical treatment of neurotic patients. [Freud then character-ises the differences between 'a medical technique' and 'psycho-analytic treat-ment', where the difficulties of the latter are deliberately stressed.] Do not be annoyed, then, if I begin by treating you in the same way as these neurotic patients. I seriously advise you not to join my audience a second time. (1916–1917/1963: 15)

The audience is expected to know 'nothing', except that psychoanalysis is a 'medical treatment'. Freud was a medical doctor, and the treatment he had developed was given credibility on that basis; but here, 'before an audience of doctors and laymen of both sexes' (9), the account is unproblematically aligned with the medical profession. Psychoanalysis is at once a field with its own distinctive label, and an extension of a well-defined institution: all that remains is to characterise the difference between their respective practices. Having performed such an alignment, and briefly characterised the distinction between medicine and psychoanalysis, Freud redescribes his 'Ladies and Gentlemen' as neurotic patients. The neurotic is told that psychoanalytic treatment is difficult, and about 'its long duration and the efforts and sacrifices it calls for'. The same must be done for members of the audience, who are 'seriously' advised not to come again: mystery is created, there is an anticipation of effort and sacrifice, and warnings are given. But not only is the reader/audience counselled against going further than the third paragraph, Freud has a psychoanalytic explanation for why such advise *must* be given: 'I will show you how the whole trend of your *previous* education and all your *habits* of thought are *inevitably* bound to *make* you into opponents of psycho-analysis' (15, emphasis mine). Along with the anticipation comes a dose of anxiety: the audience cannot help itself, it is forced by habit and pre-Freudian (previous) education to be an enemy of psychoanalysis. Thus, knowledge of this well-defined field will be withheld simply because of a fault in the history of the reader/audience: they cannot help it; education and habit will overcome any reasoned appraisal of what Freud is about to say. Hence Freud's advice: go home.

In an examination of other parts of Freud's corpus, Fish (1988) makes an argument which is relevant here. He suggests that Freud 'tars his adversaries with their own brush', such that the 'patient and critic become interchangeable' (1988: 190). The adversaries Fish refers to are critics of Freud's version of psychoanalysis, especially Jung and Adler (Fish, 1988: 189; see also Kerr, 1993). The argument is that Freud inverts the rhetoric of the critic by reinterpreting the criticism as the outcome of the critic's personal history; that Freud uses his *own* theory to explain away any objection, and defends psychoanalysis through this 'master stroke' (Fish, 1988: 190) with such an explanation.[12] Further, when Freud gives such an explanation, he does so in terms of 'psychoanalysis'; that the discipline (to which the term refers) has arrived at such an explanation, rather than Freud (the man) arriving at the explanation in order to defend himself. Freud is depicted as the representative of a collective enterprise. Or, in the terms Fish uses: Freud's description counters the possible objection that the explanation he gives (of the critic) is an example of his own 'will to power' – of which Freud is 'of course wholly innocent' (Fish, 1988: 190).

The argument from Fish is useful in an analysis of the opening of Freud's first lecture in that it provides a way of reading the opening page. Freud asks the reader/audience not to 'be annoyed' when he *treats* them as 'neurotic patients' (15): they are 'treated' both because they are naive about psychoanalysis, and because Freud *knows* (via the theory of the branch of medicine which he represents) that they will reject whatever they hear after his opening remarks. Thus, by positioning such a sentence on the first page of his (at first 15, later 28) lectures, Freud is able to treat (in one sense) possibly forthcoming objections as a direct product of the reader's 'previous' education, and at the same time treat (in the medical sense) those objections as if they were a product of a personal deficit (for which the history of the reader is responsible), rather than as an indication of wider problems produced by the theory. Freud poses the question: 'Would you like to hear how we [psychoanalysts] explain [the] fact' of the reader's 'antipathy' (22)? The answer to the question has already been given, but here it is in Freud's terms:

> . . . it is inherent in human nature to have an inclination to consider a thing untrue if one does not like it, and after that it is easy to find arguments against it. Thus society makes what is disagreeable into what is untrue. It disputes the truths of psycho-analysis with logical and factual arguments; but these arise from emotional sources . . . (Freud, 1916–1917/1963: 23)

Criticisms are a consequence of not liking something; a *post hoc* legitimation of what is 'truly' only 'emotional', arising as it does from finding psychoanalysis 'aesthetically repulsive and morally reprehensible' (23). Thus, Freud reverses any suggestion that objections come first to consciousness, and these objections then give rise to emotions. Moreover, this reversal will be understood only when the reader/audience continues with the text, struggles with their 'resistance' (22) to giving up the 'prejudice' associated with the statement 'what is mental is conscious' (22), and reads an exposition of 'the hypothesis of there being unconscious mental processes' (22).

As a result, the reader is enrolled in the text as a patient whose possible attempts at appraisal of psychoanalysis result from (a) not knowing enough about psychoanalysis (to be 'cured' by reading further), and perhaps (b) actually being neurotic (to be 'cured' by being analysed in psychoanalysis). If the present account is persuasive, it is perhaps not surprising that Freud ends his opening lecture:

Such, then, are a few of the difficulties that stand in the way of your interest in psycho-analysis. They are perhaps more than enough for a start. But if you are able to overcome the impression they make on you, we will proceed. (Freud, 1916–1917/1963: 24)

By the end of the lecture, it is the reader who must overcome any negative impression; in order to read (listen) further, it is the reader's responsibility to be 'able to overcome' the difficulties which 'stand in the way' of their own 'interest in psychoanalysis'. If the reader can manage all this, then 'we' can continue in the (now) joint effort of being faced with the matters 'of fact which we [psychoanalysts] believe we have established by our painstaking labours' (24).

The amount of rhetorical work involved in Freud's opening exposition is large for reasons already discussed. In *Principles*, the task of enrolling the reader is simpler, and James spends fewer words in setting the stage:

Psychology is the Science of Mental Life, both in its phenomena and their conditions. The phenomena are such things as we call feelings, desires, cognitions, reasonings, decisions, and the like; and, superficially considered, their variety and complexity is such as to leave a chaotic impression on the observer. (James, 1890/1950: 1)

The discipline of psychology is aligned with science, and the definition of the science (which James is about to discuss) is given in the opening sentence of the book (of 28 chapters). The object of that science is a set of phenomena, and a list of objects is immediately provided. Moreover, the list is assumed to be a familiar one such that, after listing five items, James is able to provide a partial or indefinite description ('and the like'). The opening sentence is unmitigated ('Psychology is the Science of . . .'), and the use of such rhetoric allows a comparison: if one considers the objects of the science 'superficially' (unscientifically), then the 'variety and complexity' inherent in the objects will leave 'a chaotic impression'. The term 'chaotic' is infrequently employed (and not, I suggest, by James in this context) as a positive description; rather, there is a danger being indicated. Assuming that the reader of the text actually has a 'mental life' (the importance of which was denied by Watson little more than 20 years later), the science about to be described by James will save the reader from the chaos and superficiality which James mentions. As with Freud's opening lecture, the promise of being able to provide some answers is made in the opening passages by James.

Accordingly, alternative answers are considered in the paragraphs that follow:

The most natural and consequently the earliest way of unifying the material was, first, to classify it as well as might be, and, secondly, to affiliate the diverse mental modes thus found, upon a simple entity, the personal Soul, of which they are taken to be so many facultative manifestations. . . . This is the orthodox 'spiritualistic' theory of scholasticism and of common-sense (James, 1890/ 1950: 1)

Given the rhetorical positioning of such an alternative, and the frequent use of qualifiers ('most natural', 'earliest', 'as well as might be', 'simple entity', 'orthodox'), such an approach will not do, and in the remainder of the opening paragraph, and the text continuing until page 6, other alternative approaches are also dismissed: 'associationist' and 'spiritualist' (pp. 1–5). In this way, different perspectives perhaps brought by the reader (to the text) are criticised and rejected as irrelevant to the task at hand. This tactic was used by James throughout the text, pushing aside previous work in a bid to create a reason for his own (see also Latour, 1987). James then asks:

> Can we state more distinctly still the manner in which the mental life seems to intervene between impressions made from without upon the body, and the reactions of the body upon the outer world again? Let us look at a few facts. (James, 1890/1950: 6)

The 'facts' he provides are taken from simple experiments involving iron filings, and experiments by physiologists involving frogs. Each is typical of what is to come later in the text: there is often an attempt to ground his argument in discussions of physiology. James frequently uses physical analogies employing artifacts from the physical sciences: kaleidoscopes (246), spinning tops (244) and pairs of electrodes (238). But he does not use such 'scientific' descriptions exclusively: I mentioned earlier his use of bamboo to help describe the continuity of the stream of consciousness. He also likened the working of the mind to the activities of a sculptor (288), and changes in the brain to shifts in an aurora borealis (234). In a way, James may be regarded as reproducing in his account of the mind the very processes he claims the mind uses: presenting a constant stream of images, and selecting, revising and discarding whatever analogies suit a particular purpose. He enrols the reader through this mix of the technical and the familiar: with the latter the text is made approachable, with the former, credentials are established.

James often invites the reader to identify with his introspective accounts; he gives a description which the reader is expected to recognise and agree with. For example, he uses the plural form of address in a section intended to support his claim that 'thought is in constant change' (229):

> Often we are ourselves struck at the strange differences in our successive views of the same thing. We wonder how we could have opined as we did last month about a certain matter. . . . From one year to another we see things in new lights. What was real has grown unreal, and what was exciting is insipid. The friends we used to care the world for are shrunken to shadows; the women once so divine, the stars, the woods, and the waters, how now so dull and common . . . and as for the books, what *was* there to find so mysteriously significant in Goethe, or in John Mill so full of weight? Instead of all this, more zestful than ever is the work, the work; and fuller and deeper the import of common duties and of common goods. (James, 1890/1950: 233–234)

The authority appealed to here is the wisdom of years; the ability to reflect on a long succession of states and memories (James was born in 1842, died 1910). To assent to the description is to regard change (rather than stability or repetition) as one of the primary features of the mind to be accounted for; having identified with the personalised account the reader may assent to this view of the mind in which so much is revisable: 'Experience is remoulding us every moment' (234). This style of writing has all but disappeared from psychology; it involves a kind of evidence no longer taken seriously as a method for providing facts about mental life. But James does not leave such passages unadorned: they are soon joined by descriptions of brain states as an analogy which helps to ground such introspection in the discourse of science.

James also employs several diagrams in the course of the chapter on thought. These are not given as part of some experimental report – James does not provide any new information derived from experiments – rather they offer a visual redescription of the text; a way of making the argument more concrete. The most complicated of these involves a three-dimensional representation of thought involving a wooden frame, a smooth ball and a piece of Indian rubber (283). The rubber is stretched across the frame; one side of the frame represents time, the other has the content of thought written across it (the sentence: 'I am the same I, that I was yesterday'). The ball is moved under the rubber sheet in a diagonal to represent the changing content of thought, to 'show the relative intensities, at successive moments, of the several nerve-processes to which the various parts of the thought object correspond' (283). What is interesting is the attempt to give a physical instantiation of the mental process; the assertion that something is to be gained by providing such diagrams. By implication, psychology is a practical endeavour with an object that can be mapped; the reader can see the object 'plain enough . . . to call for no more explanation' (283).

## Promissory notes

Extending the argument given in Chapter 3, it may be that a rhetorical system becomes a unified and consistent discourse partly on the basis of the 'promissory notes' issued within a text. James ends *Principles* with an account of the possibilities for continuing his form of psychological research: 'Even in the clearest parts of Psychology our insight is insignificant enough' (688). His rhetoric functions as a way of mitigating claims toward unified and 'fully explained' knowledge. However, the promise of further 'insight' is maintained, albeit with the implication that further research is called for: 'Psychology' is held to have achieved at least some 'clear parts'. Whilst he presents an 'unfinished-seeming front' (vii), psychology does have a 'scope' (1–11) with which to provide further 'explanations' of the objects James describes as forming part of further psychological enquiry. The rhetoric employed may imply that a full account of 'peculiar mental attributes' (688) will be difficult to attain, but the entire endeavour is not without promise: the rhetorical system requires and will justify further attention. The prescription is to continue in the search for useful metaphors and analogies in the pursuit of further understanding and less chaos. For example, he concludes 'The stream of consciousness':

> Descending now to finer work than this first general sketch, let us in the next chapter try to trace the psychology of this fact of self-consciousness to which we have once more been led. (290)

Although the metaphor employed relates to the work of the artist ('sketch'), the rhetoric is similar to that examined in Chapter 7: the overall account to which 'we' have been 'led' requires 'finer work' at a lower level, to which the account must now 'descend'. If the reader is, by now, enrolled in the discourse James constructs, the account assumes that more detail will be required: continued questioning of basic assumptions is no longer the rhetorical task. Instead, the promise will be, at least partially, fulfilled through further examination of the described object. But, if maintaining that consciousness as a stream is regarded as a promissory note, it needs to be asked why it wasn't more successful. James offers ways of describing what it feels like not to be able to remember a name or to have a sense of familiarity on encountering a tune or odour, and he makes suggestions which help his scientific credibility by referring to the causes of such feeling as 'sub-maximal excitement of wide-spreading associational brain-tracts' (252). He uses the stream metaphor to argue against the work of previous psychologists in an attempt to ensure 'the reinstatement of the vague to its proper place in our mental life' (254). Yet such rhetoric provides little scope for going on with experimental work (compared to, say, the metaphor in which the 'brain is a computer', or 'behaviour has a shape'); nor does it provide an account of the mind containing some hidden force to be suspicious of, and reckon with, as in the Freudian account. The Jamesian mind was perhaps neither practical nor subversive enough for the promissory note of the stream metaphor to be very influential. Rather, James highlights the importance of attempting to provide accounts of consciousness; the promissory notes he issues are more closely related to continuing the endeavour of psychology, and not to the investigation of some conceptually unifying metaphor. With the identification by the reader, with the introspective accounts which James sometimes employed to enrol his reader, may come the adoption of metaphors concerning flow, fringes and tendencies of mind, but they are merely presented as stepping stones. The stream of psychology, like the stream of thought, will go on selecting and rejecting without transcending its 'unfinished-seeming front'.

At the end of the *Lectures*, Freud also issues several promises:

> I have finished, Ladies and Gentlemen. It is more than a conventional form of words if I admit that I myself am profoundly aware of the many defects in the lectures I have given you. I regret above all that I have so often promised to return later to a topic I have lightly touched on and have then found no opportunity of redeeming my promise. I undertook to give you an account of a subject which is still incomplete and in process of development, and my condensed summary has itself turned out to be an incomplete one. . . . But I

could not pretend to make you experts; I have only tried to stimulate and enlighten you. (Part III: 463)

The unfulfilled promise referred to constructs additional promises: that the achievement of 'expertise' is attainable, that a longer account would further 'enlighten' the audience, that the psychoanalytic account is 'developing' and, therefore, promises to develop further. Thus, the enrolled reader (listener) is left expecting the fulfilment of the 'complete' account. And in psychoanalysis there is always something left undelivered and requiring further analysis (see also Forrester, 1990a). More importantly, the metaphors of mind which Freud initiated helped to create a sense of doubt concerning the reader's own mental processes, a doubt which comes from the existence of unconscious processes. Accepting such a hypothesis 'paves the way to a decisive new orientation in the world and in science' (22), while at the same time creating a mystery concerning the self; Freud's rhetoric seeks to enrol the reader through the suggestion that readers are unaware of the reasons behind their thoughts and actions. The promise he makes is to unmask such processes; to find meaning in parapraxes and dreams, and to enlighten and reorient the reader's self-understanding. The postulation of an unconscious involves issuing a promissory note, the denial of which would be regarded by someone enrolled in psychoanalysis as symptomatic of some underlying conflict.

The present chapter extended the arguments of the previous case-studies by examining the process of enrolling the reader. If the rhetoric of a psychological text is successful in issuing promises, making presuppositions and justifying the 'validity' of a general description, then the rhetorical system requires further attention to the descriptions constructed within a text. This phenomenon was described as a process of 'enrolment' in order to describe it in a way similar to the process of academic education: the student is enrolled, and taught to describe objects in particular ways and using particular rhetorical forms. When the process of education is complete or, in the present case, when the reading of a persuasive text is finished, the student is left with a way of continuing to reproduce and/or modify a particular form of description: discourse continues which remains at least partially consistent with the rhetoric of the persuasive text. To become enrolled in a text is to make its rhetoric a part of one's self, to judge other works by its criteria, to adopt its metaphors as an account of one's own inner processes: to be persuaded is to change a part of the world.

## Notes

1. The role of Freud in this process involves some difficult questions concerning the status of psychoanalysis as an academic discipline, and the influence psychoanalytic writing had on experimental psychology generally. Such issues are (unfortunately) beyond the scope of the present book, but work has been published which is relevant. Forrester (1990b) has argued, in part, that psychoanalysis had all the trappings of an academic discipline, albeit without stable university credentials, but whether or not it is regarded in the same way as the discipline of

psychology depends heavily on the definition of the term 'discipline'. On the connections between the two authors examined in detail in the present chapter: James was aware of Freud's views (Le Clair, 1966: 224, citing a letter by James dated 28 Sept. 1909), and Freud was aware of James' work (1916–1917/1963: 396). Freud also gives an account of a meeting between the two (Freud, 1925/1959: 51–52). This meeting took place in America, where Freud and Jung were invited to come to address the members of Clark University in 1909; the invitation was extended to Freud by G. Stanley Hall (see Jones, 1955: 60 ff). Hall was supervised as a graduate student (partly) by James. For an account of the connections between James and Hall, and of the formation of the American psychological discipline, see Leary (1987). Thus, there is a reasonable case to be made that there was an early mutual influence of psychology and psychoanalysis (though Freud criticised 'psychology as it is taught academically' for not giving 'adequate replies concerning our mental life', 1917/1955: 137). That the influence and the interest continued (and continues) may be seen from the citations of Freud in historical summaries such as Leary (1990b) and Koch and Leary (1985), and from overviews of issues such as Bruner (1962/1979; 1986). There have also been writers for whom the connection was more personal: see, for example, discussions of Sabina Spielrein in Appignanesi and Forrester (1992), Kerr (1993), and Soyland (1993). But it should also be noted that the 'scientific basis' of psychoanalysis has been attacked by psychologists (following Popper, e.g. 1972/1979: 38, Note 5) in terms of the extent to which it correctly predicted (and could be refuted by) aspects of human behaviour and thinking (e.g. Hebb, 1949: xii; Miller, 1962/1966: 61–62, 249–267; Eysenck, 1985). The general anti-psychoanalysis debate is summarised by Manicas (1987: 259–261), Frosh (1989), and an account of this form of attack is given by Gellner (1985: 3–5). The relationship between psychoanalysis and literature is discussed by Meltzer (1988), and (in more detail) by Brooks (1988).

2. Rose (1985: 215) gives an account of the influence of Jung on Burt. However, Spearman (Burt's senior) cites Jung's work quite often (e.g. 1923: 126, 331, 347). Jung's (1921/1971) *Psychological Types* is cited by Spearman (1927: 44, 51–52, 122, 292) using a translation from 1923. The copy of Spearman (1927) used for the present study was originally owned by Cyril Burt. Amongst other things, the copy contains several 'corrections' to the text. It is therefore possible to note that Burt wrote 'Jung' in the margin of this copy (1927: 43) just before the first mention of Jung. Further, a paper by T.L. Kelley (1928/1967: 78) discusses a relation between Jung and Spearman. Outside of the 'mental testing movement', Murphy et al. (1931/ 1937) discuss texts by Freud (e.g. pp. 313–314) and Jung (e.g. pp. 229–230): this text from the USA also cites Erich Fromm's help in their 1937 edition.

3. O'Donnell comments that the position Watson developed of an 'objective' psychology (that is, one not involving 'introspection) was announced in a letter from Watson to Yerkes in the winter of 1912 (O'Donnell, 1979: 523).

4. The symposium was published in an issue of the *British Journal of Psychology*, introduced by Still (1991).

5. But the format is not used in more general scientific journals such as *Science*, in which some psychological articles also appear.

6. Personal experience, and conversations with others.

7. The study by Peters and Ceci (1982) is an unusual one in that it involved re-submitting twelve journal articles to the journals which had published them (between 6 and 18 months) earlier. Each article was altered in two ways: slight stylistic changes (converting tables into graphs, for example), and removing and replacing the well-established author and insti-tutional names. Ten of the re-submissions went undetected, and eight were rejected, with 'statistical inadequacies' being cited as the reason for almost all of the rejections. Peters and Ceci used their paper, in part, to argue for a 'blind' reviewing system (where the journal readers who initially examine papers for possible publication aren't given access to the names of authors or institutions). Their paper appeared in the journal of *Behavioural and Brain Sciences*, which has a reviewing system for papers which is atypical (i.e. the reviewers' comments are published with an accepted paper, and the original authors are invited to reply in print).

8. Bazerman (1988) has provided a careful analysis of the rhetoric and rhetorical

development of the *APA Publication Manual*. Schaffer (e.g. 1989) and Shapin and Schaffer (1985) have provided analyses of the function that personal and scientific credibility (or 'credit') plays in the history of science.

9. It might be suggested that Broadbent is making a joke here at his own expense by referring to a list of out-of-date equipment. That is not the case. In conversation, a PhD student working with Broadbent at the time (1968–1971) argued that the Cambridge Applied Psychology Unit was using the most modern equipment available.

10. There were aspects of James' work which he used to help promote the new academic *discipline* of psychology (Leary, 1987, 1992) within the American university structure, and the role James played was crucial to the promotion of that discipline (he supervised G. Stanley Hall, who went on to become the first holder of a Chair in Psychology). However, the role James played in such a development was not one of a 'founding father', in the same way that Freud could be described as the father of psychoanalysis.

11. For an account of Freud's role in the psychoanalytic movement, see Gellner (1985); for an account of the textual development of Freud's work which places such work in the broader intellectual climate in which Freud was writing, see Forrester (1980); the 'classic' biography of Freud is Jones, in three volumes (1953, 1955, 1957).

12. It should be noted that the rhetoric employed by Fish (1988) makes it appear that he has provided a revelation concerning Freud's rebuttal of a critic; that Freud's method of equating critic with patient was something 'hidden' beneath the surface of rhetoric. However, it should be obvious from the quotation (above) from Freud's first page of Lecture One that Freud makes this rhetorical manoeuvre explicit ('I begin by treating you . . . as . . . neurotic patients', p. 15). From the present perspective, the rhetoric used by Fish may be regarded as closely directed towards his 'dedication': 'that the Wolf-Man got it right' when he claimed Freud was 'a Jewish swindler, he wants to use me from behind and shit on my head' (Fish, 1988: 184). That is, the methodology employed by Fish is asymmetric.

# 9

# Describing Psychological Objects: Concluding Discussion

One seeks a midwife for his thoughts, another someone whom he can help: origin of a good conversation.

(Nietzsche, 1886/1966: IV, 136)

'So you are saying that human agreement decides what is true and what is false?' – It is what human beings *say* that is true and false; and they agree in the *language* they use. That is not agreement in opinion but in form of life.

(Wittgenstein, 1958/1968: I, 241)

When I say 'I interpret', 'I analyse', 'I describe', 'I characterize', this, in a way, is to give a verdict, but is essentially connected with verbal matters and clarifying our exposition.

(Austin, 1962/1975: 155)

With language, we solidify the world; through rhetoric and metaphor, we shape and construct the psychological realm: memory, development, emotion, intellect, mind and beyond. This book began as an attempt to examine texts in psychology in terms of the rhetorical functions they perform: much remains to be done if such an avenue of enquiry is to be made more fruitful. In this final chapter I want to make some brief remarks concerning the methodology, scope and limitations of such work, to review the sorts of conclusions I drew earlier, and to comment on possible areas for future thought and research. An analysis of rhetoric needs to mention parts of earlier texts without using them; that is, the claims made in the texts analysed cannot be taken at face value and used to further arguments about the objects under discussion. I began some of the analytical and methodological arguments of the book by claiming that studies of rhetoric cannot privilege some texts over others, or some parts of what a text maintains over other parts. The analyst must remain agnostic about which parts of a text ought to be persuasive or not; the 'truth' of a text should not be a consideration (see also Gross, 1990). Instead, consideration is given to how a text works, how a case is made to be persuasive, and what characterisation of an object it gives. To that extent, nothing I have argued here could be considered as a contribution to debates in psychology (except, perhaps, in a critical way).

I began the book with a discussion of the distinction between philosophy and rhetoric. This was appropriate for two reasons: first, philosophy has been regarded as a kind of parent discipline of psychology. Before psychology established sufficient disciplinary credentials to be regarded as a separate institutional and practical form of enquiry, it was a sub-section of philosophy; it consisted of a range of topics about which to argue. Indeed, this was just what J.B. Watson didn't like about it: too many arguments, not enough solutions. Instead, psychology was claimed to be one of the sciences, and imported statistical methods on that basis (Gigerenzer and Murray, 1987); one was supposed to find out about the mind or about behaviour through engaging with the objects of enquiry, as if the investigation of 'brute reality' was able to decide a given question. And yet the results of such practical work must be communicated through written and verbal argument; the performance of persuasive acts will always form a part of the activities of any science (see comments in Watson, 1968/1970). Even if the authority of science is directly taken as a result of having communed with Nature, the results of that meeting have to be made intelligible and persuasive for others: the distance between philosophy and science is not all that great.

The second reason for discussing the distinction between philosophy and rhetoric was to argue against the negative connotations associated with the latter: how exactly are we to know what distinguishes a good argument from a bad one except by further argument, additional rhetoric? I suggested that engagement in rhetoric was inescapable, that the rhetoric of anti-rhetoric was self-defeating: highlighting the persuasive element in philosophical and scientific writing merely calls attention to the importance of seeing both activities as part of a collective process, one in which agreement, negotiation and consensus play important roles. The concentration on textual analysis was intended to contribute to an understanding of rhetorical construction: the claim to have described a psychological object should be seen as a rhetorical achievement, the first stage in the process of having such a description accepted by a research community. Calling attention to the amount of rhetorical work involved in giving a particular description should not suggest that there is something slippery and underhand going on – there is not some rhetoric-free practice in philosophy or science to which we should all aspire.

One way to strengthen an argument is to list or summarise a number of claims and conclusions made within a text. The object is to present a piece of writing as a kind of process with a particular outcome, a specific result. I shall now attempt to do this for the five case-studies presented here. The main claim in Chapter 3 was that metaphors function as promissory notes. I couched this claim within an argument concerning metaphors in the history of neuropsychology. Ironically, this chapter may in fact be the most fruitful in providing topics for further research: it is quite likely that scientific texts will incorporate promissory notes as a matter of routine in a bid to motivate further research in a given direction. This is not just a matter of 'showing promise' but also dismissing objections on the basis of returns expected in the 'near future'. Perhaps also ironically, the field of cognitive neuropsychology is also one of the main areas attracting the largest number of research funds – further research into the rhetorical power of texts in this area, and the ways in which the value of such research is described, could 'cast light' on the construction of a 'cutting edge' in psychology.

The object of Chapter 4 was to discuss several different ways of characterising psychological development; to engender a slight sense of aporia, to undermine any taken-for-granted character of a particular conception, to highlight the amount of rhetorical work involved in giving a particular account, and to claim that metaphors entail a number of presuppositions. The terms with which to describe the narrative of developmental change are neither natural nor obvious. Differences between theories are found in the site of theoretical investigation, the dependence on or the denial of the comparative assumption (connecting human and animal), the role of language in reflecting or initiating change, the assertion of rigid or flexible sequences, or the promotion of learning as development. The conceptual child is (re)constructed in the discourse of each theory with different practical consequences.

Chapter 5 turned the discussion to the topic of the emotions: the central argument, as an extension of the material on development, was that the emotions have a number of conflicting metaphorical constructions. While each theory claims to give an exhaustive account, the basic metaphors on which they rely work against a possible resolution between them. From the form of instinct account constructed by Darwin, and now fundamental to the way emotions are regarded, through the inversion offered by James and Lange, to the more radical theory initiated by Sartre and expanded by Soloman, the emotions become, in turn, extremely different psychological objects. As a result, the rhetoric used was claimed to be an important site of investigation: by understanding the way metaphor incorporates a network of assumptions and presuppositions, each construction could be seen as competing for persuasive effect. Once the debate can be held to be closed, the emotions have the character of their rhetorical constructions.

The consideration of the literal/metaphorical distinction given in Chapter 6 returned the discussion to debates in philosophy. I doubt that the argument in that chapter would go very far in convincing someone not already converted to the sorts of conclusions given – it relies too heavily on arguments which can at best only be worked through rather than easily summarised. But it seemed desirable to give some account which worked against a view of metaphor as something which could be translated away into literal discourse. One way of doing this is to raise some concerns about the nature of discourse regarded as literally true, and from there turn to a discussion of metaphorical discourse. I did not wish to press too hard on the claim that 'all discourse is metaphorical' because such a claim is fairly vacuous – daily practice shows that we certainly treat some aspects of discourse as being literal. Rather, the question is to consider how new sentences are raised up into literal discourse, how a description of an object is changed. Selected metaphors become literal descriptions over time, on the basis of choices between different forms of rhetoric (between, say, the mental hydraulics of psychoanalysis or the environmental mechanics of behaviourism). But the rhetorical act of defining 'metaphor' will always invoke other metaphors; thus, the distinction seems to be self-defeating. The solution I offered of maintaining the distinction for pragmatic reasons (whilst remaining sceptical about the ontological commitments which that distinction normally assumes) may seem a bit like having one's cake and eating it. As with many other parts of the book, I could have pursued this line of reasoning through other parts of the rather convoluted literature on metaphor, but fell prey to a law of minimising returns. The argument stands as background to the account of metaphor used in the book.

In Chapter 7, some consideration was given to the claim that there is a continuity of rhetoric in the IQ debate, that the arguments used in the history of the debate bear a sort of family resemblance (borrowing the term from Wittgenstein). The object in that chapter was to consider the rhetoric of this debate in isolation from discussions of the validity (or otherwise) assigned to pieces of data, and to call attention to the amount of rhetorical work involved in claiming to 'represent' the facts. While a number of different rhetorical strategies were considered, the object was not to begin a taxonomy of manoeuvres used; attempts at rhetorical closure will come in varied forms. In Chapter 8, questions were asked about how a reader is enrolled in a text and what strategies may be employed to invite a reader's acceptance of a given description. I discussed the metaphors of mind constructed by James and Freud and the way each is used to persuade the reader, through the challenges made by Freud (that one can't help resisting the truth of psychoanalysis), or the offers of introspective description given by James (that the stream flows restlessly on, revising and reformulating). To accept such rhetoric is to become a member of a discourse community, one made up of particular assumptions about what is a reasonable way of proceeding.

There are many metaphors in the texts of psychology. I hope some of the things I've pointed out in the case-studies show this to be the case (see also essays in Leary, 1990b), but I doubt that there is much point in other studies attempting to unearth more and more of them for their own sake; the existence of metaphorical discourse in the sciences is hardly a revelation. Without metaphors, meaning cannot be created or extended (see also Ricoeur, 1978) unless one is to engage in a kind of 'private language' (a practice dismissed in Wittgenstein, 1958/1968). So, metaphors are to be expected in scientific texts. However, further work which shows what function certain metaphors perform could strengthen ties between studies of rhetoric and those in the sociology of science. Thus, the analysis of scientific discourse could be used to make wider sociological points about the role of persuasion in a cultural context.

Studies of the rhetoric of science do not yet constitute an area of enquiry of the form enjoyed by, say, the sociology of scientific knowledge (SSK). That is, there does not yet exist a body of published work which could be pointed to as essential reading for the study of scientific rhetoric; there are too many disciplines which could conceivably be relevant, and little by way of previous example. These are early days in a developing area of enquiry. What Gross (1990) does at the beginning of his book is to list the work of other researchers and re-label what they do as the analysis of scientific rhetoric. A similar strategy was employed here in Chapter 2: the alignment of the present study with work in other areas of science studies, the grounding of the present in the work of the past. Nevertheless, during the course of the present project several studies became available which suggest that the analysis of rhetoric deserves consideration (for example Bazerman, 1988; Simons, 1989; Myers, 1990a; Gross, 1990; Pera and Shea, 1991; Bazerman and Paradis, 1991; Andrews, 1992; Bygrave, 1993). Such work does not present a consistent methodological or theoretical approach, nor even a unified site of investigation, and perhaps there is no compelling reason why it should do so. Perhaps, given the very wide variety of texts analysed in the works just cited, there is not yet the scope for the methodological arguments which helped shape SSK. In any case, supposing that the rhetoric of science would benefit from the spatial metaphor of describing it as a 'field', much remains to be done in debating its objects, aims and methods. A closer alliance between rhetoric and literary studies than the one attempted here could be beneficial (see, for example, essays in Christie and Shuttleworth, 1989). Gross (1990: 59ff) develops a comparison between the narrative given in *The Double Helix* and that underlying fairy tales, suggesting that there is some 'psychological force' to which the 'tale of DNA' appeals. This is an interesting reading, and there may be more to be gained from this kind of juxtaposition of texts, of understanding the form of one in terms of another. But I question the need for the psychological theory grounding the reading by Gross (he promotes a few of these); the expectation of a text having a particular form is more likely to be the product of a given context, as Bazerman's (1988) account of the *APA Publication Manual* suggests, than a product of any 'deep need'.

What constructive conclusions or 'results' could come from the analysis of scientific rhetoric? Several answers could be given to justify such work. First, the analysis of rhetoric may reveal aspects of the way authority is constructed and maintained in science (see also Latour, 1987; Myers, 1990a). The upshot of this is to suggest that the reader of a scientific text becomes more critical of the ways in which arguments are constructed, takes less for granted, and is more aware of the work involved in developing a textual construction. To that extent, the analysis of rhetoric is a way of empowering the reader. Second, some conclusion could be drawn concerning the way readers are initiated into a particular scientific culture. As an undergraduate in psychology, I was schooled into having certain expectations about what constituted knowledge in psychology, what sorts of questions were being asked within the discipline, how to write within a particular format, what methodological rules to apply, what statistical forms validated a particular argument and so on. Each of these constitutes an issue for the study of rhetoric: it offers a way of developing an ethnography of reading practices. As a result, the analysis of rhetoric offers a way into understanding the process I described earlier as enrolment. But perhaps more important than the examination of the way novices are initiated into scientific culture is the analysis of the way professional researchers are convinced to pursue a particular avenue of enquiry. What is it that persuades the members of a thought-collective that one particular way of doing things is the way to proceed? There must be particular aspects of the material such people read which decides them on an endeavour; beyond the dissection of formal criteria (see chapters in Bazerman, 1988), there are issues of content, of the way arguments are made persuasive: what is it that makes one 'language-game' seem worthwhile? I tried in Chapter 3 to suggest that the metaphors used to describe a given object were part of this process. The construction of a metaphor which other workers find fruitful in generating further ideas (see also Danziger, 1990) obviously helps in this, by-passing some problems and suggesting ways of continuing an investigation. But other aspects of the style of argument must also be involved and some general forms of persuasion were considered in Chapters 7 and 8. For example, without invoking the 'truth' of a particular claim, how is one to explain the success of psychoanalytic discourse in enrolling new members and colonising other forms of discourse (novels, plays, popularizations of psychology, etc.)? I gave an account of the way Freud's rhetoric enrols the interest of the reader, making it the reader's responsibility to overcome their 'resistances' in accepting the theory, while at the same time suggesting, on the basis of Freud's conception of the mind, that readers cannot understand themselves without recourse to psychoanalytic methods and guidance. By contrast, James could only offer a continuing stream of metaphors, introspective descriptions, and references to physiology in a bid to capture the reader's loyalty – his style of argument seems to lack the elements which may have contributed to the longevity of psychoanalysis.

Methodologically, there are several difficulties in analysing the rhetoric of science. The first is developing some level of mastery of a given technical discourse. This is not just the same problem as it is for a student learning to understand and reproduce a particular discourse. It also involves maintaining the kind of distance which an anthropologist must sustain (before 'going native'; see also Latour and Woolgar, 1986). That is, one of the important aspects of the analysis of rhetoric is the examination of what is taken for granted in a text. When a text uses particular modalisers such as 'of course', what the analyst must do is remain aware of the persuasive act which is being performed, point out the alternative constructions which are being avoided and so on. This entails the reading of a text without becoming enrolled in its discourse, of noting and explaining its persuasive force without losing an ironic distance. This analytical feat is not so easily achieved, and more remains to be done in examining the role and the position of the analyst of scientific discourse (see Woolgar, 1988a). It is, for example, all too easy to be seen as merely engaged in a debunking exercise, criticising an entire area without offering novel solutions (see Myers, 1990a: 247 ff). That is not the effect intended; the aim is not to 'degrade' science by calling attention to its textual construction. (Nor am I suggesting that the rhetoric of science could become a kind of 'master discipline' from which to evaluate the work of any other area.) A problem exists, then, in creating a style of writing in which these possibilities are minimised (a path which leads to any number of reflexive problems, hesitations and celebrations). As with so many studies, this can only lead to a call for further study.

Several points for future research may be raised. (Rhetorically, the object here is to capture the reader's interest in pursing particular questions.) It would be interesting to consider the transformations which occur between technical and popular forms of discourse (see Myers, 1990a): that would involve a discussion of the rhetorical forms which are used to maintain particular conceptions of 'science' or 'psychology', disciplines which, at least in their form of writing, deny their own use of rhetoric. Related to this could be an analysis of allegations of fraud raised against Sir Cyril Burt after his death. Here the object would be to give an account of the way psychological work is characterised, what generalisations are given about a particular area of enquiry, an analysis of any normative claims made about the way psychology should be carried out, and the way such norms are breached. A study of Burt's work which considered debates about the status of his empirical generalisations would augment the account given in Chapter 7 by calling attention to the forms of rhetoric Burt used, and with which he influenced the work of other researchers. Future work could also examine the transformations which occur between research literature and textbook accounts of original work: how is psychological research described to the novice? What sorts of information and explanation are extracted from particular texts? Frequently, students require a kind of rhetorical solidity from the material they read, the provision of answers, methods for securing knowledge, and ways of repeating forms of enquiry. An analysis of rhetoric could provide an account of how such impressions are created and maintained. In fact, the development of a tradition within a discipline relating current work to the past and giving the impression that past work has been extended or superseded – is a broad area to which the analysis of rhetoric could contribute. I made some comments related to this in Chapters 3 and 4 when discussing the way Lashley's work is described by later writers, and by noting the way writers such as Klein or Skinner describe their work as continuing on from a past master while having something new and different to contribute. An examination needs to be made of this rhetorical tension between claims of saying something novel and relating it to a tradition, between the rhetoric of 'progress' and that of defining past achievements.

Finally, an epilogue to the present study. In spending a great deal of time on a particular project, an analyst can become over-enrolled in a form of discourse; the account of a way of reasoning can take hold of the reasoner, and nothing can be seen but a confirmation of expectations. For an argument which has claimed all along that everything contained in it is only rhetoric (in the now hopefully more positive sense of the term), all that remains is to leave judgement of its overall persuasiveness in the hands of the reader.

# Appendix
## 'Proofs that P'
### (attributed to Hartry Field, courtesy of John Bigelow)

*Davidson's proof that p:* Let us make the following bold conjecture: p.

*Wallace's proof that p:* Davidson has made the following bold conjecture: p.

*Grunbaum:* As I have asserted again and again in previous publications, p.

*Morgenbesser:* If not p, what? q maybe?

*Putnam:* Some philosophers have argued that not-p, on the grounds that q. It would be an interesting exercise to count all the fallacies in this 'argument'. (It's really awful, isn't it?) Therefore p.

*Rawls:* It would be nice to have a deductive argument that p from self-evident premises. Unfortunately, I am unable to provide one. So I will have to rest content with the following intuitive considerations in its support: p.

*Unger:* Suppose it were the case that not-p. It would follow from this that someone knows that q. But on my view, no one knows anything whatsoever. Therefore p. (Unger believes that the louder you say this argument, the more persuasive it becomes.)

*Katz:* I have seventeen arguments for the claim that p, and I know of only four for the claim that not-p. Therefore p.

*Lewis:* Most people find the claim that not-p completely obvious and when I assert p they give me an incredulous stare. But the fact that they find not-p obvious is no argument that it is true: and I do not know how to refute an incredulous stare. Therefore p.

*Fodor:* My argument for p is based on three premises:
(1) q
(2) r
and
(3) p

From these, the claim that p deductively follows.
Some people may find the third premise controversial, but it is clear that if we replace that premise by any other reasonable premise, the argument would go through just as well.

*Sellars's proof that p:* Unfortunately, limitations of space prevent it from being included here, but important parts of the proof can be found in each of the articles in the attached bibliography.

*Earman:* There are solutions to the field equations of general relativity in which space-time has the structure of a four-dimensional klein bottle and in which there is no matter. In each such space-time, the claim that not-p is false. Therefore p.

*Goodman:* Zabludowski has insinuated that my thesis that p is false, on the basis of alleged counterexamples. But these so called 'counter-examples' depend on construing my thesis that p in a way that it was obviously not intended – for I intended my thesis to have no counter-examples. Therefore p.

# Bibliography

Adorno, T.W., Frenkel-Brunswik, E., Levinson, D.J. and Sanford, R.N. (1950/1969) *The Authoritarian Personality*. New York: Norton & Company.

Andrews, R. (Ed.) (1992) *Rebirth of Rhetoric: Essays in language, culture and education*. London: Routledge.

Appignanesi, L. and Forrester, J. (1992) *Freud's Women*. London: Weidenfeld & Nicolson.

Arbib, M and Hesse, M. (1986) *The Construction of Reality*. Cambridge: Cambridge University Press.

Ash, M.G. (1982) The Emergence of Gestalt Theory: experimental psychology in Germany, 1890–1920. Unpublished PhD Thesis, Harvard University (University Microfilms Edition).

Ashmore, M. (1989) *The Reflexivity Thesis: Wrighting Sociology of Scientific Knowledge*. Chicago: Chicago University Press.

Ashmore, M., Mulkay, M. and Pinch, T. (1989) *Health and Efficiency: A sociology of health economics*. Milton Keynes: Open University Press.

Austin, J.L. (1956/1979) Performative utterances. In J.O. Urmson and G.J. Warnock (Eds) *Philosophical Papers*, 3rd edn. Oxford: Clarendon Press.

Austin, J.L. (1962/1975) *How to Do Things with Words*. Oxford: Oxford University Press.

Averill, J. (1990) Inners feelings, works of the flesh, the beast within, driving force, and putting on a show: six metaphors of emotion and their theoretical extension. In D.E. Leary (Ed.) *Metaphors in the History of Psychology*. Cambridge: Cambridge University Press.

Averill, J. (1993) Putting the social in social cognition, with special reference to emotion. In R.S. Wyer and T.R. Srull (Eds) *Perspectives on Anger and Emotion. Advances in Social Cognition*, VI. Hillsdale, NJ: Lawrence Earlbaum Associates.

Ayer, A.J. (1936/1946) *Language, Truth and Logic*. Harmondsworth: Penguin.

Baldwin, J.D. and Baldwin, J.I. (1978) Reinforcement theories of exploration, play, creativity, and psychosocial growth. In E.O. Smith (Ed.) *Social Play in Primates*. New York: Academic Press.

Barnes, H.E. (1992) Sartre's ontology: the revealing and making of being. In C. Howells (Ed.) *The Cambridge Companion to Sartre*. Cambridge: Cambridge Univeristy Press.

Bazerman, C. (1988) *Shaping Written Knowledge: The genre and activity of the experimental article in science*. Madison, WI: University of Wisconsin Press.

Bazerman, C. and Paradis, J. (Eds) (1991) *Textual Dynamics of the Professions: Historical and contemporary studies of writing in professional communities*. Madison, WI: University of Wisconsin Press.

Beach, F.A., Hebb, D.O., Morgan, C.T. and Nissen, H.W. (Eds) (1960) *The Neuropsychology of Lashley*. New York: McGraw-Hill.

Beer, G. (1983) *Darwin's Plots: Evolutionary narrative in Darwin, George Eliot and nineteenth-century fiction*. London: Routledge.

Beer, G. (1989) Darwin and the growth of language theory. In J. Christie and S. Shuttleworth (Eds) *Transfiguring Nature: Science and literature, 1700–1900*. Manchester: Manchester University Press.

Beer, G. and Martins, H. (1990) Introduction. *History of the Human Sciences*, 3: 163–175.

Berlin, I. (1980) *Personal Impressions* (Ed. H. Hardy). London: Hogarth Press.

Billig, M. (1987) *Arguing and Thinking: A rhetorical approach to social psychology*. Cambridge: Cambridge University Press.

Billig, M. (1991) *Ideology and Opinions*. London: Sage.

Billig, M., Condor, S., Edwards, D., Gane, M., Middleton, D. and Radley, A. (1988) *Ideological Dilemmas: A social psychology of everyday thinking*. London: Sage.

Black, M. (1962) *Models and Metaphors*. Ithaca: Cornell University Press.

Bloor, D. (1973) Wittgenstein and Mannheim on the sociology of mathematics. *Studies in History and Philosophy of Science*, 4: 173–191.

Bloor, D. (1976) *Knowledge and Social Imagery*. London: Routledge.

Boden, M. (1982) *Piaget*. London: Fontana.

Boring, E.G. (1933/1963) *The Physical Dimensions of Consciousness*. New York: Dover.

Boring, E.G. (1950) *A History of Experimental Psychology*. New York: Appleton Century Crofts.

Boring, E.G. (1963) *History, Psychology, and Science: Selected papers* (Eds R.I. Watson and D.T. Campbell). New York: Wiley & Sons.

Bradley, B. (1989) *Visions of Infancy*. Cambridge: Polity.

Bradley, R. and Swartz, N. (1979) *Possible Worlds: An introduction to logic and its philosophy*. Oxford: Basil Blackwell.

Brand, C. (1979) The quick and the educable. *Bulletin of the British Psychological Society*, *32*: 386–389.

Brazier, M.A.B. (1988) *A History of Neurophysiology in the 19th Century*. New York: Raven Press.

Breland, K. and Breland, M. (1961) The misbehaviour of organisms. *American Psychologist*, *16*: 681–684.

Broad, C.D. (1978) *Kant: An introduction*. Cambridge: Cambridge University Press.

Broadbent, D.E. (1973) *In Defence of Empirical Psychology*. London: Methuen.

Brooks, P. (1988) The idea of psychoanalytic literary criticism. In F. Meltzer (Ed.) *The Trial(s) of Psychoanalysis*. Chicago: Chicago University Press

Brooks, P. (1991) The proffered word. *Times Literary Supplement*, *8*, 8 November: 11–12.

Bruce, D. (1986) Lashley's shift from bacteriology to neuropsychology, 1910–1917, and the influence of Jennings, Watson, and Franz. *Journal of the History of the Behavioural Sciences*, *22*: 27–44.

Bruner, J. (1962/1979) *On Knowing: Essays for the the left hand*, expanded edn. Cambridge, MA: Harvard University Press.

Bruner, J. (1974) *Beyond the Information Given: Studies in the psychology of knowing* (Ed. J.M. Anglin). London: George Allen & Unwin.

Bruner, J. (1983) *In Search of Mind: Essays in autobiography*. Cambridge, MA: Harvard University Press.

Bruner, J. (1986) *Actual Minds, Possible Worlds*. Cambridge, MA: Harvard University Press.

Bruner, J. and Feldman, C.F. (1990) Metaphors of consciousness and cognition in the history of psychology. In D.E. Leary (Ed.) *Metaphors in the History of Psychology*. Cambridge: Cambridge University Press.

Buckley, K.W. (1989) *Mechanical Man: John Broadus Watson and the beginnings of behaviorism*. New York: Guilford Press.

Burke, K. (1941/1973) *The Philosophy of Literary Form: Studies in symbolic action*. Berkeley: University of California Press.

Burt, C. (1912) The inheritance of mental characteristics. *Eugenics Review*, 4: 168–200.

Burt, C. (1923) The mental differences between individuals. *Report of the British Association for the Advancement of Science, 1923* (Presidential address to Section J, Psychology): 215–239.

Burt, C. (1937/1961) *The Backward Child*, 5th edn. London: University of London Press.

Burt, C. (1949) The structure of the mind: a review of the results of factor analysis. *British Journal of Educational Psychology*, *19*: 100–111, 176–199.

Burt, C. (1955) The evidence for the concept of intelligence. *British Journal of Educational Psychology*, *25*: 158–177.

Burt, C. (1969) Intelligence and heredity: some common misconceptions. *Irish Journal of Education*, *2*: 75–94.

Burt, C. and Howard, M. (1956) The multifactorial theory of inheritance and its application to intelligence. *British Journal of Statistical Psychology*, 8: 95–131.

Bygrave, S. (1993) *Kenneth Burke: Rhetoric and ideology*. London: Routledge.

Cairns, R.B. and Ornstein, P.A. (1979) Developmental psychology. In E. Hearst (Ed.) *The First Century of Experimental Psychology*. Hillsdale, NJ: Lawrence Erlbaum.

Callon, M. (1986) Some elements of a sociology of translation: domestication of the scallops and fishermen of St Brieuc Bay. In J. Law (Ed.) *Power, Action and Belief: A new sociology of science?* London: Routledge & Kegan Paul.

Cantor, G. (1989) The rhetoric of experiment. In G. Gooding, T. Pinch and S. Schaffer (Eds) *The Uses of Experiment: Studies in the natural sciences*. Cambridge: Cambridge University Press.

Carroll, L. (1896/1977) *Symbolic Logic* (Ed. W.W. Bartley III). Hassocks, Sussex: Harvester.

Chapman, P.D. (1988) *Schools as Sorters: Lewis M. Terman, applied psychology, and the intelligence testing movement, 1890–1930*. New York: New York University Press.

Christie, J. and Shuttleworth, S. (1989) *Transfiguring Nature: Science and literature, 1700–1900*. Manchester: Manchester University Press.

Churchland, P.S. (1986) *Neurophilosophy: Towards a unified science of the mind-brain*. Cambridge, MA: MIT Press.

Clare, A. (1976/1980) *Psychiatry in Dissent: Controversial issues in thought and practice*. London: Routledge.

Coan, R.W. (1979) *Psychologist: Personal and theoretical pathways*. New York: Irvington Publishers.

Cobb, S. (1960) Introduction: a salute from neurologists. In F.A. Beach, D.O. Hebb, C.T. Morgan and H.W. Nissen (Eds) *The Neuropsychology of Lashley*. New York: McGraw-Hill.

Cohen, D. (1979) *J.B. Watson: The founder of behaviorism*. London: Routledge & Kegan Paul.

Cohen, D. (1983) *Piaget: Critique and reassessment*. London: Croom Helm.

Cohen-Solal, A. (1985) *Sartre: A life*. London: Minerva.

Cole, M. (1975/1977) An ethnographic psychology of cognition. In P.N. Johnson-Laird and P.C. Wason (Eds) *Thinking: Readings in cognitive science*. Cambridge: Cambridge University Press.

Cole, M. and Bruner, J.S. (1971/1974) Cultural differences and inferences about psychological processes. In J.S. Bruner *Beyond the Information Given: Studies in the psychology of knowing*. London: Allen & Unwin.

Collins, H.M. (1985) *Changing Order: Replication and induction in scientific practice*. London: Sage.

Conway, D.W. (1991) Thus spoke Rorty: the perils of narrative self-creation. *Philosophy and Literature*, 15: 103–110.

Conway, J. (1958) The inheritance of intelligence and its social implications. *British Journal of Statistical Psychology*, 11: 171–190.

Cooper, D.E. (1986) *Metaphor*. Oxford: Basil Blackwell.

Cooper, D.E. (1990) *Existentialism*. Oxford: Basil Blackwell.

Corbin, A. (1982/1986) *The Foul and the Fragrant: Odor and the French social imagination*. Leamington Spa: Berg.

Costall, A. (1985) Specious origins? Darwinism and developmental theory. In G. Butterworth, J. Rutkowska and M. Scaife (Eds) *Evolution and Developmental Psychology*. Brighton: Harvester Press.

Costall, A. (1991) Are 'stage theories' of depiction really stage theories? In P.J. Beek, R.J. Bootsma and P.C.W. van Wieringen (Eds) *Studies in perception and action: Posters presented at the VIth International Conference on Event Perception and Action*. Amsterdam: Rodopi. (pp. 12–14).

Crick, B. (1980/1992) *George Orwell: A life*. Harmondsworth: Penguin.

Danziger, K. (1990) Generative metaphor and the history of psychological discourse. In D.E.

Leary (Ed.) *Metaphors in the History of Psychology*. Cambridge: Cambridge University Press.

Danziger, K. (1991) Editorial introduction (to special issue on 'new developments in the history of psychology'). *History of the Human Sciences*, *4*: 327–333.

Darwin, C. (1859/1968) *The Origin of the Species by Means of Natural Selection*, 1st edn. Harmondsworth: Penguin.

Darwin, C. (1872/1890) *The Expression of the Emotions in Man and Animals*, 2nd edn. London: John Murray.

Day, W.F. (1969) Radical behaviourism in reconciliation with phenomenology. *Journal of the Experimental Analysis of Behaviour*, *12*: 315–328.

Dear, P. (1985) *Totius in verba*: rhetoric and authority in the early Royal Society. *Isis*, *76*: 145–161.

De Beauvoir, S. (1981/1984) *Adieux: A farewell to Sartre*. London: Andre Deutsch.

Defoe, D. (1719/1965) *Robinson Crusoe*. Harmondsworth: Penguin.

De Man, P. (1978) The epistemology of metaphor. *Critical Enquiry*, *5*: 13–30.

Dennett, D. (1979) *Brainstorms: Philosophical essays on mind and psychology*. Hassocks, Sussex: Harvester Press.

Derrida, J. (1967/1976) *Of Grammatology* (Trans. G.C. Spivak). Baltimore: Johns Hopkins University Press.

Derrida, J. (1972/1982) White mythology: metaphor in the text of philosophy. In J. Derrida *Margins of Philosophy* (Trans. A. Bass). Hemel Hempstead: Harvester-Wheatsheaf.

Derrida, J. (1978/1979) *Spurs: Nietzsche's styles* (Trans. B. Harlow). Chicago: Chicago University Press.

Derrida, J. (1983) The Time of a Thesis: Punctuations. In A. Montefiore (Ed.) *Philosophy in France Today* (Trans. K. McLaughlin). Cambridge: Cambridge University Press.

Desmond, A. and Moore, J. (1991) *Darwin*. Harmondsworth: Penguin.

Doty, R.W. (1982) Lashley as iconoclast in the temple of neuroscience: some thrusts he would have enjoyed today. In J. Orbach (Ed.) *Neuropsychology after Lashley: Fifty years since the publication of 'Brain Mechanisms and Intelligence'*. Hillsdale, NJ: Lawrence Erlbaum.

Douglas, M. (1975) *Implicit Meanings: Essays in anthropology*. London: Routledge.

Dunlap, K. (Ed.) (1922/1967) *The Emotions*. New York: Hafner.

Durant, J. (1991a) Review of Alan Gross, 'The Rhetoric of Science'. *Times Literary Supplement, no. 4589*, 15 March.

Durant, J. (1991b) Letter to the editor. *Times Literary Supplement, no. 4595*, 26 April.

Eacker, J.N. (1983) *Problems of Metaphysics and Psychology*. Chicago: Nelson-Hall.

Eaton, J. and Soyland, A.J. (1994) Lacan and the rhetoric of the master. Paper presented to the Science/Text/Discourse Seminar, Lancaster University.

Eco, U. (1979/1981) *The Role of the Reader: Explorations in the semiotics of texts*. London: Hutchinson.

Ellis, A.W. and Young, A.W. (1988) *Human Cognitive Neuropsychology*. London: Lawrence Erlbaum Associates.

Emerson, R.W. (1881) *The Works of Ralf Waldo Emerson, Volume 1*. London: George Bell & Sons.

Enos, R.L. (1991) Socrates questions Gorgias: the rhetorical vector of Plato's 'Gorgias'. *Argumentation*, *5*: 5–15.

Euler, L. (1956) The seven bridges of Koenigsberg. In J.R. Newman (Ed.) *The World of Mathematics*. New York: Simon & Schuster.

Eysenck, H.J. (1982) *Personality, Genetics and Behaviour: Selected papers*. New York: Praeger.

Eysenck, H.J. (1985) *Decline and Fall of the Freudian Empire*. New York: Penguin Viking.

Eysenck, H.J. versus Kamin, L. (1981) *Intelligence: The battle for the mind*. London: Macmillan Press and Pan Books.

Feyerabend, P. (1984) The lessing effect in the philosophy of science: comments on some of my critics. *New Ideas in Psychology*, *2*: 127–136.

Finocchiaro, M.A. (1990) Varieties of rhetoric in science. *History of the Human Sciences*, *3*: 177–193.

Fish, S. (1988) Withholding the missing portion: psychology and rhetoric. In F. Meltzer (Ed.) *The Trial(s) of Psychoanalysis*. Chicago: Chicago University Press.

Flew, A. (Ed.) (1979) *Dictionary of Philosophy*. London: Pan Books.

Fodor, J.A. (1983) *Modularity of Mind*. Cambridge, MA: MIT Press.

Forrester, J. (1980) *Language and the Origins of Psychoanalysis*. London: Macmillan.

Forrester, J. (1990a) *The Seductions of Psychoanalysis: Freud, Lacan and Derrida*. Cambridge: Cambridge University Press.

Forrester, J. (1990b) The notion of a scientific discipline. Paper presented to the Intellectual History Group Seminar, King's College, Cambridge.

Foucault, M. (1954/1976) *Mental Illness and Psychology* (Trans. A. Sheridan). New York: Harper & Row.

Foucault, M. (1961/1971) *Madness and Civilization: A history of insanity in the age of reason* (Trans. R. Howard). London: Tavistock Publications.

Foucault, M. (1975/1977) *Discipline and Punish: The birth of the prison* (Trans. A. Sheridan). Harmondsworth: Penguin.

Franz, S.I. (1912) The new phrenology. *Science*, *35*: 321–328.

Franz, S.I. (1932) Autobiography. *A History of Psychology in Autobiography*, *2*: 89–133.

Freud, S. (1905/1953) Three Essays on the Theory of Sexuality. In J. Strachey (Ed.) *The Standard Edition of the Complete Psychological Works of Sigmund Freud, Volume VII (1901–1905)*. London: Hogarth Press.

Freud, S. (1911/1970) Letter to Else Voigtlander. In E.L. Freud (Ed.) *Letters of Sigmund Freud, 1873–1939*. London: Hogarth Press.

Freud, S. (1916–1917/1963) Introductory lectures on psychoanalysis. In J. Strachey (Ed.) *The Standard Edition of the Complete Psychological Works of Sigmund Freud, Volume XV (1915–1916) and XVI (1916–1917)*. London: Hogarth Press.

Freud, S. (1917/1955) A difficulty in the path of psycho-analysis. In J. Strachey (Ed.) *The Standard Edition of the Complete Psychological Works of Sigmund Freud, Volume XVII (1917–1919)*. London: Hogarth Press.

Freud, S. (1925/1959) An autobiographical study. In J. Strachey (Ed.) *The Standard Edition of the Complete Psychological Works of Sigmund Freud, Volume XX (1925–1926)*. London: Hogarth Press.

Freud, S. (1930/1961) Civilization and its Discontents. In J. Strachey (Ed.) *The Standard Edition of the Complete Psychological Works of Sigmund Freud, Volume XXI (1927–1931)*. London: Hogarth Press.

Fromm, E. (1942/1960) *The Fear of Freedom*. London: Routledge & Kegan Paul.

Frosh, S. (1989) *Psychoanalysis and Psychology: Minding the gap*. London: Macmillan.

Fuller, S. (1991) Disciplinary boundaries and the rhetoric of the social sciences. *Poetics Today*, *12*: 301–325.

Galton, F. (1869) *Hereditary Genius: An enquiry into its laws and consequences*. London: Macmillan.

Gellner, E. (1982/1985) The scientific status of the social sciences (*und leider auch Sociologie*). In *Relativism and the Social Sciences*. Cambridge: Cambridge University Press.

Gellner, E. (1985) *The Psychoanalytic Movement*. London: Paladin.

Gephart, R.T. (1988) *Ethnostatistics*. London: Sage.

Gergen, K.J., Hepburn, A. and Fisher, D.C. (1986) Hermeneutics of personality description. *Journal of Personality and Social Psychology*, *50*: 1261–1270.

Gieryn, T.F. and Figert, A.E. (1986) Scientists protect their cognitive authority: the status degradation ceremony of Sir Cyril Burt. In G. Bohme and N. Stehr (Eds) *The Knowledge Society: The growing impact of scientific knowledge on social relations*. Dordrecht: D. Reidel Publishing.

Gieryn, T.F. and Figert, A.E. (1990) Ingredients for a theory of science in society: O-rings, ice water, C-clamp, Richard Feynman and the Press. In S.E. Cozzens and T.F. Gieryn (Eds) *Theories of Science in Society*. Bloomington: Indiana University Press.

Gigerenzer, G. and Murray, D.J. (1987) *Cognition as Intuitive Statistics*. Hillsdale, NJ: Erlbaum.

Gilbert, N. and Mulkay, M. (1984) *Opening Pandora's Box: A sociological analysis of scientists' discourse*. Cambridge: Cambridge University Press.

Giorgi, A. (1975) Convergences and divergences between phenomenological psychology and behaviorism. *Behaviorism, 3*: 200–212.

Gould, S.J. (1977) *Ontogeny and Phylogeny*. Cambridge, MA: Harvard University Press.

Grayling, A.C. (1982) *An Introduction to the Philosophy of Logic*. Hassocks, Sussex: Harvester.

Gross, A.G. (1990) *The Rhetoric of Science*. Cambridge, MA: Harvard University Press.

Gross, A.G. (1991) Letter to the editor. *Times Literary Supplement, no. 4594*, 19 April.

Haack, S. (1978) *Philosophy of Logics*. Cambridge: Cambridge University Press.

Harré, R. (1986) Social sources of mental content and order. In J. Margolis, P.T. Manicas, R. Harré and P.F. Secord *Psychology: Designing the discipline*. Oxford: Blackwell.

Harrington, A. (1987) *Medicine, Mind, and the Double Brain: A study in nineteenth-century thought*. Princeton: Princeton University Press.

Harwood, J. (1977) Heredity, environment, and the legitimation of social policy. In B. Barnes and S. Shapin (Eds) *Natural Order: Historical studies of scientific culture*. London: Sage.

Hatfield, G. (1988) Neuro-philosophy meets psychology: reduction, autonomy, and physiological constraints. *Cognitive Neuropsychology, 5*: 723–746.

Hearnshaw, L.S. (1979) *Cyril Burt: Psychologist*. London: Hodder & Stoughton.

Heatherington, E.M. and Parke, R.D. (1986) *Child Psychology: A contemporary viewpoint*. New York: McGraw-Hill.

Hebb, D.O. (1949) *The Organization of Behavior: A neuropsychological theory*. New York: John Wiley & Sons.

Heidegger, M. (1936/1949) Hölderlin and the essence of poetry (Trans. D. Scott). In M. Heidegger *Existence and Being*. London: Vision Press.

Heidegger, M. (1949 [no original publication date given]) On the essence of truth (Trans. R.F.C. Hull and A. Crick). In M. Heidegger *Existence and Being*. London: Vision Press.

Heidegger, M. (1961/1991) *Nietzsche, Volume I: The will to power as art*. New York: Harper Collins.

Henle, M. (1962/1968) On the relation between logic and thinking. In P.C. Wason and P.N. Johnson-Laird (Eds) *Thinking and Reasoning: Selected readings*. Harmondsworth: Penguin.

Hesse, M. (1974) *The Structure of Scientific Inference*. London: Macmillan.

Hesse, M. (1980) *Revolutions and Reconstructions in the Philosophy of Science*. Bloomington: Indiana University Press.

Hillner, K.P. (1985) *Psychological Reality: Advances in psychology, 26*. Amsterdam: North-Holland.

Hirschon, T. (1991) Letter to the editor. *Times Literary Supplement, no. 4593*, 12 April.

Hoffman, R.R., Cochran, E.L. and Nead, J.M. (1990) Cognitive metaphors in experimental psychology. In D.E. Leary (Ed.) *Metaphors in the History of Psychology*. Cambridge: Cambridge University Press.

Holton, G. (1981) Thematic presuppostions and the direction of scientific advance. In A.F. Heath (Ed.) *Scientific Explanations*. Oxford: Clarendon Press.

Holub, R.C. (1984) *Reception Theory: A critical introduction*. London: Methuen.

Howe, M. (1990) Does intelligence exist? *The Psychologist, 3*: 490–493.

Howells, C. (Ed.) (1992) *The Cambridge Companion to Sartre*. Cambridge: Cambridge University Press.

Hughes, J.M. (1989) *Reshaping the Psychoanalytic Domain: The works of Melanie Klein, W.R.D. Fairbairn, and D.W. Winnicott*. Berkeley: University of California Press.

Hume, D. (1739/1962) *A Treatise of Human Nature: Book 1*. London: Fontana.

Hume, D. (1739/1972) *A Treatise of Human Nature: Books 2 and 3*. London: Fontana.

Hume, D. (1779/1948) *Dialogues Concerning Natural Religion*. New York: Hafner Press.

Inhelder, B. and Piaget, J (1958) *The Growth of Logical Thinking: From childhood to adolescence* (Trans. A. Parsons and S. Milgram). London: Routledge & Kegan Paul.

Ivamy, E.R.H. (1988) *Mozley and Whiteley's Law Dictionary*, 10th edn. London: Butterworths.

James, W. (1884) What is an emotion? *Mind*, *9*: 188–205.

James, W. (1890/1950) *Principles of Psychology: Volumes 1 & 2*. New York: Dover.

James, W. (1899/1920) *Talks to Teachers on Psychology: And to students on some of life's ideals*. London: Longmans, Green & Co.

James, W. (1907/1978) *Pragmatism and the Meaning of Truth*. Harvard: Harvard University Press.

Jardine, N. (1991) Demonstration, dialectic and rhetoric in Galileo's Dialogue. In D.R. Kelley and R.H. Popkin (Eds) *The Shapes of Knowledge from the Renaissance to the Enlightenment*. Dordrecht: Kluwer.

Jensen, A.R. (1969) How much can we boost IQ and scholastic achievement? *Harvard Educational Review*, *39*: 1–123.

Jones, E. (1953) *Sigmund Freud, Life and Work: Volume I, the young Freud, 1856–1900*. London: Hogarth Press.

Jones, E. (1955) *Sigmund Freud, Life and Work: Volume II, years of maturity, 1901–1919*. London: Hogarth Press.

Jones, E. (1957) *Sigmund Freud, Life and Work: Volume III, the last phase, 1919–1939*. London: Hogarth Press.

Jordanova, L. (1989) *Sexual Visions: Images of gender in science and medicine between the eighteenth and twentieth centuries*. Hemel Hempstead: Harvester-Wheatsheaf.

Joynson, R.B. (1989) *The Cyril Burt Affair*. London: Routledge.

Jung, C.G. (1921/1971) *Psychological Types*. Princeton, NJ: Princeton University Press.

Kahlbargh, P.A. (1993) James Mark Baldwin: a bridge between social and cognitive theories of development. *Journal for the Theory of Social Behaviour*, *23*: 79–103.

Kamin, L.J. (1974) *The Science and Politics of IQ*. Maryland: Erlbaum.

Kaufmann, W. (1974) *Nietzsche: Philosopher, psychologist, antichrist*, 4th edn. Princeton: Princeton University Press.

Keller, E.F. (1991) Fractured images of science, language and power: a postmodern optic or just bad eyesight? *Poetics Today*, *12*: 227–243.

Kelley, T.L. (1928/1967) The boundaries of mental life. In S. Wiseman (Ed.) *Intelligence and Ability: Selected readings*. Harmondsworth: Penguin.

Kellogg, W.N. and Kellogg, L.A. (1933) *The Ape and the Child: A study of environmental influence upon early behaviour*. New York: McGraw-Hill.

Kendall, G. and Soyland, A.J. (1993) Abusing Foucault: methodology, critique and subversion. Unpublished manuscript, Lancaster University (under review).

Kerr, J. (1993) *A Most Dangerous Method: The story of Jung, Freud and Sabina Spielrein*. New York: Knopf.

Kevles, D.J. (1985) *In the Name of Eugenics: Genetics and the uses of human heredity*. Harmondsworth: Penguin.

Kierkegaard, S. (1841/1989) *The Concept of Irony: With continual reference to Socrates*. Princeton, NJ: Princeton University Press.

Kimble, G. (1984) Psychology's two cultures. *American Psychologist*, *39*: 833–839.

Kimmel, A.J. (1991) Predictable biases in the ethical decision making of American psychologists. *American Psychologist*, *46*: 786–788.

Klein, M. (1935/1975) A contribution to the psychogenesis of manic-depressive states. In *Love, Guilt and Reparation, and other works, 1921–1945*. London: Hogarth Press.

Klein, M. (1940/1975) Mourning and its relation to manic-depressive states. In *Love, Guilt and Reparation, and other works, 1921–1945*. London: Hogarth Press and the Institute of Psycho-Analysis.

Klein, M. (1946/1975) Notes on some schizoid mechanisms. In *Envy and Gratitude and Other Works, 1946–1963*. London: Hogarth Press and the Institute of Psycho-Analysis.

Klein, M. (1952a/1975) The origins of transference. In *Envy and Gratitude and Other Works, 1946–1963*. London: Hogarth Press and the Institute of Psycho-Analysis.

Klein, M. (1952b/1975) On observing the behaviour of young infants. In *Envy and Gratitude and Other Works, 1946–1963*. London: Hogarth Press and the Institute of Psycho-Analysis.

Klein, M. (1956/1986) A study of envy and gratitude. In J. Mitchell (Ed.) *The Selected Melanie Klein*. Harmondsworth: Penguin.

Kneale, W. and Kneale, M. (1962/1984) *The Development of Logic*, 2nd edn. Oxford: Clarendon Press.

Koch, S. (1981) The nature and limits of psychological knowledge: lessons of a century qua 'science'. *American Psychologist*, 36: 257–269.

Koch, S. and Leary, D.E. (1985) *A Century of Psychology as Science*. New York: McGraw-Hill.

Kolenda, K. (1991) Misreading Rorty. *Philosophy and Literature*, 15: 111–117.

Kozulin, A. (1986) Vygotsky in context: introduction. In L.S. Vygotsky *Thought and Language*. Cambridge, MA: MIT Press.

Kuhn, T.S. (1962/1970) *The Structure of Scientific Revolutions*, 2nd edn. Chicago: Chicago University Press.

Kvale, S. and Grenness, C.E. (1967) Skinner and Sartre: towards a radical phenomenology of behavior? *Review of Existential Psychology and Psychiatry*, 7: 128–150.

Lacan, J. (1975/1988) *The Seminar of Jacques Lacan, Book I: Freud's papers on technique, 1953–1954*. (Ed. J-.A. Miller; Trans. J. Forrester). Cambridge: Cambridge University Press.

Laing, R.D. (1960/1965) *The Divided Self: An existential study in sanity and madness*. Harmondsworth: Penguin.

Lange, C.G. (1885/1967) The emotions. (Facsimile of the 1922 edn. Trans. I.A. Haupt) In K. Dunlap (Ed.) *The Emotions*. New York: Hafner.

Lashley, K.S. (1929/1963) *Brain Mechanisms and Intelligence: A quantitative study of injuries to the brain*. New York: Dover.

Lashley, K.S. (1950/1960) In search of the engram. In F.A. Beach, D.O. Hebb, C.T. Morgan and H.W. Nissen (Eds) *The Neuropsychology of Lashley*. New York: McGraw-Hill.

Lashley, K., Chow, K. and Semmes, J. (1951) An examination of the electrical field theory of cerebral integration. *Psychological Review*, 58: 123–136.

Latour, B. (1987) *Science in Action: How to follow scientists and engineers through society*. Milton Keynes: Open University Press.

Latour, B. (1988) The politics of explanation: an alternative. In S. Woolgar (Ed.) *Knowledge and Reflexivity: New frontiers in the sociology of knowledge*. London: Sage.

Latour, B. and Woolgar, S. (1986) *Laboratory Life: The construction of scientific facts*, 2nd edn. Princeton: Princeton University Press.

Laudan, L. (1977) *Progress and its Problems*. Berkeley: University of California Press.

Lawrence, C. and Shapin, S. (1991) Letter to the editor. *Times Literary Supplement, no. 4594*, 19 April.

Lazarus, R.S. (1991) Progress on a cognitive-motivational-relational theory of emotion. *American Psychologist*, 46: 819–834.

Leach, E. (1976) *Culture and Communication: The logic by which symbols are connected*. Cambridge: Cambridge University Press.

Leary, D.E. (1987) Telling likely stories: the rhetoric of the new psychology, 1880–1920. *Journal of the History of the Behavioural Sciences*, 23: 315–331.

Leary, D.E. (1990a) Psyche's muse: the role of metaphor in the history of psychology. In D.E. Leary (Ed.) *Metaphors in the History of Psychology*. Cambridge: Cambridge University Press.

Leary, D.E. (Ed.) (1990b) *Metaphors in the History of Psychology*. Cambridge: Cambridge University Press.

Leary, D.E. (1992) William James and the art of human understanding. *American Psychologist*, 47: 152–160.

Le Clair, R.C. (Ed.) (1966) *The Letters of William James and Theodore Flournoy*. Madison: University of Wisconsin Press.

Lévi-Strauss, C. (1958/1967) *Structural Anthropology*. New York: Anchor.

Lewontin, R.C. (1991) *Biology as Ideology: The doctrine of DNA*. New York: HarperCollins.

Lorenz, K. (1963/1966) *On Aggression* (Trans. M. Latzke). London: Methuen.

Luria, A.R. (1973/1984) *The Working Brain: An introduction to neuropsychology*. Harmondsworth: Penguin.

Lutz, C.A. and Abu-Lughod, L. (Eds) (1990) *Language and the Politics of Emotion*. Cambridge: Cambridge University Press.

Lynch, M. (1985) *Art and Artifact in Laboratory Science: A study of shop work and shop talk in a research laboratory*. London: Routledge.

MacKenzie, D. (1978) Statistical theory and social interests: a case study. *Social Studies of Science*, *8*: 35–83.

Manicas, P.T. (1987) *A History and Philosophy of the Social Sciences*. Oxford: Basil Blackwell.

McCloskey, D.N. (1990) Reply to Munz. *Journal of the History of Ideas*, *51*: 143–147.

McDowell, J.J. (1975) Behavior modification's existential point of departure. *Behaviorism*, *3*: 214–220.

McGovern, T.V., Furumoto, L., Halpern, D.F., Kimble, G.A. and McKeachie, W.J. (1991) Liberal education, study in depth, and the arts and sciences major – psychology. *American Psychologist*, *46*: 598–605.

McReynolds, P. (1990) Motives and metaphors: a study of scientific creativity. In D.E. Leary (Ed.) *Metaphors in the History of Psychology*. Cambridge: Cambridge University Press.

Mead, M. (1928/1943) *Coming of Age in Samoa: A study of adolescence and sex in primitive societies*. Harmondsworth: Penguin.

Meltzer, F. (1988) *The Trial(s) of Psychoanalysis*. Chicago: Chicago University Press.

Melville, H. (1851) *Moby-Dick, or The Whale*. London: Oxford University Press.

Merleau-Ponty, M. (1960/1964) The child's relations with others (Trans. W. Cobb). In M. Merleau-Ponty *The Primacy of Perception*. Evanston: Northwestern University Press.

Merton, R.K. (1965) *On the Shoulders of Giants: A Shandean postscript*. New York: Free Press.

Merton, R.K. (1973) *The Sociology of Science: Theoretical and empirical investigations*. Chicago: University of Chicago Press.

Meyer, M. (1985/1987) *Strindberg: A biography*. Oxford: Oxford University Press.

Miller, G.A. (1962/1966) *Psychology: The science of mental life*. Harmondsworth: Penguin.

Mitchell, J. (Ed.) (1986) *The Selected Melanie Klein*. Harmondsworth: Penguin.

Mitroff, I. (1974) *The Subjective Side of Science: A philosophical inquiry into the psychology of the Apollo moon scientists*. Amsterdam: Elsevier Scientific Publishing.

Mulkay, M. (1985) *The Word and The World: Explorations in the form of sociological analysis*. London: Allen & Unwin.

Murphy, G., Murphy, L.B. and Newcomb, T.M. (1931/1937) *Experimental Social Psychology: An interpretation of research upon the socialization of the individual*, revised edn. New York: Harper & Brothers.

Myers, G. (1988) Every picture tells a story: illustrations in E.O. Wilson's 'Sociobiology'. *Human Studies*, *11*: 235–269.

Myers, G. (1990a) *Writing Biology: Texts in the social construction of scientific knowledge*. Madison: Wisconsin University Press.

Myers, G. (1990b) The rhetoric of irony in academic writing. *Written Communication*, *7*: 419–455.

Myers, G. (1991a) Politeness and certainty: The language of collaboration in an AI project. *Social Studies of Science*, *21*: 27–73.

Myers, G. (1991b) Scientific speculation and literary style in a molecular genetics article. *Science in Context*, *4*: 321–346.

Myers, G. (1992) History and philosophy of science seminar, 4:00 Wednesday, Seminar room

2, 'Fictions for facts: the form and authority of the scientific dialogue'. *History of Science*, *30*: 221–247.

Napoli, D.S. (1981) *Architects of Adjustment: The history of the psychological profession in the United States*. Port Washington, NY: Kennikat Press.

Nehamas, A. (1982) Can we ever quite change the subject? Richard Rorty on science, literature, culture, and the future of philosophy. *Boundary 2, 10*: 395–413.

Nehamas, A. (1985) *Nietzsche: Life as literature*. Cambridge, MA: Harvard University Press.

Nelson, J.S., Magill, A. and McCloskey, D.N. (Eds) (1987) *The Rhetoric of the Human Sciences: Language and argument in scholarship and public affairs*. Madison: Wisconsin University Press.

Nettelbeck, T. (1990) Intelligence does exist. *The Psychologist, 3*: 494–497.

Nietzsche, F. (1873/1979) On the truth and lies in a nonmoral sense. In D. Breazeale (Ed.) *Philosophy and Truth: Selections from Nietzsche's notebooks of the early 1870s*. London: Humanities Press International.

Nietzsche, F. (1874/1983) On the uses and disadvantages of history for life. In F. Nietzsche *Untimely Meditations* (Trans. R.J. Hollingdale). Cambridge: Cambridge University Press.

Nietzsche, F. (1878/1986) *Human, All Too Human: A book for free spirits* (Trans. R.J. Hollingdale). Cambridge: Cambridge University Press.

Nietzsche, F. (1879/1986) *Assorted Opinions and Maxims*. In Nietzsche, F. (1878/1986) *Human, All Too Human: A book for free spirits* (Trans. R.J. Hollingdale). Cambridge: Cambridge University Press.

Nietzsche, F. (1881/1982) *Daybreak: Thoughts on the prejudices of morality* (Trans. R.J. Hollingdale). Cambridge: Cambridge University Press.

Nietzsche, F. (1886/1966) *Beyond Good and Evil* (Trans. W. Kaufmann). New York: Vintage.

Nietzsche, F. (1887/1969) *On the Genealogy of Morals*. (Trans. W. Kaufmann). New York: Vintage.

Nietzsche, F. (1887/1974) *The Gay Science* (Trans. W. Kaufmann). New York: Vintage.

Oatley, K. (1985) Representations of the physical and social world. In D.A. Oakley (Ed.) *Brain and Mind*. London: Methuen.

O'Connor, W.J. (1988) *Founders of British Physiology: A biographical dictionary, 1820–1885*. Manchester: Manchester University Press.

O'Donnell, J.M. (1979) The origins of behaviorism: American psychology, 1870–1920. Unpublished PhD Thesis, University of Pennsylvania. (University Microfilms International edition.)

Orbach, J. (1982) *Neuropsychology after Lashley: Fifty years since the publication of 'Brain Mechanisms and Intelligence'*. Hillsdale, NJ: Lawrence Erlbaum.

Papineau, D. (1978) *For Science in the Social Sciences*. London: Macmillan.

Papineau, D. (1988) Does the sociology of science discredit science? In R. Nola (Ed.) *Relativism and Realism in Science*. Dordrecht: Kluwer.

Pepper, S.C. (1942) *World Hypotheses: A study in evidence*. Berkeley, CA: University of California Press.

Pera, M. and Shea, W.R. (Eds) (1991) *Persuading Science: The art of scientific rhetoric*. Canton, MA: Science History Publications.

Peters, D.P. and Ceci, S.J. (1982) Peer-review practices of psychological journals: the fate of published articles, submitted again. *The Behavioural and Brain Sciences, 5*: 187–255.

Peters, J.D. and Rothenbuhler, E.W. (1989) The reality of construction. In H.W. Simons (Ed.) *Rhetoric in the Human Sciences*. London: Sage.

Phillips, M. (1992) Artificial intelligence – commentary. *The Guardian*, 28 February.

Piaget, J. (1926/1959) *The Language and Thought of the Child*, 3rd edn. (Trans. M. Gabain). London: Routledge & Kegan Paul.

Piaget, J. and Inhelder, B. (1975) *The Origin of the Idea of Chance in Children*. (Originally published, 1951, Trans. L. Leake, P. Burrell and H.D. Fishbein). London: Routledge & Kegan Paul.

Pinter, H. (1965/1978) *The Homecoming*. London: Methuen.

Plato (1956) *Protagoras and Meno* (Trans. W.K.C. Guthrie). Harmondsworth: Penguin.

Plato (1974) *The Republic*, 2nd edn. (Trans. D. Lee). Harmondsworth: Penguin.

Popper, K. (1972/1979) *Objective Knowledge: An evolutionary approach*, revised edn. Oxford: Clarendon Press.

Potter, J. (1988a) What is reflexive about discourse analysis? The case of reading readings. In S. Woolgar (Ed.) *Knowledge and Reflexivity: New frontiers in the sociology of knowledge*. London: Sage.

Potter, J. (1988b) Cutting cakes: a study of psychologists' social catagorizations. *Philosophical Psychology*, 1: 19–33.

Potter, J., Stringer, P. and Wetherell, M. (1984) *Social Texts and Contexts: Literature and social psychology*. London: Routledge.

Potter, J. and Wetherell, M. (1987) *Discourse and Social Psychology: Beyond attitudes and behaviour*. London: Sage.

Pratt, V. (1978) *The Philosophy of the Social Sciences*. London: Methuen.

Pribram, K. (1969) The neuropsychology of remembering. *Scientific American*, 220: 73–86.

Pribram, K. (1982) Localization and distribution in the brain. In J. Orbach (Ed.) *Neuropsychology after Lashley: Fifty years since the publication of 'Brain Mechanisms and Intelligence'*. Hillsdale, NJ: Lawrence Erlbaum.

Pribram, K. (1990) From metaphors to models: the use of analogy in neuropsychology. In D.E. Leary (Ed.) *Metaphors in the History of Psychology*. Cambridge: Cambridge University Press.

Priest, G. (1987) *In Contradiction: A study of the transconsistent*. Dordrecht: Nijhoff.

Quine, W.V.O. (1991) Two dogmas in retrospect. *Canadian Journal of Philosophy*, 21: 265–274.

Ramsey, F.P. (1925/1990) Epilogue. In D.H. Mellor (Ed.) *Philosophical Papers*. Cambridge: Cambridge University Press.

Reber, A.S. (1985) *The Penguin Dictionary of Psychology*. Harmondsworth: Penguin.

Ree, J. (1987) *Philosophical Tales*. London: Methuen.				.

Ree, J. (1988) History, philosophy and interpretation: some reactions to Jonathan Bennett's study of Spinoza's 'Ethics'. In P.H. Hare (Ed.) *Doing Philosophy Historically*. Buffalo, NY: Prometheus Books.

Renner, M.J. and Rosenzweig, M.R. (1986) Object interactions in juvenile rats (*rattus norvegicus*): Effects of different experiential histories. *Journal of Comparative Psychology*, 100: 229–236.

Ribot, T.H. (1897) *The Psychology of the Emotions*. London: Walter Scott, Ltd.

Richards, G. (1989) *On Psychological Language and the Physiomorphic Basis of Human Nature*. London: Routledge.

Richards, G. (1991) James and Freud: two masters of metaphor. *British Journal of Psychology*, 82: 205–215.

Richards, M. and Light, P. (1986) *Children of Social Worlds*. Cambridge: Polity Press.

Ricoeur, P. (1971) The model of the text: meaningful action considered as a text. *Social Research*, 38: 529–562.

Ricoeur, P. (1978) *The Rule of Metaphor: Multi-disciplinary studies of the creation of meaning in language* (Trans. R. Czerny). London: Routledge.

Riese, W. (1959) *A History of Neurology*. New York: MD Publications.

Roberts, J. (1988) *German Philosophy: An introduction*. Cambridge: Polity Press.

Rorty, R. (1980) *Philosophy and the Mirror of Nature*. Oxford: Basil Blackwell.

Rorty, R. (1982) Philosophy as a kind of writing. In R. Rorty *Consequences of Pragmatism: Essays: 1972–1980*. Minneapolis: University of Minnesota Press.

Rorty, R. (1989) *Contingency, Irony and Solidarity*. Cambridge: Cambridge University Press.

Rorty, R. (1991a) *Objectivity, Relativism and Truth: Philosophical papers, volume 1*. Cambridge: Cambridge University Press.

Rorty, R. (1991b) *Essays on Heidegger and Others: Philosophical papers, volume 2*. Cambridge: Cambridge University Press.

Rose, N. (1985) *The Psychological Complex: Psychology, politics and society in England 1869–1939*. London: Routledge & Kegan Paul.

Rose, N. (1990) *Governing the Soul: The shaping of the private self*. London: Routledge.

Rumelhart, D.E. and McClelland, J.L. (1986) *Parallel Distributed Processing, Volume 1*. Cambridge, MA: MIT Press.

Russell, B. (1917/1986) *Mysticism and Logic*. London: Allen & Unwin.

Russell, B. (1948/1961) *History of Western Philosophy*, 2nd edn. London: Allen & Unwin.

Russell, J. (Ed.) (1988) *Philosophical Perspectives on Developmental Psychology*. Oxford: Clarendon Press.

Ryle, G. (1949/1973) *The Concept of Mind*. Harmondsworth: Penguin.

Sampson, E.E. (1977) Psychology and the American ideal. *Journal of Personality and Social Psychology*, *35*: 767–782.

Sampson, E.E. (1991) The democratization of psychology. *Theory and Psychology*, *1*: 275–298.

Sampson, E.E. (1993) *Celebrating the Other: A dialogic account of human nature*. Hemel Hempstead: Harvester Wheatsheaf.

Sarbin, T.R. (1990) Metaphors of unwanted conduct: a historical sketch. In D.E. Leary (Ed.) *Metaphors in the History of Psychology*. Cambridge: Cambridge University Press.

Sartre, J.-P. (1939/1990) The emotions: outline of a theory. In J.-P. Sartre *Essays in Existentialism*. New York: Citadel Press.

Sartre, J.-P. (1940/1972) *The Psychology of the Imagination*. Secaucus, NJ: Citadel Press.

Sartre, J.-P. (1943/1966) *Being and Nothingness: A phenomenological essay on ontology*. New York: Washington Square Press.

Sartre, J.-P. (1948/1990) What is writing? In J.-P. Sartre *Essays in Existentialism*. New York: Citadel Press.

Sartre, J.-P. (1964/1965) Merleau-Ponty. In J.-P. Sartre *Situations* (Trans. B. Eisler). London: Hamish Hamilton.

Schaffer, S. (1989) Glass works: Newton's prisms and the uses of experiment. In D. Gooding, T. Pinch and S. Schaffer (Eds) *The Uses of Experiment: Studies in the natural sciences*. Cambridge: Cambridge University Press.

Schaffer, S. (1991) The Eighteenth Brumaire of Bruno Latour. *Studies in History and Philosophy of Science*, *22*: 174–192.

Schaffer, S. (1992) Utopia Limited: on the end of science. *Strategies* (spring).

Schrift, A.D. (1990) *Nietzsche and the Question of Interpretation: Between hermeneutics and deconstruction*. London: Routledge.

Scribner, S. (1977) Modes of thinking and ways of speaking: culture and logic reconsidered. In P.N. Johnson-Laird and P.C. Wason (Eds) *Thinking: Readings in cognitive science*. Cambridge: Cambridge University Press.

Secord, P.F. (1986) Social psychology as a science: philosophical, psychological and sociological perspectives. In J. Margolis, P.T. Manicas, R. Harré and P.F. Secord (Eds) *Psychology: Designing the discipline*. Oxford: Basil Blackwell.

Segal, H. (1975) *Introduction to the Work of Melanie Klein*. London: Hogarth Press.

Shallice, T. (1988) *From Neuropsychology to Mental Structures*. Cambridge: Cambridge University Press.

Shapin, S. (1979) The politics of observation: cerebral anatomy and social interests in the Edinburgh phrenology disputes. In R. Wallis (Ed.) *On the Margins of Science: The social construction of rejected knowledge*. *Sociological Review Monograph*, *27*. Keele: University of Keele.

Shapin, S. (1984) Pump and circumstance: Robert Boyle's literary technology. *Social Studies of Science*, *14*: 481–520.

Shapin, S. and Schaffer, S. (1985) *Leviathan and the Air Pump: Hobbes, Boyle, and the experimental life*. Princeton, NJ: Princeton University Press.

Shostakovich, D. (1979) *Testimony: The memoirs of Dmitri Shostakovich*. (Ed. S. Volkov; Trans. A.W. Bouis). London: Faber and Faber.

Shotter, J. (1975) *Images of Man in Psychological Research*. London: Methuen.

Shuttleworth, S. (1989) Psychological definition and social power: phrenology in the novels of Charlotte Brontë. In J. Christie and S. Shuttleworth (Eds) *Nature Transfigured: Science and literature, 1700–1900*. Manchester: Manchester University Press.

Signorile, V. (1989) Buridan's ass: the statistical rhetoric of science and the problem of equiprobability. In H.W. Simons (Ed.) *Rhetoric in the Human Sciences*. London: Sage.

Simons, H.W. (1989) Introduction. In H.W. Simons (Ed.) *Rhetoric in the Human Sciences*. London: Sage.

Sinha, C. (1988) *Language and Representation: A socio-naturalistic approach to human development*. Hemel Hempstead: Harvester-Wheatsheaf.

Sinha, C. (1989) Reading Vygotsky. *History of the Human Sciences*, 2: 309–331.

Skinner, B.F. (1948/1976) *Walden Two*, 2nd edn. New York: Macmillan.

Skinner, B.F. (1953) *Science and Human Behavior*. New York: Free Press.

Skinner, B.F. (1966) The phylogeny and ontogeny of behavior. *Science*, *153*: 1205–1213.

Skinner, B.F. (1967) Autobiography. In C. Murchison (Ed.) *A History of Psychology in Autobiography, Volume 5*. Worchester, MA: Clark University.

Skinner, B.F. (1971) *Beyond Freedom and Dignity*. Harmondsworth: Penguin.

Skinner, B.F. (1974) *About Behaviorism*. London: Jonathan Cape.

Skinner, B.F. (1985) Cognitive science and behaviorism. *British Journal of Psychology*, *76*: 291–301.

Skinner, Q. (1984) The idea of negative liberty: Philosophical and historical perspectives. In R. Rorty, J.B. Schneewind and Q. Skinner (Eds) *Philosophy in History*. Cambridge: Cambridge University Press.

Slife, B.D. and Barnard, S. (1988) Existential and cognitive psychology: contrasting views of consciousness. *Journal of Humanistic Psychology*, *28*: 119–136.

Smith, D. (1978) 'K is mentally ill': the anatomy of a factual account. *Sociology*, *12*: 23–53.

Smith, L.D. (1990a) Metaphors and knowledge and behaviour in the behaviourist tradition. In D.E. Leary (Ed.) *Metaphors in the History of Psychology*. Cambridge: Cambridge University Press.

Smith, L.D. (1990b) Models, mechanisms, and explanation in behaviour theory: the case of Hull versus Spencer. *Behaviour and Philosophy*, *18*: 1–18.

Smith, R. (1988) Does the history of psychology have a subject? *History of the Human Sciences*, *1*: 147–177.

Smith, R. (1992) *Inhibition: History and meaning in the sciences of mind and brain*. London: Free Association Press.

Solomon, R. (1976) *The Passions*. New York: Anchor Press/Doubleday.

Soyland, A.J. (1991a) Common sense in clinical discourse. *Text*, *11*: 223–240.

Soyland, A.J. (1991b) Review of D. Leary (Ed.) (1990) 'Metaphors in the history of psychology'. *History of the Human Sciences*, *4*: 452–454.

Soyland, A.J. (1992) Review of P.D. Chapman (1988) 'Schools as Sorters: Lewis M. Terman, applied psychology, and the intelligence testing movement, 1890–1930'. *Social History of Medicine*, *5*: 167–168.

Soyland, A.J. (1993) Sabina Spielrein and the hidden psychoanalysis of psychologists. *BPS History and Philosophy of Psychology Newsletter, No. 17* (Nov.): 5–13.

Soyland, A.J. (1994a) Functions of the psychiatric case-summary. *Text*, *14* (1) (in press).

Soyland, A.J. (1994b) The fate of 'K is mentally ill'. Unpublished manuscript, Lancaster University.

Soyland, A.J. (1994c) Presuppositions and methodologies in psychology. Unpublished manuscript, Lancaster University (under review).

Soyland, A.J. (1994d) Review of R. Smith (1992) 'Inhibition: History and meaning in the sciences of mind and brain'. *British Journal for the History of Science* (in press).

Soyland, A.J. (1994e) Developmental theory: surveying the forerunners. *Early Development and Parenting*, *3* (in press).

Soyland, A.J. (1994f) Authority, role and status in psychiatric discourse. *Discourse and Society*, *5* (in press).

Soyland, A.J. (1994g) After Lashley: neuropsychology, metaphors, promissory notes. *Theory and Psychology*, 4: 227–244.

Soyland, A.J. (forthcoming a) Commonsense and necessity: is Smedslund's vocabulary necessary? (manuscript under review).

Soyland, A.J. (forthcoming b) *Discourse and Clinical Identity*. London: Sage.

Spearman, C. (1923) *The Nature of 'Intelligence' and the Principles of Cognition*. London: Macmillan.

Spearman, C. (1927) *The Abilities of Man*. London: Macmillan.

Spivak, G.C. (1976) Translator's Preface. In J. Derrida (1967/1976) *Of Grammatology*. Baltimore: Johns Hopkins University Press.

Staats, A.W. (1983) *Psychology's Crisis of Disunity: Philosophy and method for a unified science*. New York: Praeger.

Star, S.L. (1983) Simplification in scientific work: an example from neuroscience research. *Social Studies of Science*, 13: 205–228.

Star, S.L. (1989) *Regions of the Mind: Brain research and the quest for scientific certainty*. Stanford, CA: Stanford University Press.

Still, A. (1991) Introduction to a centenary symposium of William James' 'The Principles of Psychology'. *British Journal of Psychology*, 82: 191–193.

Stimson, D. (1949) *Scientists and Amateurs: A history of the Royal Society*. London: Sigma Books.

Stove, D.C. (1982) *Popper and After: Four modern irrationalists*. Oxford: Pergamon Press.

Stove, D.C. (1984) Paralytic epistemology, or the soundless scream. *New Ideas in Psychology*, 2: 21–24.

Stretton, H. (1987) *Political Essays*. Melbourne: Georgian House.

Swanson, G.E., Newcomb, T.M. and Hartley, E.L. (Eds) (1952) *Readings in Social Psychology*, revised edn. New York: Henry Holt & Company.

Swartz, M. (1978) *Physiological Psychology*, 2nd edn. London: Prentice-Hall.

Thompson, R. (1982) Functional organization of the rat brain. In J. Orbach (Ed.) *Neuropsychology after Lashley: Fifty years since the publication of 'Brain Mechanisms and Intelligence'*. Hillsdale, NJ: Lawrence Erlbaum.

Tobach, E., Aronson, L.R. and Shaw, E. (Eds) (1971) *The Biopsychology of Development*. New York: Academic Press.

Travis, G.D.L. (1981) Replicating replication? Aspects of the social construction of learning in planarian worms. *Social Studies of Science*, 11: 11–32.

Turner, G.W. (1973) *Stylistics*. Harmondsworth: Penguin.

Valentine, E.R. (1982) *Conceptual Issues in Psychology*. London: Allen & Unwin.

Valentine, E.R. (1991) William James's 'The Principles of Psychology': 'A seemingly inexhaustible source of ideas'. *British Journal of Psychology*, 82: 217–227.

Valsiner, J. and van der Veer, R. (1988) On the social nature of human cognition: an analysis of the intellectual roots of George Herbert Mead and Lev Vygotsky. *Journal for the Theory of Social Behaviour*, 18: 117–136.

Vasta, R. (Ed.) (1992) *Six Theories of Child Development: Revised formulations and current issues*. London: Jessica Kingsley Publications.

Vygotsky, L. (1934/1986) *Thought and Language*. Cambridge, MA: MIT Press.

Vygotsky, L. (1978) *Mind in Society: The development of higher psychological processes*. Cambridge, MA: Harvard University Press.

Wahl, J. (1946/1990) The roots of existentialism: an introduction. In J.-P. Sartre *Essays in Existentialism*. New York: Citadel Press.

Walkerdine, V. (1988) *The Mastery of Reason*. London: Routledge.

Wann, T.W. (Ed.) (1964) *Behaviorism and Phenomenology – Contrasting Bases for Modern Psychology*. Chicago: Chicago University Press.

Watson, J.B. (1913) Psychology as the behaviorist views it. *Psychological Review*, 20: 158–177.

Watson, J.B. (1916) Behavior and the concept of mental disease. *Journal of Philosophy, Psychology, and Scientific Method*, 13: 589–596.

Watson, J.B. (1917) Does Holt follow Freud? *Journal of Philosophy, Psychology, and Scientific Method*, *14*: 85–92.

Watson, J.B. (1924/1930) *Behaviorism*. Chicago: Chicago University Press.

Watson, J.B. (1925/1926) What the nursery has to say about instincts. In C. Murchison (Ed.) *Psychologies of 1925: Powell lectures in psychological theory*, 2nd edn. Worchester, MA: Clark University.

Watson, J.B. and McDougall, W. (1928) *The Battle of Behaviorism: An exposition and an exposure*. London: Kegan Paul, Trench, Trubner & Co.

Watson, J.D. (1968/1970) *The Double Helix: A personal account of the discovery of the structure of DNA*. Harmondsworth: Penguin.

Weatherall, M. (1991) Letter to the editor. *Times Literary Supplement, no. 4591*, 29 March.

Weimer, W.B. (1979) *Notes on the Methodology of Scientific Research*. Hillsdale, NJ: Lawrence Erlbaum.

Wertsch, J.V. (1985) *Vygotsky and the Social Formation of Mind*. Cambridge, MA: Harvard University Press.

Wilkes, K.V. (1988) *Real People: Personal identity without thought experiments*. Oxford: Clarendon Press.

Winnicott, D.W. (1957/1964) *The Child, the Family, and the Outside World*. Harmondsworth: Penguin.

Wittgenstein, L. (1958/1968) *Philosophical Investigations*. Oxford: Basil Blackwell.

Wooffitt, R. (1992) *Telling Tales of the Unexpected*. London: Harvester-Wheatsheaf.

Woolfolk, R. and Sass, L.A. (1988) Behaviorism and existentialism revisited. *Journal of Humanistic Psychology*, *28*: 108–119.

Woolgar, S. (1976) Writing an intellectual history of scientific development: the use of discovery accounts. *Social Studies of Science*, *6*: 395–422.

Woolgar, S. (1981) Interest and explanation. *Social Studies of Science*, *11*: 504–14.

Woolgar, S. (1983) Irony in the social study of science. In K.D. Knorr-Cetina and M.J. Mulkay (Eds) *Science Observed: Perspectives on the social study of science*. London: Sage.

Woolgar, S. (Ed.) (1988a) *Knowledge and Reflexivity: New frontiers in the sociology of knowledge*. London: Sage.

Woolgar, S. (1988b) *Science: The very idea*. London: Tavistock.

Wundt, W. (1897) *Outlines of Psychology* (Trans. C.H. Judd). Leipzig: Wilhelm Engelmann.

Young, J.Z. (1987) *Philosophy and the Brain*. Oxford: Oxford University Press.

Young, R. (1970) *Mind, Brain, and Adaptation in the Nineteenth Century*. Oxford: Clarendon Press.

Zajonc, R.B. (1980) Thinking and Feeling. *American Psychologist*, *35*: 151–175.

# Index

Actor-Network Theory 26, 139, 142
anthropology 19, 25, 88
anti-rhetoric (the rhetoric of) 13–15, 52, 84, 155
Aristotle 44, 106, 107, 113
Ash, M.G. 59, 87
Ashmore, M. 16, 27–31, 33, 34, 121, 122
Austin, J.L. 5–7, 23, 53, 54, 105, 120, 154
Averill, J. 91
Ayer, A.J. 5–6

Barnes, H. 29
Bazerman, C. 19, 21, 24, 27–29, 33, 86, 89, 143, 152, 158–159
Beer, G. 2, 24–25, 27
behaviourism 19, 87, 88, 97, 98–99, 139–140, 157
Berlin, I. 5–6
Billig, M. 2, 9, 24, 33, 55, 81
Binet, A. 79, 80, 81
Black, M. 94–95, 117–119
body (the)
    and development 56–90
    and emotion 91, 97, 100
Boring, E.G. 18, 19, 41, 53, 54, 58, 140
Broadbent, D.E. 53, 81, 115, 140, 143–144, 153
Bruner, J. 4, 19, 53, 62, 64, 77, 80, 81, 87, 88, 91, 138, 140, 152
Burke, K. 53
Burt, Sir C. 19, 20, 123–131, 133–134, 152, 160
Bygrave, S. 53, 158

Callon, M. 26, 38, 139
Carroll, L. 122
Chapman, P. 19, 87, 136–137
Churchland, P.S. 43–44, 51, 113
Clare, A. 88
closure (rhetorical) 16, 18, 70, 86, 156, 157
Collins, H.M. 18, 22, 26, 33, 137
Cooper, D. 81, 82, 90, 94, 106, 109, 111–112, 118

Danziger, K. 52, 87, 159
Darwin, C. 24, 37, 92, 93–95, 156

Dennett, D.C. 17, 58
Derrida, J. 105–107, 111, 112–117, 120–121, 122
development (theories of) 56–90
    and developmental noise 87
    and the ego 58, 60, 61–62, 66
    and ego-centric speech 76–77, 81
    and the environment 62, 64, 69–70, 72, 80, 82
    and instinct 62–64, 66, 69
    and language 60, 76, 79–81
    and learning 61, 71–72
    and zone of proximal development 80
discourse analysis 23, 26–27
dismissing (an argument) 3–6, 8–15, 41–42, 54, 72, 77, 81, 130, 135, 147–148
distinctions
    degree versus kind 3, 59, 103, 133–134
    growth versus conditioning 72
    is versus ought 3
    literal versus metaphorical 86, 94–95, 102, 105–122, 156–157
    nature versus nurture 58, 68, 87
    public versus private 115–117
Douglas, M. 25
Durkheim, E. 25, 33

Eco, U. 94, 13
Emerson, R.W. 105, 123
emotion (theories of) 99, 101
    and anthropology 99, 101
    and behaviour 96–99
    and choice 82
    and Darwin 92, 93–95
    and discourse 94–101
    and instinct 93, 95–96, 146
    and James 96–98
    and learning 99, 101
    and Sartre 93, 99–101
enrolment (rhetorical) 26, 38, 138–153, 159
ethnomethodology (ethnological) 16, 18, 19, 22, 159
Eysenck, H.J. 124, 126, 130–133, 152

fallacy 5, 7

Fish, S. 14, 145–146, 153
Fodor, J.A. 42, 49
Forrester, J. 55, 63, 65, 66, 88, 89, 140,
	151, 152, 153
Foucault, M. 18, 27, 57, 91, 106
Franz, S.I. 41–42, 54
Frenkel-Brunswik, E. 83, 90
Freud, S. 32, 59, 61–64, 67–68, 76, 81, 83,
	88–89, 90, 94, 138–153, 157

Gall, 41, 49, 54
Galton, Sir F. 87
Gellner, E. 4, 62, 66, 70, 86, 88, 140, 144,
	152–153
Gigerenzer, G. 19, 38, 55, 165
Gilbert, G.N. 13, 17, 18, 22–23, 24, 27, 33
Gross, A. 13, 18, 22, 24, 27, 124, 143, 154,
	158

Hall, G.S. 87, 152
Harrington, A. 41, 42, 53, 54, 89
Hearnshaw, L.S. 123–131
Hebb, D.O. 39–40, 46, 54, 89
Heidegger, M. 105, 106, 107–110, 111, 112,
	120–121, 152
Hesse, M. 32, 94, 118
Hume, D. 10–11, 17, 103–104

instincts 62–64, 66, 69, 70, 93, 95–96
interest theory 26, 33
IQ (intelligence quotient) 55, 123–137
	and Burt 123–131

James, W. 4, 19, 53, 72, 79, 97–98, 100,
	138–153, 156–157
Jordanova, L. 18, 27, 86
Joynsen, R.B. 126, 130–131, 137
Jung, C. 138, 145, 152

Kamin, L. 126, 130–133
Kaufmann, W. 4, 23, 106
Kevles, D. 124–125, 137
Kierkegaard, S. 105
Klien, M. 64–68, 76, 83–84, 160
Koch, S. 87
Kuhn, T. 28–29, 53

Lacan, J. 53, 84, 88, 91
Laing, R.D. 90
Lashley, K. 14, 35–53, 113, 140, 160
Latour, B. 24, 25, 26, 29, 33, 38, 86, 109,
	139, 148, 159
Leary, D. 16, 38, 43, 53, 152, 153, 157, 158
Lewontin, R.C. 87, 126
lexicon 56, 57, 65, 67, 68, 72, 77, 91, 142

Lorenz, K. 18
Luria, A.R. 19, 46, 53, 54, 55

Manicas, P. 19, 81, 152
Mead, M. 87, 88
memory 35–53, 60, 66
Merleau-Ponty, M. 58, 81–84, 88
Merton, R.K. 25, 33, 46
metaphor 1–161
	and Derrida 112–117
	and 'is' 106–107
	and the literal 86, 94–95, 102, 105–122,
		156–157
	and Nietzsche 106, 112, 115, 122
	and philosophy 105–122
metaphors
	boxes in the brain (modularity) 38,
		45–46, 48
	containment 113
	empty organism 72–74, 98–99
	divisibility 73
	holographic 36–37, 40–41, 43–47, 119
	logic 75
	shaping 69–71, 73–74, 79
	social interaction 82, 84
Miller, G.A. 19, 53, 54, 152
mind (constructions of)
	and Freud 142
	and James 140–141
Mitchell, J. 61–62, 65, 68
mitigation 16, 19, 40, 42, 72, 126, 132, 147,
	149
Mulkay, M. 13, 17, 18, 22–23, 30
Myers, G. 4, 18, 22, 24, 25, 26, 54, 71, 86,
	122, 137, 143, 158, 160

nature/nurture dichotomy (the) 58, 68, 87
Nehamas, A. 23, 111, 121, 122
Nettelbeck, T. 55, 134–135
neuropsychology 35–55
Nietzsche, F. 1, 13, 21, 23, 35, 91, 106,
	112, 115, 122, 123, 138, 154

parallel distributed processing 46–50, 55
philosophers (and rhetoric) 3–12, 162–163
philosophical tools 21,
	acceptable 3–5, 7
	unacceptable 3–5, 7, 131–132
philosophy 2–12, 70
phrenology 41, 49
Piaget, J. 4, 14, 19, 53, 64, 74–77, 79, 82,
	84, 90, 137
Pinter, H. 122
Plato 8, 13

Potter, J. 19, 23
presuppositions 22, 56–90
Pribram, K. 43–46, 49
principle
  of equipotentiality 39, 40, 46, 48, 50
  of verification 5–6, 7
promissory notes 3, 35–55, 62, 88, 129, 136,
  149–151
psychoanalysis 57, 61–68, 138–153, 157
  and the breast 66–68
  and the ego 61
  and fundamental experiences 63–64, 65,
    83
  and sexuality 61–64
  and transference 65, 88
psychology 1–161
  and animals 53–54, 59, 69, 71, 79, 80, 96
  definitions of 15–16, 19–20, 87
  and physiology 59–60, 71, 148
  and publishing 142–143
  and relations to other disciplines 70,
    130–133
  and textbooks 59
  and unification 87

Quine, W.V.O. 11

Ree, J. 10, 11, 24, 33, 122
reflexivity 17, 19, 25, 29–31
reinforcement (see also behaviourism) 69,
  72, 73–74
repertoires 17
repetition
  of argument 6
  of numbers 129–131
rhetoric 1–178
  and history 2, 9–12, 22, 33, 36, 46–47,
    59, 60–61, 138
  and philosophy 3–12
  and science 13–20
  of validity 77, 90, 123–137, 157
Richards, G. 87, 140
Ricoeur, P. 19, 44, 53, 94, 106, 114, 157
Roberts, J. 33, 107, 117
Rorty, R. 4, 19, 21, 23, 38, 105–106, 107,
  111, 112, 115–117, 120–122
Rose, N. 15, 19, 88, 123, 137
Rumelhart, D.E. 46–50
Russell, B. 4, 11–12

Ryle, G. 17

Sarbin, T. 106
Sartre, J.-P. 19, 81, 84, 90, 93, 99–101,
  137, 156
Schaffer, S. 18, 24, 26, 33, 137, 153
Schrift, A. 106, 107
Segal, H. 65, 67
Shallice, T. 50–51
Shapin, S. 18, 26, 153
sexuality 27, 61–64
Shostakovich, D. 103
Skinner, B.F. 15, 19, 53, 58, 72–74, 76,
  98–99, 140, 160
Smith, R. 16, 53, 87, 91–92, 95
sociology (of scientific knowledge) ix, 17,
  18, 22–23, 158
Soloman, R. 99, 101, 156
sophists (rhetoritians) 2, 8–9
Soyland, A.J. ix–x, 23, 33, 53, 66, 68, 86,
  88, 90, 92, 106, 121, 137, 152
Spearman, C. 19, 55, 87, 124–125, 137,
  152, 153
speech-acts (see also Austin) 7
statistics 55, 77
Strindberg, A. 103
strong programme (the) 25–31
style 15, 21, 23, 73, 114, 142–143
symmetry 25–29, 123–137, 154
symptoms 60, 75, 76, 82, 88

transference 65, 88–89
translations (the use of) 32

validity 34, 123–137
  and margin of error 129
  and statistics 129–131
Vygotsky, L. 19, 32, 57–58, 59, 60, 75, 76,
  77–81, 84, 88, 137

Watson, J.B. 19, 54, 58, 69–72, 76, 79, 81,
  89, 139–140, 147, 152, 155
Wetherell, M. 19, 23
Wittgenstein, L. 23, 35, 117–119, 138, 154,
  157
Woolgar, S. 18, 22, 26, 122, 137, 159, 160
Wundt, W. 59–60, 64

Young, J.Z. 36–37